・ ・ ・

BOLIVIA AND COCA

Sᴛᴜᴅɪᴇꜱ ᴏɴ ᴛʜᴇ Iᴍᴘᴀᴄᴛ ᴏꜰ ᴛʜᴇ Iʟʟᴇɢᴀʟ Dʀᴜɢ Tʀᴀᴅᴇ
LaMond Tullis, Series Editor

●　　●　　●

A Project of the
United Nations Research Institute
for Social Development (UNRISD)
and the
United Nations University (UNU)

BOLIVIA AND COCA

• • •

A Study in Dependency

James Painter

LYNNE RIENNER PUBLISHERS • BOULDER & LONDON

Published in the United States of America in 1994 by
Lynne Rienner Publishers, Inc.
1800 30th Street, Boulder, Colorado 80301

and in the United Kingdom by
Lynne Rienner Publishers, Inc.
3 Henrietta Street, Covent Garden, London WC2E 8LU

Library of Congress Cataloging-in-Publication Data
Painter, James.
    Bolivia and coca : a study in dependency / by James Painter.
        p.   cm.—(Studies on the impact of the illegal drug trade :
    v. 1)
    Includes bibliographical references and index.
    ISBN 1-55587-490-8 (alk. paper)
    1. Coca industry—Bolivia. 2. Cocaine industry—Bolivia.
3. Narcotics, Control of—Bolivia. 4. Bolivia—Economic policy.
5. Bolivia—Rural conditions. I. Title, II. Series.
HD9019.C632B6458   1994
363.4'5'0984—dc20   93-32723
                                                              CIP

British Cataloguing in Publication Data
A Cataloguing in Publication record for this book
is available from the British Library.

The United Nations University Press has exclusive rights
to distribute this book in Japan and Southeast Asia:
United Nations University Press
The United Nations University
53-70, Jingumae 5-chome
Shibuya-ku, Tokyo 150
ISBN 92-808-0856-7

To Sophia, Maya, and Cassie

Contents

. . .

Tables and Figures

• • •

Tables

Figure

Foreword

. . .

LaMond Tullis

James Painter's excellent book is part of a multicountry study of the socioeconomic and political impact of the production, trade, and use of illicit narcotic drugs. The project is sponsored by the United Nations Research Institute for Social Development (UNRISD), the United Nations University (UNU), and Brigham Young University (BYU).

The first phase of the project, a review monograph and annotated bibliography entitled *Handbook of Research on the Illicit Drug Traffic: Socioeconomic and Political Consequences* (Westport, Conn.: Greenwood Press), was issued in 1991. The second phase is a series of country-specific books that both describe and analyze the interplay of economics, politics, society, and illicit drugs and drug-control policies through a careful analysis of causes and consequences of production, trade, consumption, and control.

Since the early 1980s the national and international traffic in and consumption of cannabis, opiate, and coca derivatives have exploded, perhaps now tapering off in the United States but vigorously expanding in Western and Eastern Europe and the former Soviet Union. Consumption has also rapidly increased in the principal so-called producer countries (for example, Peru, Bolivia, Colombia, Mexico, Myanmar, Afghanistan).

The socioeconomic and political costs of consumption and efforts to suppress it have mounted. Policy initiatives to reduce those costs have, in the worst cases, simply aggravated the problem. In the best cases the initiatives have apparently had only a marginal impact.

Although the literature on illicit drugs is now rapidly expanding, most of it has focused on consumption and drug-control problems in major industrialized countries. Less attention has been paid to the developing countries. This is highly unfortunate, because illicit-drug-control initiatives have concentrated mostly on supply-reduction efforts in developing countries. In the wake of a general failure of these supply-reduction strategies to control consumption anywhere, a strong shift is now expected in international drug-control efforts.

The purpose of the country studies in this series is to increase the level of information and awareness about costs and consequences of the present policies and to consider the implications of proffered new solutions for developing areas. We desire to contribute to an enhanced quality of policy review discussions by bringing together a rich array of historical and contemporary information and careful analyses regarding specific countries.

James Painter's book makes a substantial contribution to this effort. Bolivia is a principal producer of coca, the agricultural precursor to cocaine. Painter describes the coca boom in Bolivia, the development of a cocaine industry in the country, and the catastrophic surrender of the Bolivian economy to that industry. He also looks into the costs and benefits of the industry and the impact of various policies to curb the drug trade. Among the latter he examines "alternative development," the present prospective solution to reduce crop production.

Although alternative development has not received a fair shake in Bolivia, Painter is not optimistic that even its success would materially alter Bolivian coca production or the availability of cocaine for the international market. Nevertheless, he concludes with the following challenge: "Even if a successful policy did little to stop the availability of cocaine in the United States, at least policymakers favoring alternative development could be left with the honorable objective of contributing to Bolivia's efforts to escape underdevelopment and helping poor farmers in their efforts to escape poverty —which was, after all, why most of them started growing coca in the first place."

Painter shows how coca and cocaine are inextricably linked to Bolivia's long-term development problems, to its economic stabilization prospects, to incipient militarization of the society, to internal political dynamics, and to a frantic search—involving everyone from peasants to elites—for a solution to the underlying problems of poverty in the country. Readers will be pleased with his lucid style and intimate familiarity with Bolivia as he shows us, step by step, how a country struggling to survive in today's world becomes beholden to and integrated into an international illegal economy.

Aside from acknowledging the financial support of UNRISD, UNU, and BYU, we thankfully acknowledge the excellent support from Chelita Pate and her BYU staff of assistants in preparing the country-study manuscripts. Lani Gurr, in particular, has provided matchless service for this project, for which we are truly grateful.

Acknowledgments

. . .

The research for this book was carried out during a period of three years, from October 1988 to December 1991, while I was working and living in Bolivia as a journalist. During that time, many people helped me to a deeper understanding of the complexities of Bolivia's coca and cocaine production. However, special thanks are due to the United Nations Fund for Drug Abuse Control (UNFDAC), now called the United Nations International Drug Control Programme (UNDCP), and particularly Giovanni Quaglia and Jaime Idrovo. Various officials of the Bolivian and U.S. governments went out of their way to find time to speak to me, including representatives of SUBDESAL, PDAR, UMOPAR, the DEA, the NAU, and USAID. Most of them talked on condition of anonymity, so they shall remain nameless. Representatives of the coca federations and nongovernmental organizations in Cochabamba (particularly Alberto Rivera from CERES) and La Paz were also most helpful. Among those providing detailed and insightful comments on the text, I should like to thank Solon Barraclough, Carlos Pérez-Crespo, Francisco Thoumi, and LaMond Tullis. But the responsibility for any errors or dubious interpretations remains mine.

J. P.

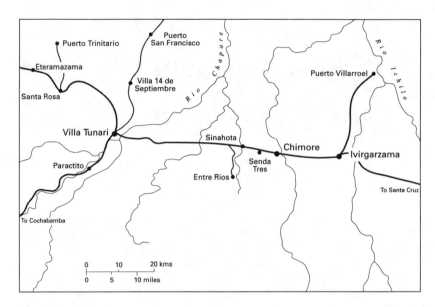

The Chapare

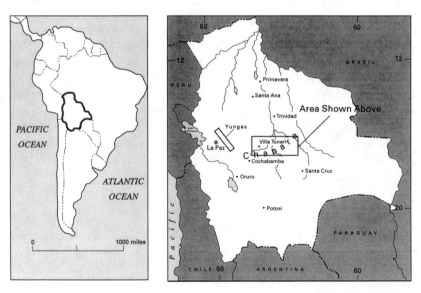

South America   Bolivia

. . . 1 . . .

The Rise of Coca

The Coca Boom

In the early 1980s, Roberto Suárez Gómez, probably Bolivia's best-known cocaine trafficker, presented a highly ambitious plan to the government of General Luis García Meza. Basing his vision on studies carried out by Spanish and Japanese academics, Suárez Gómez imagined it would be feasible to finance a new multinational corporation capable of transforming Bolivia's excess coca leaf production into medicinal products for a mass market. History relates that Suárez Gómez's idea was dismissed perfunctorily by a government already deeply aware of the financial benefits to be won by coca's better-known derivative, cocaine.

However unlikely Suárez Gómez's apparent conversion from trafficker to healer may seem, his vision stemmed from a centuries-old tradition in Bolivia of the use of the coca leaf for medicinal, cultural, and religious purposes. Its first use can be traced back to at least 3000 BC.[1] During the colonial period, Quechua and Aymara Indian laborers in the silver mines consumed coca—or the *hoja sagrada,* as it is commonly known in Bolivia—as a stimulant and as protection against altitude, hunger, and cold.[2] Five hundred years later, the practice known as *acullico,* in which the coca leaf is chewed and held in a wad in the cheek, is still regularly adopted by at least one million Bolivians, mostly Indian peasants and miners.[3] Some observers believe the chewing of coca supplies some of the vitamins and minerals missing from poor peoples' diet, particularly calcium, iron, and phosphorous.[4] Moreover, coca remains an integral part of indigenous community life, used extensively in rituals, as a natural medicine, and as a highly valued gift in the *mink'a* system of reciprocal favors.

The original version (invented at the end of the last century) of what we now know as Coca-Cola drew on the medicinal benefits of coca before any of its fourteen alkaloids are removed. This was perceived to be the only way to compete with a popular tonic of the time, vino Mariani, a favorite of such notables as the author H. G. Wells, Pope Benedict XV, and U.S. president William McKinley. Now, as the Coca-Cola Company is keen to stress, any trace of an addictive drug has been taken out of its product, but the company still buys coca from Bolivia to be used as flavoring.[5]

Such stories are a salutary reminder that the illicit production of cocaine—which few Bolivians consume—stems from a long period of legal consumption and production of coca in Bolivia. Such was the legitimacy of coca and the importance of coca production to the economy that the government passed a decree in 1940 declaring coca "an article of prime necessity" and ordering its compulsory sale in mining and railway companies (unless otherwise noted, all translations are the author's).[6] The Bolivian government did ratify the 1961 United Nations Convention on Drugs, which included not only cocaine but the coca leaf on its list of proscribed products, but the narcotics law passed a year later did not include coca. (According to the UN convention, the acullico was technically typified as an illegal use of drugs, and even the act of picking coca leaf constituted producing a drug.)[7]

It was regarded as a major triumph for Bolivia when the 1988 UN Vienna convention recognized in its Article 14 the "traditional legal uses" of coca leaf in its natural state, a change that was apparently greeted by a standing ovation by the convention delegates.[8] Even though coca remained a proscribed drug under the 1961 convention, the Bolivians felt the addition—though vaguely worded—was at least one step on the path toward the "rehabilitation" of coca. It was only with the passing of the Ley del Régimen de la Coca y Sustancias Controladas (Law Regulating Coca and Controlled Substances, or law 1008) in July 1988 that a Bolivian law specifically prohibited the growing of coca outside "traditional zones." Even now, it remains legal to grow coca within most of these zones under certain conditions (see pp. 77–80).

Until the 1940s most of Bolivia's coca was grown in a region known as the Yungas, a 11,000-square-kilometer area of deep, plunging valleys three hours' drive northeast of the capital, La Paz. During the colonial period, production levels in the Yungas boomed and slumped largely in response to the fortunes of the silver mines, where most of the coca was consumed. Most of the production was carried out on large, terraced, commercial plantations, or *haciendas*, in sharp contrast to contemporary small-scale peasant production. To this day, most of the 10,000 to 20,000 tonnes of coca consumed each year in Bolivia are grown in the Yungas, partly because its coca is regarded as sweeter than that grown in the Chapare.

According to the agrarian census of 1937, the Yungas accounted for 97 percent of the country's coca fields, with the remainder found in Cochabamba (2 percent) and Santa Cruz (1 percent). By the time of the 1950 census, the share of the Yungas had dropped to 67 percent, and the balance was coming principally from the Chapare, a subtropical rainforest area in the eastern lowlands of the department of Cochabamba.[9] By 1967 the Chapare had overtaken the Yungas, accounting for over half the total hectares (ha) under coca cultivation (see Table 1.1).

The rapid consolidation of the Chapare as the country's main coca-growing region—before the real boom in international demand for cocaine—was a product both of its natural advantages and state colonization policies. Farmers in the Chapare did not have to build steep terracing and could expect higher annual yields, partly because of the richer nutrients in the soil and partly because of the Chapare's four harvests every year compared to the three most common in the Yungas. As early as 1963, the Chapare was producing nearly 3,500 tonnes of coca from only 1,300 hectares compared to the 1,400 tonnes from the 1,700 hectares in the Yungas. By 1970 the Chapare accounted for 83 percent of national production (of 8,500 tonnes) from just 850 hectares more of coca.[10]

In the 1930s and 1940s governments gave a major impetus to a long-held desire to thin out highland areas by relocating farmers to the warmer eastern lowlands. Roads began to penetrate the low-lying areas of Cochabamba to encourage colonization in part as a protection against predatory neighboring countries.[11] More important, the government hoped the resettlement program would forge stronger political and economic links with outlying tropical areas and thereby build a stronger sense of the Bolivian nation, increase domestic food production to achieve food self-reliance, and create an escape valve for demographic pressures elsewhere in the country.[12]

Migration to the Chapare was given a further impetus in the 1960s and early 1970s with the onset of internationally funded colonization projects and the building of a paved road to the area financed by USAID (United States Agency for International Development).[13] By the time international demand for cocaine exploded in the mid-1970s, the Chapare was producing all but 1,300 tonnes of Bolivia's national production of 27,000 tonnes of coca. Its vast, flat lands with a myriad of small paths and roads running off a main artery compared sharply with the steep terrain of the Yungas, where no small airplane could land and whose main entry point from La

Paz was (and remains) an extremely hazardous road easily monitored by checkpoints.

According to figures from the Bolivian research institute UDAPE (Unidad de Análisis de Políticas Económicas), national coca production grew from an average of 9,000 tonnes a year between 1963 and 1975 to an average of 79,000 tonnes from 1976 to 1988 (see Table 3.1). This expansion was mostly due to new areas being cultivated with coca rather than improved productivity from existing areas.[14] New coca areas, mostly in the Chapare but also in the Yungas, expanded every year from an average of 690 hectares in the earlier period to 3,747 hectares a year in the latter period.[15] The gross value of coca production as a percentage of total national agricultural production increased from 8 percent in 1980 to 17 percent in 1983 and 19 percent in 1988.[16]

The population of the Chapare grew accordingly. Between 1967 and 1981, the number of colonies in the Chapare increased from 54 with a settler population of 24,000 inhabitants, to 247 and a population of 84,000 inhabitants. By 1987 this population had probably more than doubled again to around 200,000, including residents and transients (i.e., those resident for only part of the year with primary residence elsewhere, particularly day laborers, coca stompers, and small traders).[17] As early as 1981, an estimated 400,000 people and 29,000 vehicles were moving in and out of the region, making an accurate breakdown of the resident versus transient population very difficult. Government estimates from 1989 suggest that as much as 60 percent of the population in the Chapare may have been transient.[18] Some recent calculations of more than 300,000 for the population of the Chapare now seem exaggerated,[19] and the increase in the total population is probably closer to the estimates outlined in Table 1.2, which clearly shows the dramatic rise in the early 1980s. New research by the Bolivian sociologist Alberto Rivera suggests that the population dropped dramatically in late 1989 when coca prices collapsed, causing the mass exodus of thousands of people, particularly from the transient population.[20] However, many analysts and representatives of the coca unions deny the extent of the exodus. They suggest that many, but not all, returned after coca prices began to improve in mid-1990 and beyond.

An extensive survey of more than 10,000 Chapare farmers carried out between 1985 and 1989 by the state eradication agency, DIRECO (Dirección de Reconversión Agrícola), shows that of the settler farmers, 19 percent arrived in the second half of the 1970s and a massive 43 percent in the first five years of the 1980s (see Table 1.3).[21]

The same survey shows that of the 10,000 questioned, nearly two-thirds came from within the Cochabamba department, twelve percent from the department of Potosí and a further four percent from Oruro, for decades two of Bolivia's poorest areas (see Table 1.4). Land scarcity in the highlands was the major motive for migrating. A study carried out by the Cochabamba-based research institute CERES (Centro de Estudios de la Realidad Económica y Social) in the early 1980s indicated that 62 percent of the farmers in the Chapare at that time had no land in their highland communities prior to migration, and of those who did have land, half of them owned one hectare or less.[22] These results broadly coincide with a later study by CERES of 180 Chapare farmers in 1989, which concluded that only 40 percent of the landowners in the Chapare also had land in their home areas. Of these, 64 percent owned less than 1 hectare.[23]

There was nothing new in large-scale migration. The Chapare was simply the latest chapter in a long history of migration and settlement by rural people from the *altiplano* (highland areas) looking for off-farm income for their survival.[24] Although rural-urban migration is the most usual pattern, rural-rural migration is also common, as peasants seek off-farm employment during the harvest season of cash crops, particularly in the Santa Cruz department, Argentina, and Chile. This ubiquitous search for employment away from rural homes has its roots in a complex interplay of factors including increases in the rural population; a government emphasis on export-oriented agriculture (which tends to employ fewer peasants) at the cost of domestic food production; the lack of agro-ecological sustainability of excessively parcelized land in large areas of the altiplano; and government credit, investment, and pricing policies that prejudiced the small producer.

Much of this was true of the Cochabamba department. A 1990 study of the population of Cochabamba showed that more than forty percent had migrated at least once before 1983 and nearly half before 1988.[25] The main attraction of the Chapare was not only the immediate financial gain but also its geographical proximity and a long history of close production relations between the upland and lowland areas of the department. Temporary migration was facilitated by the complimentary seasons—and therefore periods of high and low labor demand—between the two zones of Cochabamba. A 1984 study also shows the strong links maintained between the Chapare and highland home communities. Half the people questioned said they continued to own houses in their home towns or villages of the Cochabamba valley, while more than half sent money back to invest.[26]

The structural factors causing frequent permanent or temporary migration were compounded in the early 1980s by climatic disruption and a national economic slump, which undoubtedly gave a huge fillip to the exodus to the Chapare. The conjunctural "push factors" have been well documented,[27] and they include a widespread and sustained drought in 1983–1984 in central and southern parts of the country and the virtual collapse of the formal economy throughout the whole country.

The drought was widely regarded as Bolivia's worst this century, causing a major drop in the availability of staple crops (particularly potatoes and maize), a drastic fall in rural incomes, and the death of large numbers of livestock. All these factors pushed even more rural families to migrate for survival. Ironically, a credit relief program sponsored by USAID designed to help families bear the effects of the drought in the upper Cochabamba area encouraged migration to the Chapare. Farmers forced by credit institutions to repay their loans before the drought was over responded by migrating temporarily to the Chapare to acquire the ready cash to meet repayment demands. In some cases, their numbers included farmers who had not visited the Chapare before.[28]

The boom in the demand from abroad for cocaine coincided with Bolivia's worst economic slump this century, caused essentially by government mismanagement but compounded by falling commodity prices and growing debt-service payments. The crisis started in the early 1980s and was hardly resolved by the beginning of the next decade. GDP declined by an average 2.2 percent annually from 1980 to 1986 and barely outstripped population growth until 1991, when good rains reversed years of poor agricultural output to push the overall growth rate over 4.0 percent (see Table 1.5). From 1980 to 1985 per capita consumption declined by over 30 percent, family income by 38 percent, and the purchasing power of wages by 50 percent.

Bolivia became synonymous with hyperinflation, which spiraled out of control to exceed 8,000 percent in 1985, by repute the seventh highest ever recorded in the world. It was mainly caused by the unwillingness of the government of President Hernán Siles Zuazo (1982–1985) to cut government spending in the face of the demands of organized labor, high debt servicing, falling tax revenues, and a rapid decline in new dollar loans from abroad. The Siles Zuazo government proved incapable of following a consistent set of macroeconomic policies, at times favoring orthodox deflationary measures harming labor, and at other times attempting stabilization policies while maintaining wage indexation.[29]

Official unemployment jumped from 5.8 percent in 1980 to more than 21 percent in 1985, as at least 60,000 people were sacked in the manufacturing and mining sectors. The best documented of these were 27,000 miners who lost their jobs as a result of a tin price slump in October 1985 and a government response to it of closing seventeen state mines.[30] Tin had formed the backbone of the country's formal export economy for most of the century, but a price fall from U.S. $12,000 a ton to U.S. $5,000 a ton virtually overnight compounded a more gentle decline in production and export value already apparent from the early 1980s. In 1980 Bolivia produced 28,000 tonnes of tin worth U.S. $378 million, but by 1986 its high-cost, low-grade mines could only produce 6,000 tonnes worth a meager U.S. $48 million. Tin exports, worth 40 percent of exports in 1980, fell to only 8 percent in 1987.

It is not clear how many of these sacked miners actually migrated permanently from mining districts such as Potosí and Oruro to the Chapare. Certainly, press reports in 1986 suggested that at least in the early stages, their numbers were significant.[31] Of all the settlers interviewed in the DIRECO survey, 7.9 percent said they arrived after 1985, and 16.4 percent said they came from Potosí and Oruro, which would give a figure of nearly 800 arriving from those two departments after the tin crash (assuming a population of 60,000 permanent settlers in the Chapare). Anecdotal evidence suggests that some ex-miners have remained, but reports from church-based organizations working with mining communities in the late 1980s suggested that many others had already returned to their mining communities after encountering difficulties with the new lifestyle, different climate, and unaccustomed diseases in the Chapare. Others stayed in the lowlands as miners, looking for gold in the rivers of the Beni, Pando, and tropical regions of La Paz department.

It hardly needs stating that the national economic slump and the virtual collapse of the tin mining industry worsened many of Bolivia's social statistics, which for years have kept Bolivia rooted near or at the bottom of the Latin American poverty league. In 1989, 165 out of every 1,000 children born died before their fifth birthday, and 105 before their first birthday—both rates are the worst in Latin America, including Haiti.[32] The same report indicated that more than half of Bolivian children between ages two and five have stunted growth due to malnutrition. UNICEF (United Nations International Children's Emergency Fund) statistics showed Bolivia to have registered a slower rate of improvement since 1960 than virtually all other Latin American countries. As recently as 1991, a World Bank report compared the conditions of Bolivia's poor to those more publicized cases in sub-Saharan Africa.[33]

It comes as no surprise to learn that permanent settlers and temporary workers in the Chapare blame poverty—and particularly the lack of land, money, and employment—in their zones of origin for their migration. Of the 176 settlers questioned in the CERES survey, 42 percent said lack of land, and 41 percent pointed to insufficient income in their home areas. Although there are important differences between settlers and laborers, these are the same reasons given by most rural inhabitants seeking to migrate to cities.[34]

The attraction of the Chapare for many migrant settlers was inextricably linked to the dominant system of land tenure, which is almost exclusively small peasant plots. There is not one large-scale plantation of over 20 hectares dedicated to coca in the Chapare. The DIRECO survey suggests that the mean-size plot is between 9 and 12 hectares, of which 1.25 to 4 hectares are under cultivation. Coca is only one crop in a diversified cropping system, but it is the most important, representing an average 0.9 hectares (a range of 0.5 to 1.25). The rest of the plot is dedicated to bananas, cassava, corn, rice, citrus fruits, or other minor crops (see Table 1.6). SUBDESAL (Subsecretaría de Desarrollo Alternativo) calculated that by 1988 coca represented 46.9 percent of the total area under cultivation in the Chapare. It is interesting to note that, regardless of how much property farmers have, they rarely dedicate more than 1.5 hectares to coca.[35] Coca fields are found very close to the houses where farmers live, thus making it very difficult to use herbicides or defoliants without damaging people and other crops.

It should be stressed that life in the Chapare is a long way from the utopia conjured up by some writers. Surveys suggest that migrants would prefer not to have to travel there if suitable job opportunities existed in their home areas and even if the local wage were lower than the rates in the Chapare.[36] One study suggests that Chapare wages have to be higher than 1.6 times the going rate at home to attract farmers or workers.[37] Fear of police violence and of disease (particularly yellow fever, tuberculosis, and various lung diseases) are common reasons cited by interviewees for their dislike of the Chapare.

The Chapare is also one of the wettest areas in the world, mainly because of a sharp drop in elevation of more than 4,000 meters in less than 100 kilometers. It registers a rainfall of between 2,700 and 4,900 millimeters (mm) a year (and once in 1982 of 7,500 mm), and an average temperature of 22 degrees Centigrade—not conditions familiar to highland dwellers. What is familiar is the lack of social services. In 1989 no town could count on drinking water, proper drainage, or an electricity supply (Chimore alone had some water and locally generated electricity). Although the Chapare has no electricity, high-voltage lines carry electricity generated in the higher regions of the Chapare to Santa Cruz. This is another symbol of the outward-looking development of the Chapare.[38]

Schools are sparse and poorly attended, partly because many family heads are known to travel without their children and remit their money to their families in their home communities. Ministry of Education figures in 1988 suggested that only 9,000 students were enrolled in schools in the Chapare, while informal conversations give the impression most children study outside the Chapare, primarily in Cochabamba.[39] And there are insufficient medical posts to cope with widespread yellow fever, tuberculosis and other lung diseases, and others such as measles and skin infections.[40] Anemia, vitamin deficiencies, and malnutrition are endemic among children, causing some to estimate infant mortality under one year of age to be as high as 50 percent. Venereal diseases are also particularly acute among the young female population.[41]

Although the Chapare has a number of diverse microregions, the region as a whole is not particularly suitable for growing other crops due to heavy erosion, the excessively high rainfall, and the high level of acidity and aluminum toxicity. Lime could help to neutralize the acidity and toxicity of the soil to allow plants to absorb nutrients more readily, but lime is one of the controlled substances in the Chapare because it is used in the manufacture of coca paste, the first stage in the manufacture of cocaine.

The Income from Coca

Undoubtedly the major pull factor to the Chapare was the expectation of higher income levels. Although it has almost become a truism that coca is the "green gold of the Andes," against which other crops could hardly compete, there are surprisingly few detailed studies of just how much income coca generates compared to its rivals. However, anecdotal evidence and the studies that are available do point to the spectacular gains to be made from coca, particularly in the boom period of the early 1980s when migration to the Chapare was at its highest. What is certainly true is that the expectation of good incomes, even after the price had begun to fall, encouraged people to move to the Chapare.

Basing their figures on the estimates of others, two economists at Harvard University, Mario de Franco and Ricardo Godoy, have made the following comparison between the 1960s and the early part of the 1980s:

The return a farmer obtains per hectare from selling coca leaves and coca paste has increased fifteen fold in real terms since 1960. In 1960 a farmer could expect to earn 12,000 bolivianos (in 1966 bolivianos) per year . . . by 1985 a farmer earned 178,842 bolivianos (in 1966 bolivianos). Put in real growth rate terms, during 1960–1985 the returns from coca cultivation grew by 11 percent per year. In contrast, the real price of potatoes, the principal food and cash crop in the highlands, has declined steadily . . . since 1936.[42]

De Franco and Godoy use a midpoint value of U.S. $1,000 per year for the net annual income from one hectare of coca in the 1960s, and U.S. $5,000 for 1985.[43] This latter figure is low compared to the findings of a study carried out by the OAS (Organization of American States) for 1984, which suggests an annual income of U.S. $9,000 from 1 hectare of coca, nineteen times higher than the income of U.S. $500 from the second most profitable crop in the Chapare at that time, citrus fruit. However, a study by the Bolivian research institute CERES in Cochabamba suggests a lower figure, between U.S. $5,000 and U.S. $6,000 per hectare in 1982–1983.[44]

Much depends on the price of coca at the time of the calculation of income, as prices throughout the 1980s fluctuated widely. Figure 1.1 shows the sharp variations in price even from month to month for the period from April 1986 to July 1991. Until November 1989 the price dropped only twice below the U.S.-calculated break-even point of U.S. $30 a *carga*, the 100-pound bag used throughout the Chapare as the universal measurement for coca. Prices fell sharply in July 1986 as a result of a much-publicized antidrug operation known as Blast Furnace from July to November 1986, when U.S. troops were deployed in support of the Bolivian antidrug police. Prices climbed back again soon after the U.S. troops left, but they are yet to recover the levels prior to the operation.

The variations in coca prices may account for a figure calculated by USAID in the mid-1980s of only U.S. $2,600 a year from one hectare of coca. This figure is only four times greater than the revenue from avocados or citrus fruits, with which USAID hoped to replace coca at the time, but is also four times USAID's calculation of the 1986 per capita income.[45]

Although prices registered high variations in the late 1980s, there was an inexorable drop from the highs of U.S. $300 a carga in the earlier part of the decade. Even though coca prices were apparently locked into a downward trend, and more frequently falling below U.S. $30 a carga, the advantages of coca—of which higher income was only a part—were still self-evident. The study of the Chapare carried out in 1990 by Alberto Rivera suggests that even when coca prices were at their lowest sustained rate for a decade from November 19, 1989, to January 22, 1990 (between U.S. $8 and $30 a carga), farmers were still receiving an income between U.S. $204 and $735 per *cosecha* (harvest).[46] Assuming four cosechas a year, this would have given the farmer with 1 hectare of coca (slightly above the average farm size in the Chapare) a gross annual income between U.S. $816 and $2,940.

Rivera calculates that the costs of production at the time amounted to U.S. $582 per hectare, broken down into $28 for the purchase of coca plants (24,000), $117 each for the purchase of insecticides and herbicides, and $320 for contract labor.[47] These assumptions would give a net annual income of between U.S. $200 and $2,300 if those prices remained low for an entire twelve-month period (which, in fact, they were not).

However, Rivera points out that the labor costs can be reduced to U.S. $160 if the owner of a farm takes on daily labor instead of maintaining the more normal practice of shared contracts with outsiders. Interviews carried out in the Chapare at the time of the price slump at the end of 1989 suggested that owners were indeed shedding labor or not contracting outside labor in order to counter cash flow problems.

Calculations by a former chief economist for USAID in Bolivia, Clark Joel, suggest lower income figures from a hectare of coca, mainly because he assumes lower yield figures. Rivera works on the assumption of a yield of 24.5 cargas per harvest, giving an annual production of 9,800 pounds of coca. USAID assumes a yearly output of 2.2 tonnes from a hectare of coca (an average of its upper estimate of 2.76 tonnes and lower estimate of 1.6 tonnes), equivalent to a production of only 4,851 pounds. The UNDCP (United Nations Drug Control Program) unofficial figure is for a similar annual output of around 5,000 pounds. The different yield figures reveal different net incomes for a hectare of coca, depending on the price of a carga and the estimates of production costs (see Table 1.7). Joel assumes production costs of U.S. $1,455 a hectare, which gives him lower net incomes.

The UNDCP does not publish official figures for its estimates of income, but conversations with top UNDCP officials suggested that in 1991 they used a working figure of around U.S. $3,000 for gross income from a hectare of coca, assuming an average price of around U.S. $40 a carga for the year.[48]

It has to be remembered that Table 1.8 only shows expected income for a price range for coca of between U.S. $20 and $60 a carga. Until November 1989, prices were, on average, well above the U.S. $60 mark and often were sustained at over $100 for the first five years of the decade. In the second half, they peaked at U.S. $120 in August 1988, which, using Rivera and Joel's methodologies, would have given a net income range of between $5,000 and $10,000.

The figures for incomes from coca even in a slump compare favorably with the 1989 average annual income in Bolivia of just over U.S. $500 and a minimum wage of around U.S. $300.[49] When times were good in the early 1980s, and farmers could expect at least U.S. $5,000 a year, income from coca represented as much as fifty times the average income from a plot smaller than 5 hectares elsewhere in the country. On plots less than 1 hectare per capita, income was estimated to be a meager U.S. $63, and for farmers with land ranging from 5.0 to 9.9 hectares, the figure was $120. Although there were important regional variations, only rural households with more than 10 hectares—or 13 percent of the total number of rural households—rose above critical poverty levels.[50]

But coca's advantage is not simply that of income. A farmer can expect to have some sort of income within twelve months of planting coca, full production after two to three years, and an average plant lifespan of fifteen years (in some cases twenty-five years). Coca gives four crops a year, requires less attention and investment than other crops once it has been planted, and requires only manual labor to pick. It is also easy to pack and transport (often on the back of a bicycle) and has a virtually assured nearby market right through the year. In many cases, *comerciantes* (merchants) will even come to the farm to buy the coca. It is also a crop with which generations of rural Bolivian families are familiar. In short, as many development economists have pointed out, in other circumstances it would be the ideal income-generating crop to alleviate poverty and underdevelopment.

This is not to say that there are no financial risks associated with growing coca. Once the coca is picked, it has to be spread out and dried in the sun, and sold usually within three days. If the leaves are not dried in three days (for example, if it rains) the coca leaves turn black. But even then the product is still marketable, although at a lower price. Rivera points out that in not one of his interviews (even during the great price collapse) did a farmer report a case of having to return from the local coca market with his coca unsold.[51] And this perhaps is the most overlooked benefit of coca: It can provide ready and guaranteed liquidity virtually at any time of the year—a type of instant convertibility into cash when times are good or bad. That is to say, returns over a period are less significant than the immediate effect coca has on easing cash flow.

It is illustrative to compare the difficulties associated with the production and sale of the other common crops grown in the

Chapare, namely rice, citrus fruits, cassava, bananas, and papaya. All the crops suffer from quick spoilage and the absence of a good infrastructure to get them quickly to market. Rice, for example (which gives an average yield of around 1.5 tonnes/hectare a year in the Chapare), has to be transported rapidly to the nearest *peladora* (dehusking plant) because there are few silos to store the rice in the area. The transport charge plus the costs of the peladora can amount to half the final costs, and even then a rice producer has to compete with imported or contraband rice, which keep prices low.[52]

A hectare of cassava could yield an income of as much as U.S. $400 in 1990, but it is more costly and difficult to transport (usually to markets outside the Chapare) and gives only a "one-off" income in the year compared to the regular income from coca throughout the year.[53]

Bananas and papaya are highly perishable, and transport costs very high. One hectare of papaya will yield twice a year around eight to ten crates of about 100 papayas each. Of the market price (in 1990) of around U.S. $7 a crate, $5 goes on transport to markets either in Cochabamba or the capital, La Paz.[54] A farmer is fortunate to achieve a profit of U.S. $50 after six months of labor. Similarly, bananas can be profitable (see discussion on p. 117), but, again, transport costs are the key obstacle. Bananas, too, usually have to be sent by truck to urban centers, and truck drivers (in 1990) were charging between U.S. $70 and $80 for each trip to La Paz.

The Chapare is full of rotting oranges, lemons, and grapefruit. Oversupply, high transport costs, and long distances to markets mean that often it is simply not worth a farmer's even picking them up off the ground where they fall. In 1990 a truckload of oranges fetched around U.S. $75 in La Paz, roughly the same as transporting them there.[55]

USAID frequently carries out studies of the relative profitability of alternatives to coca. If we assume an average price of U.S. $40 a carga for 1991, and take the average of the Rivera, Joel, and UNDCP estimates ($3,338; $485; and $2,000 respectively) to arrive at a net income per hectare of $1,940, then only macadamia nuts and rubber out of eleven products chosen by a 1990 USAID study would have given a farmer a greater income than coca that year (see Table 1.8). But farmers would have had to make the risky decision to grow those two crops a number of years previously. There is a wait of seven years before macadamia nuts are ready for commercial production (and nine years for full production), or a wait of ten years for rubber to start producing (or fifteen years for full production). In fact, no farmers were receiving any income from either macadamia nuts or rubber in 1990, though some had planted macadamia seeds.

It is also important to stress that these calculations of income do not take into account that more and more coca farmers in the late 1980s and early 1990s were involved in the early stages of coca paste manufacture, in some cases near or on their farm sites, which would have maintained their income levels during hard times.

The attractions of coca are of course not confined to owning a coca farm. Thousands of unemployed farmers or farm laborers—and particularly young males—are also involved in picking coca, or the early stages of cocaine manufacture, particularly as *pisacocas* (coca stompers), for which they either received a fixed daily wage or part of the gross earnings. It is calculated that work as an unskilled laborer in cocaine production in the mid-1980s paid twenty times more than the work as a public employee.[56] One report in a Cochabamba newspaper article suggested that in late 1984 70 percent of schoolteachers in the region, whose monthly salaries then averaged U.S. $15 to $20, were working in cocaine factories.[57]

The consensus view is that in the mid-1980s rural laborers in the Chapare earned three to five times more than what they could have earned in their homelands.[58] Despite the price collapse in late 1989, day workers on coca farms could still earn between U.S. $1.60 and $4.0, or, as stompers at night, between $5 and $6.60.[59] This is a sharp drop from the peak of U.S. $40 a day a pisacoca could earn in 1986 but still compares favorably with the earnings of a rural teacher or a junior member of the antidrug police (UMOPAR, or Unidad Móvil de Patrullaje Rural) of less than $2.0 a day in the early 1990s.

Table 1.1   Area Under Coca Cultivation in Bolivia, 1963–1991 (in hectares)

	La Paz Department (Yungas)	Cochabamba Department (Chapare)	Total	U.S. State Department Estimate
1963	1,700	1,300	3,000	
1964	1,800	1,300	3,100	
1965	1,900	1,297	3,197	
1966	1,900	1,289	3,189	
1967	1,900	2,080	3,980	
1968	1,500	1,100	2,600	
1969	1,500	1,100	2,600	
1970	1,800	2,650	4,450	
1971	1,800	3,630	5,340	
1972	1,800	4,340	6,140	
1973	1,800	5,360	7,160	
1974	1,800	6,100	7,900	
1975	1,600	9,685	11,285	
1976	2,000	10,000	12,000	
1977	2,300	10,000	12,300	
1978	3,795	15,065	18,860	
1979	4,933	15,900	18,860	
1980	6,418	16,370	22,788	
1981	4,392	23,312	27,704	
1982	4,902	26,558	31,459	
1983	5,452	30,023	35,475	
1984	6,043	33,707	39,750	
1985	6,675	37,611	44,286	33,165
1986	7,348	41,734	49,082	35,612
1987	8,912	51,798	60,710	40,360
1988	8,885	49,005	57,890	48,925
1989	8,467	46,983	55,450	52,900
1990	8,206	39,438	47,644	50,300[a]
1991[b]				47,900

Sources: SUBDESAL, *Superficie y Producción de Coca en el Chapare y Yungas,* Mimeo (La Paz, Bolivia: SUBDESAL, 1991). U.S. State Department figures are from U.S. Department of State, Bureau of International Narcotics Matters, *International Narcotics Control Strategy Report,* Statistical Tables (for 1987–1991), and March 1988 for previous years.

Notes: a. This is broken down into the Chapare, 35,230 hectares; the Yungas, 14,100; and Apolo in the Santa Cruz department, 1,000.

b. Projection estimate.

Table 1.2 Population Estimates for the Chapare and Carrasco Provinces of Cochabamba, 1967–1990

Year	Population	Of which transient
1967[a]	24,000	n.a.
1976[a]	33,000	n.a.
1980[b]	40,000	n.a.
1981[a]	84,000	n.a.
1983[c]	142,000	n.a.
1987[d]	215,000	n.a.
1988[e]	208,000	n.a.
1990[f]	63,700	27,300

Sources: Carlos Pérez-Crespo, *Why Do People Migrate?* 22.

a. José Blanes and Gonzalo Flores, *Campesino, migrante y colonizador* (La Paz: CERES, 1982).

b. Organization of American States, *Integrated Regional Development Planning: Guidelines and Case Studies from OAS Experience* (Washington, D.C.: OAS, 1984).

c. José Blanes and Gonzalo Flores, *¿Dónde?*

d. An average figure of the range of between 196,000 and 235,000 found in J. Durana et al., *Population Estimate for the Chapare Region, Bolivia* (Washington, D.C.: Desfil, 1987).

e. CIDRE, *Estrategia y plan de acción para la formulación de un plan de desarrollo del trópico cochabambino* (Cochabamba: CIDRE, 1988).

f. A. Rivera, *Diagnóstico socioeconómico.*

Table 1.3 Chapare Farmers by Year of Arrival

	Percentage
Pre-1960	4.1
1960–1964	4.8
1965–1969	8.3
1970–1974	13.2
1975–1979	19.2
1980–1984	42.5
1985–1989	7.9
Total	100.0

Source: Adapted from M. Painter and E. Bedoya Garland, *Socioeconomic Issues,* 12, using DIRECO database (Bolivian state coca eradication agency).

Table 1.4 Origin of Chapare Farm Population

Department	Percentage
Cochabamba	65.2
Potosí	12.3
Oruro	4.1
Chuquisaca	2.9
La Paz	1.4
Santa Cruz	0.6
Others	0.3
No response	13.2
Total	100.0

Province of Origin of Those from Cochabamba Department

Province	Percentage
Chapare	28.8
Quillacollo	15.0
Arani	7.0
Ayopaya	7.0
Capinota	5.9
Punata	5.2
Arque	4.2
Tapacari	4.0
Cercado	3.6
Carrasco	3.1
Esteban Arce	2.8
Mizque	1.9
Campero	0.8
Jordán	0.7
Bolívar	0.0
No response	9.7
Total	100.0

Source: Adapted from M. Painter and E. Bedoya Garland, *Socioeconomic Issues,* 19–20, based on DIRECO database of interviews with 10,531 farmers (of which 6,867 were from Cochabamba).

Table 1.5 Economic Indicators, 1980–1990

	1980	1981	1982	1983	1984	1985	1986	1987	1988	1989	1990
1. GDP growth	(1.4)	(0.9)	(4.4)	(4.5)	(0.6)	(1.0)	(2.5)	2.6	3.0	2.7	2.6
2. GDP per capita growth	(4.5)	(1.8)	(7.0)	(7.1)	(3.3)	(3.0)	(5.1)	(0.2)	0.2	(0.1)	(0.2)
3. External debt (U.S. $billion)	2.53	2.65	2.80	3.18	3.21	3.29	3.64	4.29	4.07	3.49	3.77
4. Debt as percentage of exports	28.4	29.3	31.3	38.4	42.1	33.1	29.2	25.6	35.5	26.1	23.4
5. Inflation (percent)	24	25	297	328	2,275	8,269	66.0	10.7	21.5	16.5	18.0
6. Public sector Def (percentage of GDP)	9.0	7.8	14.7	19.1	27.4	9.1	4.0	n.a.	n.a.	n.a.	n.a.
7. Open Unemployment (percentage of EAP)	5.8	9.7	10.9	13.0	15.5	21.2	11.5	n.a.	n.a.	n.a.	n.a.

Sources: All the data for rows 1–5 are found in Muller Associates, *Estadísticas económicas*, La Paz, 1990 and 1991. Data in rows 6–7 are found in James Dunkerley, *Political Transition*, 1990, Appendix II, quoting Muller Associates, *Estadísticas económicas*, 1989; and Juan Antonio Morales, "Inflation Stabilization in Bolivia," in M. Bruno, G. Di Tella, R. Dornbusch, and S. Fischer, eds., *Inflation Stabilization: The Experience of Argentina, Brazil, Bolivia, Israel and Mexico* (Cambridge, Mass.: MIT Press, 1988).

Table 1.6   Mean Area per Farm Dedicated to Coca and Other Crop Production in the Chapare (in hectares)

	Regions						
	1	2	3	4	5	6	7
Crop							
Coca	1.04	1.57	1.08	1.22	0.88	1.28	0.91
Bananas	0.78	0.32	0.25	0.11	0.22	0.25	0.89
Cassava	0.18	0.25	0.18	0.22	0.13	0.20	0.29
Corn	0.09	0.16	0.05	0.03	0.04	0.07	0.16
Rice	0.24	0.59	0.32	0.44	0.13	0.32	1.77
Citrus	1.03	0.61	0.30	0.31	0.21	0.45	0.22
Others	0.20	0.13	0.11	0.06	0.13	0.09	1.28

Source: Adapted from M. Painter and E. Bedoya Garland, *Socioeconomic Issues*, 41, using DIRECO database.

Table 1.7   Estimates of Net Income from 1 Hectare of Coca in 1990

	Production (pounds/yr)	Gross Income (U.S. dollars)	Production Costs (U.S. dollars)	Net Income (U.S. dollars)
Rivera[a]				
Price of coca (carga)				
U.S. $60	9,800	5,880	582	5,298
U.S. $40	9,800	3,920	582	3,338
U.S. $30	9,800	2,940	582	2,358
U.S. $20	9,800	1,960	582	1,378
Joel[b]				
Price of coca (carga)				
U.S. $60	4,850	2,910	1,455	1,455
U.S. $40	4,850	1,940	1,455	485
U.S. $30	4,850	1,455	1,455	0
U.S. $20	4,850	970	1,455	(485)

Sources: a. A. Rivera, *Diagnóstico socioeconómico*, 33–35.

b. C. Joel, "At What Price of Coca Is Our Compensation and Credit Program Effective in Inducing Eradication? And What Is the Relative Profitability of Alternative Crops?" (U.S. Embassy, La Paz, May 1990, Table 1).

Note: Rivera does not include the costs of harvesting the coca. Joel uses the customary Bolivian government and U.S. assumption of U.S. $30 per carga. This includes all the investment costs and operating costs of producing coca, but not the "marginal costs of production," which are mainly harvesting (estimated by USAID to be between U.S. $12 and $15 a carga).

Table 1.8   Net Annual Incomes of Alternative Crops and Coca in 1990 (U.S.$)

	Gross Revenue Per Hectare	Costs of Production Per Hectare	Net Income Per Hectare
Coca[a]	2,953	1,012	1,940
Macadamia nuts	4,640	1,000	3,640
Rubber	2,750	736	2,104
Pineapple	3,750	2,071	1,679
Black pepper	3,360	2,143	1,217
Oranges	1,980	824	1,156
Hearts of palm	2,200	1,129	1,071
Coffee	2,250	1,343	907
Cacao	1,500	912	588
Annatto	720	308	412
Bananas	560	403	157
Corn	447	301	146

Source: C. Joel, "At What Price of Coca," Table A, using figures from USAID personnel.

Notes: There are a number of assumptions behind the calculations of income from other crops. For example, it is assumed that prices are maintained despite an increase in production, and that the USAID credit program covers the full initial costs of planting.

a. These figures are taken as an average of the estimates of Rivera, Joel, and the UNDCP, at a price of U.S. $40 a carga.

Figure 1.1 Coca Prices, April 1986–July 1991

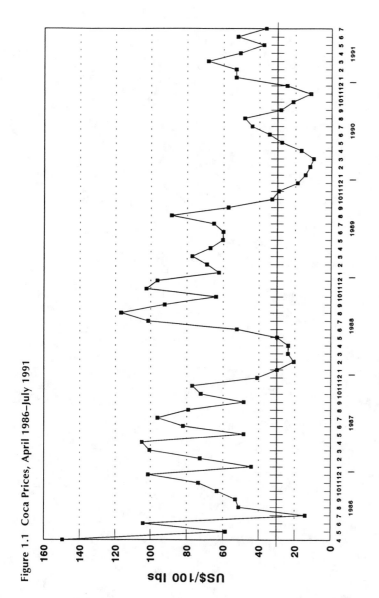

Source: DIRECO, using average price figures from three Chapare markets—Ivirgarzama, Sinahota, and Eteramazama.

. . . 2 . . .

From Coca to Cocaine

Coca Farmers, Rural Elites, and Paste Production

Turning coca leaves into cocaine is a three-stage process. In the first stage, the dried leaves are usually treated with an alkaline solution (lime, sodium carbonate, or potash), which begins to break down the fourteen alkaloids contained in the leaf, one of which is cocaine. The leaves are then usually stomped in large plastic vats full of kerosene, the blackened leaves removed, and sulfuric acid added to the mix. The substance left at the bottom of the vat is known as cocaine paste (*sulfato* or *pasta base*).

In the second stage the base is usually washed in kerosene again, dissolved in sulfuric acid, and mixed with potassium permanganate and ammonium hydroxide to get a purer form of the cocaine alkaloid known as cocaine base (*sulfato base*). In the final stage the base is dissolved in ether, hydrochloric acid is added, and the mixture is then dried and filtered until it reaches the final stage, known variously as HCL, hydrochloride, or pure cocaine (*clorhidrato de cocaína*).

The assumption of the U.S. State Department in 1991 was that between 75 and 110 kilograms (kg) of coca leaves yielded 1 kg of coca paste, between 2 and 4 kg of paste yielded 1 kg of base, and 1 kg of base yielded 1 kg of cocaine HCL.[1]

Until the early to mid-1980s, Bolivians essentially grew coca, processed it into paste and base, and then exported it to Colombia, which had the necessary technology for the more complicated later stage of HCL production.[2] While coca was grown almost exclusively in the Chapare and the Yungas, the processing, storage, and transport of paste and base were—and remain—spread over large areas of the northern and eastern departments of Bolivia, mainly in Santa Cruz, the Beni, and Pando. Hundreds, possibly thousands, of clandestine airstrips scattered throughout these departments facilitate

the easy transport of the drug from the Chapare to further processing points either within Bolivia or on to Colombia.

At the bottom end of the coca-cocaine process are the thousands
of coca farmers. Five peasant federations (*federaciones*) account for all
but a small portion of coca production. In 1989 the five represented
around 40,000 peasant farmers (or between 150,000 and 200,000
people) in the Chapare, divided into the FETCTC (Federación Especial de Trabajadores Campesinos del Trópico de Cochabamba, the
FCCT (Federación de Colonizadores de Carrasco Tropical), the
FECCh (Federación Especial de Colonizadores de Chimoré), the
FUCU (Federación Única de Centrales Unicas), and the FEYCh
(Federación Especial de Yungas-Chapare). Of these, by far the most
important are the FETCTC and the FCCT, which have an estimated
membership of 23,000 and 8,300 respectively, representing 78 percent of the unionized farmers in the Chapare.

Each of the federations is broken down into subdivisions of *centrales* (central bodies) and *sindicatos* (unions). The sindicatos are a
form of local government, with the power to establish land bound-
aries for new colonists; set road taxes; and collect taxes on coca-leaf
markets, which are used for small-scale local public works programs.
In some towns in the Chapare, the centrales and not the Bolivian
state control the coca markets. Members typically pay between U.S.
$1 and $3 a month for membership dues, and a fining system (of
$0.70 per missed meeting in 1989) helps to assure a heavy turnout
at union meetings.

In the 1980s the federaciones grew to be probably the most powerful pressure group from the popular sectors in the country, partly
filling the gap left by the decline of the traditionally most militant
miners' union.[3] There have been important political differences between the federations (for example, in their degree of acceptance of
government and international alternative development projects), but
the two main organizations, the FETCTC and the FCCT, have maintained a virtually uninterrupted opposition to coca eradication unless it is preceded by the introduction of realistic alternative crops
and economic opportunities.

In recent years the federations have focused their opposition on
two key government policies—the approval of law 1008 in July 1988
and the introduction of the Bolivian army into the antidrug war in
1991 (see Chapter 5). In both cases they could point to moderate
successes. The new law 1008 recognized the legitimacy of traditional
uses of coca; called for voluntary, not forced eradication of coca
plants; and linked eradication to progress on finding substitutes for
coca—all three were demands of the coca farmers. And in constant

negotiations with the government in 1991, the federations managed to secure assurances that the army would only carry out operations against cocaine traffickers and not coca farmers.

The principal means of protest adopted by the coca growers is mass-based and nonviolent, relying usually on the road blockade (*bloqueo*).[4] In a space of seven years in the late 1980s and early 1990s, they organized six major roadblocks, numerous hunger strikes, mass marches and public demonstrations against government policy, and several acullicos (chew-ins) in defense of the cultural values of coca.[5] However, the state's response to their protests has often been violent, most notably in May 1987 when five peasants were killed by UMOPAR troops in Parotani, Cochabamba; and in June 1988 when at least ten were killed at Villa Tunari in the Chapare after UMOPAR opened fire on protesting farmers.

The coca unions can count on the support of some left-wing parties and deputies, and have also gained ground within the main national peasant organization, the CSUTCB (Confederación Sindical Unica de Trabajadores Campesinos de Bolivia), and the main labor umbrella organization, the COB (Central Obrera Boliviana).[6] The unions' relationship with both the CSUTCB and the COB is complex, but coca farmers have learned quickly to forge alliances with these and other groups to, at the very least, slow down the pace of eradication demanded by national and foreign governments.

The coca lobby, of which the coca unions are the most important force, should of course be sharply distinguished from a lobby in favor of cocaine. The coca growers maintain that they are as different from the producers and distributors of paste and base as coca is different from cocaine. They strongly defend the cultural and medicinal properties of coca. But critics say the weakness of their position is that because only a small proportion of coca is consumed or used for "natural" purposes, they are abnegating responsibility for what happens to most of the coca, particularly that from the Chapare.

The distinction between coca and cocaine is one that has been promoted by many Bolivian governments, whose ambassadors often like to point out that cocaine is only the end product of processing coca, as whisky comes from barley, or wine from the grape.[7] In May 1992, President Jaime Paz Zamora's government launched a plan aimed at developing an international market for the coca leaf, particularly for medicinal teas. The government had clearly been insulted by the Spanish government's seizure in April of a display of coca leaves on the Bolivian stall at the Expo '92 World Fair in Seville, on the grounds that the leaves were a narcotic and still technically banned under the 1961 Vienna convention.[8]

The *cocaleros* (coca farmers) stress that growing coca in the Chapare and the Yungas remains a legal activity (the planting of new coca in the Chapare is illegal), although the production of paste, base, and HCL is not. In recent years they admit that more cocaleros may have been tempted to process the coca into the first stage of cocaine paste in an attempt to maintain income as coca prices showed a slow but steady decline from the mid-1980s. It is hard to deny that more *pozos* (maceration pits used to process the leaves into paste) are appearing close to coca farms. But there is yet to be one reported case of a major processing operation being found under peasant ownership.

Most studies agree that it was traditional rural elite groups and particularly ranchers who controlled the country's manufacture and distribution of paste and base in the boom period from the mid-1970s to the early 1980s.[9] Of these, two groups are usually identified. According to a study by Kevin Healy:

> Two principal groups of this economic elite included owners of large cattle ranches and merchants (e.g., exporters of cattle, rubber and Brazil nuts) in the eastern department of the Beni, and the agro-business elite (whose wealth and income derived primarily from sugar cane, cotton, soybeans, cattle production, commerce and agro-industries such as sugar and rice mills) in the Santa Cruz region. Their multiple economic interests . . . extend into import houses, banks, automobile dealerships, retail stores and money exchange houses.[10]

The members of these landowning elites had not been affected by Bolivia's sweeping agrarian reform program in 1953 but had benefited from the generous tax concessions, investment and credit policies, and general government policy of boosting agro-exports in the late 1960s and 1970s.

A widely quoted study by Bolivian journalist René Bascopé Aspiazu identified a number of distinct groups within the rural elite separated by geography, and, to a lesser extent, by their distinct roles in the production chain. The most important of these was the group ADEPA (Asociación de Productores de Algodón), based in the rich farming lands north of Santa Cruz, which had apparently moved into the lucrative cocaine business after the collapse of cotton prices in 1975/76. The state-owned Banco Agrícola (Agriculture Bank) was also singled out as a major partner in the cocaine boom, as it had lent heavily to Santa Cruz cotton growers prior to the cotton crash and stood to lose as much money as its clients.[11]

A second group, probably more concerned with transport than production, centered around the geographical axis of San Javier, San

Ramón, Santa Ana de Yacuma, and Paraparu in the Beni. Because several senior military officials had received land concessions in the Beni during the 1970s, it can be surmised that this group probably included significant numbers of military personnel. The ranch at Paraparu originally belonged to the army development corporation, COFADENA (Corporación de las Fuerzas Armadas para el Desarrollo Nacional).

Kevin Healy adds a separate, third group made up of some—but not all—military officers who became directly involved in trafficking in the late 1970s and early 1980s under the leadership of Gen. Luis García Meza and Col. Luis Arce Gómez.[12] The two came to power in a coup in June 1980, which many observers believe was partly financed by drug traffickers.[13] During their twelve-month regime, they and others used control of the state to forge an impressive network of private airstrips, guards, and depots under military protection, which even included the vaults of the Central Bank in La Paz as a storage facility.[14] There was, as one author put it, "a virtual symbiosis between drug traffickers and the state."[15]

Care should be taken not to see these groups as too distinct; a large degree of overlap and collaboration undoubtedly existed. The most important point is that the ranchers in particular had the necessary advantages to facilitate the shift into the cocaine business: small isolated airstrips, the capital and credit to invest in the necessary chemical inputs, infrastructure and transport, and a local political and economic power base that could be used to bribe or control members of the police or politicians.

Until his capture in July 1988, Roberto Suárez Gómez was regarded as Bolivia's "king of cocaine."[16] He was a traditional *latifundista* (large landowner) of Spanish descent, with extensive property around Santa Ana and an impressive fleet of small aircraft, originally used to fly meat from the Beni and Santa Cruz to La Paz. He was also the cousin of Luis Arce Gómez. Although other traffickers would undoubtedly help him make up orders, Suárez Gómez was regarded by the DEA as the largest collector of base and paste to sell to Colombians, particularly the Medellín cartel. His most extravagant claim (in 1984) was that he had accrued sufficient economic resources to pay off two-thirds of Bolivia's debt, then standing at U.S. $3 billion, in exchange for government tolerance.[17] When he was finally arrested in 1988 in a raid by the antidrug police on one of his ranches in the Beni, it was the first time that any major Bolivian trafficker had been captured.[18]

Suárez Gómez and his ilk clearly had a different social background from the predominately lower-middle-class "new breed" of

Colombian traffickers, who drew on the tough business and smuggling skills of the Colombian city of Medellín to dominate the Medellín cartel in the mid-1980s.[19] DEA officials also considered that the Bolivian traffickers' close family and business links contributed to the low level of violent resolution to any disputes—in marked contrast to their Colombian counterparts.

From Paste to Cocaine

For as long as Bolivia remained primarily a cultivator of coca and an exporter of coca paste or base to Colombia, Bolivian drug trafficking merely supplemented the Colombian drug trade. In the early 1980s, however, Bolivians—and Colombians working in Bolivia—slowly started to manufacture more and more of the base into the final product, cocaine HCL. U.S. drug officials estimate that by 1990 as much as one-third of Bolivian coca paste—or between 150 and 200 tonnes of cocaine—was being processed into HCL within Bolivia. U.S. officials were adamant that Bolivia had become the world's second-largest cocaine producer after Colombia, a world ranking the Bolivian government never accepted.[20]

The motive for Bolivian traffickers was partly the desire to engineer some minimum amount of independence from the Colombian Medellín and Cali cartels, in order to capture more of the profits from the more lucrative later stages of production and distribution. Colombian and the smaller Bolivian organizations also faced a profit squeeze at the lower end of the production chain because wholesale prices at every stage of production and distribution declined while operating costs remained stable. As a result, traffickers started to integrate their operations vertically, from wholesale paste purchase to cocaine refining and export, leaving the less-profitable paste production to farmers and middlemen.[21]

Colombians were also reported to be facing a production glut in the mid-1980s, which encouraged some of them to move part of their operations to Bolivia, where costs were cheaper, operations at times safer, and the supply of coca and coca paste more assured.[22] This process of vertical integration involved the exporting of technological know-how to Bolivia, including chemicals, processing equipment, chemists, bodyguards, airplanes, radio equipment, and weapons. As a result, more Colombians started to work in Bolivia on the final processing stages.

At the same time, there was evidence that Bolivian traffickers were attempting to diversify their markets and, to a limited extent, bypass the Colombians. While it was still true that the United States remained the main destination for Bolivian cocaine, new and more lucrative markets, particularly in Europe and the Pacific Rim countries (mainly Japan), were opening up via new routes through Argentina, Paraguay, Uruguay, or Brazil.

U.S. and European police and customs officials maintained that by the end of the 1980s the U.S. market was leveling out and gave regular warnings that traffickers—including Bolivians—were now targeting Europe as the main alternative to the saturated U.S. markets. Cocaine prices in Europe were at least twice as high as those in the United States. The *Financial Times* reported in 1989 that the price difference was even higher—between U.S. $10,000 and $15,000 a kilo in Miami, compared to as much as $60,000 in Madrid.[23]

U.S. drug officials estimated that in the early 1990s Bolivia probably accounted for around 25 percent of the U.S. cocaine market, and perhaps a larger portion of the European market. Whereas the cocaine used to be transported in single suitcases or on or in the carrier or "mule," now the trend ran to much larger shipments carried by commercial aircraft or cargo ship, often from cities like Buenos Aires or Rio de Janeiro.

DEA figures estimated that fourteen tonnes of cocaine were seized in Europe in 1990, up from virtually nothing in 1985. Another 200 tonnes probably entered undetected. By early 1992 police in Britain, Belgium, and Holland were making record seizures, usually from ships, of between 650 and 950 kilograms. A seizure of nearly a ton of cocaine—worth U.S. $250 million—on Britain's Merseyside in March 1992 was discovered to have come from Venezuela, prompting speculation that cocaine now made its way along a new route from Bolivia through north Brazil to Venezuela and on to Europe.[24]

By mid-1991 Interpol was becoming increasingly concerned not only that Bolivia (and Peru) were producing more of the final product, but also that Bolivian organizations were forging new links with European organized crime groups such as the mafia and the British underworld. As evidence, Interpol pointed to the increasing number of Bolivians and Peruvians being arrested in Europe.[25]

In 1990 the U.S. State Department and the DEA estimated that of the thirty or forty organizations controlling Bolivia's drug trade, most now had the capacity to produce cocaine. A small number of "broker" operations bought paste only for resale, but the rest had access to facilities in Bolivia to process the paste into base or HCL. DEA intelligence suggested that representatives of these organizations—around forty buyers—would meet twice a year in the city of Cochabamba to set the price for coca and coca paste.[26] (However,

DEA sources suggested that in late 1991 only four to six significant organizations were operating as a result of a large raid carried out in June 1991 on the town of Santa Ana in the Beni.)

It should be stressed that Bolivian trafficking organizations were never capable of becoming truly independent of their Colombian masters and probably continued to sell the vast majority of their product—either base or HCL—to Colombian buyers for further sales to U.S. markets. Drug analysts say that the Bolivians' geographical isolation, their smaller financial capacity, and perhaps their lack of the necessary marketing aggression meant that even when they could find new routes or bypass the Colombians, they usually did so with the tacit permission of the Colombians. For example, there were reports in 1991 that in the previous three years, while the Colombians maintained control over larger U.S. cities like New York and Los Angeles, Bolivian organizations had successfully established distribution networks for their cocaine via Mexico and Central America to cities in Texas like Houston and Dallas.[27] This may have been the case, but DEA officials were keen to stress that the Colombian organizations remained in sufficient control to take over whenever they chose.

U.S. drug officials say that Bolivian traffickers often fail to get the Colombians to pay the asking price and end up "fronting" base and HCL. Lack of finance apparently often causes the Bolivian trafficking organizations to purchase as much as 80 percent of their paste on credit from intermediaries.

Jorge Roca Suárez, the nephew of Roberto Suárez Gómez and his apparent heir, is widely credited with initiating the process of both producing more cocaine within Bolivia and establishing Bolivian-controlled routes, particularly to the United States. By the mid-1980s Roca Suárez had clearly eclipsed his uncle, and the DEA and Bolivian antidrug officials identified him as the country's number-one trafficker.

Some analysts argue that Roca Suárez was the first to set up major cocaine-processing factories within Bolivia, specifically at Huanchaca in northern Santa Cruz and La Floresta in the Beni, using chemists from Cali.[28] Some of the paste manufactured in the Chapare was apparently redirected toward these two laboratories and possibly others. Some time in 1986 Roca Suárez was thought to have left Bolivia to live in Los Angeles, California, but this did not prevent him from running a huge network of intermediaries, corrupt officials, front organizations, and cocaine-processing factories that came to be known as "the corporation" or the "Bolivian line" supplying cocaine via Mexico to the United States. When he was finally arrested in California in December 1990, he was accused of running a number of secret laboratories in the Bolivian jungle. His organization was, in the words of one DEA official, larger than that of the convicted Colombian trafficker Carlos Lehder.[29]

The top suspected traffickers of the late 1980s, such as Bismark Barrientos, Gerardo "Yayo" Rodríguez, William "Pato" Pizarro, and Hugo Rivero Villavicencio were all regarded by the DEA as major collaborators of Roca Suárez. But *Techo de Paja* (straw-hair) as Roca Suárez came to be known for his blond hair, could also count on the support of his extended family. It was described by the DEA as the *clan de los techos* and boasted at least ten of his close relatives.[30] His brother, José Luís Roca Suárez, suspected of being a major paste buyer, was arrested (and then released) a number of times in the Chapare. And in June 1991 three members of his family—his mother (Blanca Suárez de Roca), brother (Rafael), and sister (Asunta Beatriz)—were the first Bolivian traffickers the U.S. government had ever formally asked the Bolivian government to extradite.

Techo de Paja was also regarded as the leader of probably the largest drug-trafficking group in Bolivia, the so-called "Santa Ana clan,"[31] which later included other traffickers like Erwin Guzmán (a pilot), Hugo Rivero Villavicencio (a rancher), Oscar Roca Vásquez (a former popular folksinger and a cousin of Jorge Roca Suárez), and Jorge Flores Moisés (another pilot).[32] Santa Ana, and two other towns in the Beni named San Ramón and San Joaquín, were particularly suitable for trafficking. They were remote and inaccessible, relatively near the Brazilian border (for chemical inputs), and served by airstrips that were no more than clearings in the jungle; and they could count on a loyal local population long neglected by the state.

Santa Ana's traffickers enjoyed close links with the Medellín and Cali cartels, to whom they supplied base and the final product, and also with each other. Photographs on the walls of their houses in Santa Ana showed many of them enjoying parties or celebrations together, which suggested the close-knit nature of their "family operations." U.S. officials described their clan as the "most aggressive traffickers, most interested in producing cocaine, rather than just . . . base for the Colombians, and the people most interested in expanding independent networks into Europe and the U.S."[33]

In early 1989 the then subsecretary for social defense (the junior minister responsible for antidrug operations), Dr. Jorge Alderete, identified thirteen traffickers who controlled between 75 and 85 percent of the country's drug trade. Alderete maintained that the thirteen still "depended on other international contacts, be they Colombians, Brazilians or others, who had the links with the mafia controlling the world drug trade."[34] Techo de Paja headed the list, and two of his close associates—Humberto Gil and Bismark Barrientos—came second and third, followed by two members of the Santa Ana clan, Hugo Rivero Villavicencio and Winston Rodríguez. Three others—Mario Araoz, Carmelo Nuñez del Prado, and Rosa Romero de Humerez (the *Chola Rosa*)—were accused of being major paste buyers in the Chapare.[35] A later list of six traffickers that circulated among Bolivian journalists in early 1990 included Roca Suárez, Rivero Villavicencio, and Gil, but added Guzmán (described as having good links with the Brazilian mafia), Roca Vasquez, and Flores Moisés, all from the Santa Ana clan.[36]

These lists of top *narcos*, as they are known locally, tend to feature different names and different rankings, which is partly to be explained by the timing and the source (usually the DEA or the Bolivian antidrug police).[37] Top names mysteriously appear and disappear because undoubtedly the names are leaked or kept off the list as and when it suits the police's priorities. For example, Gerardo Yayo Rodríguez from San Ramón never appeared on a published list, and yet he was regarded by the DEA in 1990 as one of the country's top three traffickers and a target of sufficient importance to justify spending thousands of dollars to capture him.[38]

Yayo Rodríguez has been described as a "typical Bolivian drugs trafficker," as he was "not involved in distribution, which required expertise in smuggling, marketing and international connections . . . [but] concentrated on cocaine production."[39] Like Techo de Paja, he used as the basis of his organization members of his extended family (specifically his daughter and grandson, who flew in paste from the Chapare), who were middle-class ranchers of Spanish ancestry who had diversified into cocaine from cattle ranching. Rodríguez apparently employed a Colombian chemist and pilot, controlled the local airport hangar and tower in San Ramón, used a handful of small, mobile laboratories and six safe houses in Santa Cruz, and relied on a paid mole in the local antidrug police to ward off his capture.[40] In November 1989 a huge DEA-planned raid on San Ramón called "Operation Tandem" failed to capture Yayo Rodríguez despite the deployment of virtually the entire Bolivian antidrug police, every U.S. agent in the country, and three Bolivian air force C-130 airplanes. Yayo Rodríguez had apparently left the town the night before. (He was reported to have eventually been arrested in June 1991.)

Yayo Rodríguez was said to be a close associate and friend of both Erwin Guzmán and Hugo Rivero Villavicencio of the Santa Ana clan. By mid-1991 Guzmán was regarded by the DEA as the "godfather of them all," having usurped Roca Suárez as Bolivia's number-one trafficker.[41] Guzmán, Rivero, and Flores Moisés were, according to the Americans, the top three; several newspaper reports described them as supplying cocaine from Santa Ana to Oscar Escobar (cousin of the better-known Pablo Escobar) in Colombia.

By December 1991 the government could boast that no fewer than seven top members of the Santa Ana clan were under lock and key. But not one of the seven was actually captured, as they all volunteered to give themselves up to take advantage of a new government decree, no. 22881, passed on July 29, 1991. The Decreto de Arrepentimiento, or "decree of repentance," as it came to be known, allowed traffickers 120 days to surrender in return for a government guarantee that they would not be extradited to the United States to stand trial[42] (see pp. 80–85).

Erwin Guzmán was the first to offer himself up (actually before the decree was passed, on July 11), followed by Winston Rodríguez and Antonio Naciff (August 7), Hugo Rivero Villavicencio (September 16), Oscar Roca Vásquez (September 19), Jorge Flores Moisés (September 22), and finally Hugo Rivero Villavicencio's brother Rafael "Ico" on December 5 (after the decree had expired on November 26). The DEA claimed that Erwin Guzmán had enjoyed sufficient weight within the clan to persuade the others to give themselves up, which, if true, reveals much about the way Bolivian traffickers continued to operate in close-knit, family-oriented, geographical units.[43] Local press reports speculated that most of them had even met in Guzmán's house in Santa Ana to make the decision collectively.[44]

In his first declaration to a judge, Guzmán admitted to lending money to traffickers, although he denied being directly involved in storing or transporting cocaine. He did, however, admit to owning U.S. $350,000 in capital, 1,500 head of cattle, and four ranches, which he claimed to have acquired from his legitimate activities as a pilot. Naciff followed a similar line, saying he was principally a rancher.[45]

The first reaction of the government to the mass surrender was ecstatic, as ministers claimed that the major Bolivian trafficking organizations were now headless and links with the Colombians had been broken.[46] Later, the triumphant note was toned down as officials accepted that there had been no letup in the drugs trade, that the clan could still direct its operations from prison, and that Colombians were moving in quickly to fill the void left by the Bolivians. Indeed, the DEA reported that Colombian traffickers were "fighting it out like the old Wild West" in the Beni, bringing in whole organizations in an attempt to get laboratories back into action and reestablish air routes. The Bolivians were, in the words of the DEA chief in

Bolivia, "getting blown aside."[47] By mid-1992, the DEA believed that the old Bolivian trafficking organizations had "withered on the vine," and that the Colombians had succeeded in dominating the operations by supplying the necessary aircraft and finance.[48] Perhaps more significantly, it seemed that, temporarily at least, cocaine trafficking was returning to its old international division of labor. DEA intelligence suggested that Bolivians were being forced by the Colombians to return to their previous role of supplying just base and paste and not the final product.

... 3 ...

The Coca-Cocaine
Economy

Production and Value

Unfortunately, the cocaine traffickers described in Chapter 2 have yet to publish quarterly bulletins of statistics on their activities. Therefore enormous, but not insuperable, difficulties surround any calculation of the value of Bolivia's coca-cocaine economy. The illicit nature of cocaine production and trafficking; different methods of achieving raw data; and differing yield figures, prices, and conversion factors all combine to put obstacles in the way of even the most general agreement on values.

Bolivia shares all these problems and more, as nationalist interests can and do obstruct objective calculations. Officials of the U.S. government are often inclined to make lower estimates, and Bolivian officials higher estimates, as they are involved in constant and delicate negotiations over the levels of international aid, or compensation, to be paid for coca eradication. For example, a 1991 internal U.S. embassy calculation summarized the direct value of the coca-cocaine industry at U.S. $375–550 million, of which $150–300 million remained in Bolivia; and between 97,000 and 100,000 people spent a quarter of their working time in the coca industry. Samuel Doria Medina, former president Paz Zamora's chief economic adviser from 1989–1990 and a key figure in negotiations with the United States over levels of economic aid, calculated the total value of the industry at U.S. $1.5 billion, of which $600 million stayed in the economy; and 300,000 people participated in some aspect of the coca-cocaine production chain. Both sides were using the same figure of around 50,000 hectares (ha) under coca cultivation. Some commentators also suggest that the U.S. government increases its estimates of the number of hectares under cultivation when it is opting for a repressive or militarized strategy and drops them when Bolivia is pushing for economic compensation for the reduction of its coca.[1]

It is therefore hardly surprising to find that studies carried out in recent years have produced wide discrepancies, particularly on the value of coca and cocaine production, the size of the labor force involved, and the number of dollars remaining within the country.[2] Figures for the value of coca-cocaine production range from as little as U.S. $300 million (an estimate of USAID in 1988) to $5.7 billion (an estimate of Doria Medina in 1986). Similarly, estimates of direct employment generated by the coca-cocaine economy range from 120,000 to 500,000.

Most of the discrepancies can be explained by the different methodologies used, the different starting figures, and the different years for which the calculations have been done. However, more recent studies are increasingly sophisticated and reliable and consequently the differences between the statistical results are less marked.

In the mid-1980s a common way to guess the value of the Bolivian coca-cocaine economy was to look at the "Errors and Omissions" column in the current account balance of the Central Bank and assume that this figure was probably coca-dollars. This amounted to U.S. $282 million in 1986, although the figure has dropped considerably in recent years. The main problem with this method is the difficulty of knowing with any certainty what percentage of the figure corresponds to revenue from cocaine dollars.

The availability of more reliable figures on prices and production has led most coca statisticians to reject this method in favor of a detailed breakdown of the value of the various stages of coca and cocaine production. They usually start from virtually the only given that exists—the amount of land under coca cultivation—and assume all but 10,000 tonnes for licit consumption will be used to manufacture cocaine. Even with this method disagreements persist, as U.S. government estimates have tended to trust U.S. aerial surveys, while the Bolivian government and UN figures tend to rely on ground-based surveys. As recently as 1986, a preliminary U.S. State Department figure for total coca cultivation in Bolivia was 37,000 hectares, while the Bolivian Ministry of Agriculture suggested a preliminary figure of 71,000 hectares, nearly twice as much. This type of variance is usually explained by the inability of U.S. aerial surveys to detect coca grown under trees. However, one of the most notable differences continues to occur in the Yungas, where U.S. aerial surveys suggest a high figure of 14,000 hectares. On-the-ground surveys by the Bolivian government and the UNDCP suggest a more conservative figure of around 8,000 hectares.

However, in recent years U.S., UNDCP, and Bolivian figures of the total hectares under coca cultivation have diverged much less. By

1989 the U.S. State Department and the Bolivian government estimates came to within 3,000 hectares of each other (52,900 and 55,450 hectares, respectively). This small range of discrepancy was virtually maintained the following year. Table 1.1 shows the evolution of the estimated surface area under coca production since 1963.

After estimating hectares under calculation, the next step coca statisticians take is to assume a fixed yield per hectare of coca, which gives an estimate of the volume of coca produced. Here some of the major divergences occur. Until 1991, USAID officials assumed a yield of between 1.2 metric tonnes (for the Yungas) and 1.6 metric tonnes (for the Chapare) per hectare of coca, whereas Bolivian officials used a more realistic figure of between 0.81 and 0.94 metric tonnes/ hectare (mt/ha) for the Yungas, and between 1.91 and 2.45 mt/ha for the Chapare. Toward the end of 1991, U.S. embassy officials had begun to use an average figure of 2.2 mt/ha, as it was recognized that their original working figures were low. As the U.S. embassy itself argued, tea yields 5–8 mt/ha in the Yungas, and conservative estimates of coca yields in the Upper Huallaga Valley in Peru use 4.0 mt/ha.[3] Table 3.1 shows the estimates of the U.S. State Department and the Bolivian SUBDESAL (Subsecretaría de Desarrollo Alternativo) for the annual volume of coca produced from 1963.

The difference in the yield assumptions is probably the major factor behind wildly divergent figures for the total value of the coca-cocaine economy. As recently as 1990, the U.S. State Department used the figure of 64,400 tonnes of coca produced in Bolivia, which gave it market share of 27.4 percent of a total world production of 235,000 tonnes, compared to Peru's 58.9 percent (138,300 tonnes), and Colombia's 13.7 percent (32,100 tonnes).[4] The SUBDESAL figure for the same year is 117,000 tonnes (including licit consumption), almost twice the State Department's figure. The SUBDESAL figure would boost Bolivia's world market share to 40.7 percent.

The figures for coca production provide the estimates for the next three stages in the production chain, namely paste (pasta base), base (sulfato base), and HCL or hydrochloride (clorhidrato de cocaína). Obviously, if low coca production figures are the starting point, low production figures will be achieved for the three next stages and finally for the total value of the coca-cocaine economy. Tables 3.2 and 3.3 show the likely upper and lower ends of the ranges (Table 3.2 shows high ranges of coca yields/ha; Table 3.3 shows low ranges of coca yields/ha.) Table 3.2 is adapted from a study by Jeffrey Franks for the independent Bolivian research group, Muller Associates, and uses the conversion rate of 2.45 mt/ha for 1990. In Table 3.3 the State Department study uses an average 1.27 mt/ha for the same year. Similarly, the Franks study uses a conversion rate of 50–57 kilos of coca leaf for 1 kg of coca paste, compared to the U.S. estimates of 75–110 kilos per kg of paste.

Both the Franks and the U.S. State Department studies use the same data as the basis for all calculations, namely the figures for total coca cultivation found in the final column of Table 1.1 (with the exception of 1986). Yet the two studies end up with remarkably different figures for the amount of cocaine HCL produced in 1990—662 metric tonnes and 205 metric tonnes, respectively. At a Miami street price of U.S. $15,000 a kilo, this would represent a staggering difference of $7 billion.

The same problem of conversion rates hampers any calculation of the total value of the coca-cocaine economy. Most studies derive their figures from the sum of the values of the volumes produced at each of the four stages of production. Two of the most recent and most detailed studies, one carried out in 1991 by an independent economist working for USAID in La Paz and the above-mentioned Franks study, used roughly the same methodology. Their results for the total value of coca and cocaine production in 1990 are summarized in Table 3.4.

As can be seen from the table, Franks emerges with a slightly higher figure than USAID (U.S. $911 million compared to $591–801 million), principally because he uses a higher yield rate of 2.45 mt/ha (widely accepted by Bolivian government statisticians) compared to USAID's 1.6 mt/ha. In a separate calculation Franks emerges with a lower figure of U.S. $405 million when he uses a yield rate of 1.49 mt/ha.[5] Given that some U.S. embassy officials have now changed to using a figure of 2.2 mt/ha, it would seem reasonable to assume that Franks's figures using the higher yield estimate are nearest the mark.

Table 3.5 shows Franks's upper estimates of coca-cocaine exports (which he estimates to be the value of base and HCL production, i.e., lines 9 and 12 in Table 3.4) compared to the value of other legal exports from 1986 to 1990. Since 1986, coca-cocaine exports have represented between 28 and 53 percent of the value of total exports that include the value of coca-cocaine exports, or between 39 and 112 percent of those that exclude them. Only in 1986 did any other single export (gas) exceed the value of coca-cocaine. Even the total value of minerals combined could not match coca-cocaine for all of the five years. It is also worth noting that even though the price of coca leaves has suffered a historical decline since 1986, the value of the coca-cocaine economy has increased because U.S. drug analysts estimate that more HCL is produced within the country and that less paste is needed to make a kilo of base (4.0 kg in 1986, compared to 2.8 kg in 1990).

If we take Franks's lower estimate, coca-cocaine production represents 5.7 percent of GDP (including coca) in 1990, or 12.9 percent according to his higher estimate. This compares with contribution of the manufacturing and trade sectors at 11.4 and 11.2 percent respectively. Only legal agricultural production at 18.1 percent is more important than coca.[6] The share of manufacturing, oil, and gas has declined from 1970 to 1988, while the share of agriculture (including coca production, but not cocaine processing) has increased from 18 percent to 22 percent.[7]

The USAID study emerges with a slightly lower figure of 11.9 percent of legal GDP, using a median figure of U.S. $501 million for the value of the coca-cocaine economy.[8] Bolivian government figures put the figure at 12 percent of GDP in 1989, a drop of 12 percent from 24 percent in 1987.[9]

Both the Franks and the USAID studies also make a "guesstimate" of the amount of money actually staying in the country in 1990 (see Table 3.6)—for many observers, the most relevant statistic, as it comes closest to assessing how much the coca-cocaine economy is worth to Bolivians. Franks assumes that all the income from coca production, 80 percent of paste income (because paste production is small-scale and labor intensive), 20 percent of base income, and 10 percent of HCL income remain in Bolivia. These assumptions give a range of U.S. $106–$216 million, a significant drop from the 1989 range of U.S. $198–373 million (see Table 3.7). This is due to the abrupt fall in coca and coca-paste prices (from an average U.S. $1.27/kg of coca in 1989 to $0.52/kg in 1990, and from $175/kg of paste to $75/kg). The USAID study assumes 100 percent of the value of coca and paste, 40 percent of base, and 15 percent of HCL remains in Bolivia. This gives a range for 1990 between U.S. $150 million and $208 million, which falls within that of Franks. It is worth stressing that neither study seems to take into account the coca revenues returning to the country through contraband financed with narco-dollars (described on pp. 60–63). If these revenues are not included, then obviously the total value of the coca-cocaine economy is considerably higher.

Finally, it is worth making a crude calculation of how little of the total end-value of coca-cocaine production is retained by the coca growers. If we take Franks's figure of U.S. $64 million for the value of the coca production in 1990, then each of the 122,000 coca farmers (see Table 3.8) would have received an average U.S. $525 from the sale of their coca over the year. The money earned by the coca farmers represents only 7 percent of the total value of coca-cocaine production in Bolivia in 1990 (U.S. $911 million) (see Table 3.4). If one takes the amount of HCL the coca is capable of producing (between 205 and 662 mt, according to Tables 3.2 and 3.3) and assumes a low U.S. street price for cocaine of U.S. $15,000 a kilo, then the coca farmers share between 0.65 percent and 2.1 percent of the final street value of their product once fully processed. That is to say, even though coca provides a higher income than other crops, the level of exploitation by intermediaries of coca producers is sufficiently entrenched to deny producers a large share of the profits. And Bolivia, as with so many of the commodities it has produced in the past, is not the major beneficiary of the raw materials it produces.

Employment

The coca-cocaine economy is equally important as a provider of labor, particularly at times of severe recession in the early 1980s and of slow growth in the late 1980s. Not only are there about 60,000 farmers growing coca,[10] but thousands more are involved in picking, selling, and transporting the coca and in processing and distributing the paste. The principal types of employment are as *propietarios* (owners of a plot of land), *partidarios* (farmers who do not own land, but who make deals with propietarios to work part of their land), *jornaleros* (day laborers), pisacocas or *pisadores* (stompers), *zepe(dore)s* (carriers), *compradores* (buyers of coca), and various types of comerciantes (buyers of coca paste, suppliers of chemical inputs, and owners of transport).[11]

Again, there is wide disagreement on the total number of people employed in the coca-cocaine chain, with recent estimates ranging from a low of 120,000 (UDAPE in 1989) to a maximum of 500,000.[12] Much depends on how many members of each family are assumed to work on coca production on each farm. Franks assumes two per family, while the Bolivian sociologist Federico Aguiló assumes five per family.[13] Starting from roughly the same number of families (60,000), Franks therefore has 120,000 workers growing coca, whereas Aguiló has 300,000. This is the major factor accounting for the differing totals outlined in Table 3.8. Aguiló calculates nearly 450,000, while Franks has a more conservative 207,000.

Franks uses Aguiló's figure of 830 buyers at each of the country's fifteen coca markets but not unreasonably assumes that each buyer will visit two different markets, giving him a total of 6,725 buyers when nonmarket-based buyers and carriers within each market are included.[14] But Aguiló assumes that each buyer consists of a family of five, giving him a total of 74,250 buyers when nonmarket-based buyers, carriers within each market, and markets in the Yungas are included.[15] The two studies assume similar figures for the number of paste laboratories (4,500) in the country, but Aguiló again estimates each owner of a laboratory will employ all family members, whereas Franks assumes just two. Both studies also assume five stompers and ten carriers per paste laboratory.

Neither study seems to admit the possibility that many of the workers may double up. For example, since the late 1980s more and more producers in the Chapare moved into paste refining to maintain income as the price of coca fell.[16] Moreover, anecdotal evidence suggests that a stomper can double up as a carrier, or a supplier of precursors as a buyer of paste or base. However, neither study includes in its calculation the full reach of the coca-cocaine industry, which depends not only on protection and legal and financial services, but also food and refreshments from local suppliers.

A 1990 USAID study reports a higher figure than Franks, though it is achieved by a different methodology.[17] The study assumes 60,000 families working in the Chapare, for whom between 1.5 and 3.0 members are actively growing coca. After weighting, this gives a total of 162,000 workers, which is then multiplied by an employment factor of 1.5 (to include indirect employment) which gives a final figure of 243,000 workers.

Another calculation carried out internally by the U.S. embassy in La Paz in 1991 assumes that in 1990 82,000 workers were involved in the leaf stage and 15,000–18,000 in the paste stage, giving a final range of 97,000–100,000.[18] With the same multiplier effect of 1.5 for indirect employment, the final figure for total employment ranges between 145,000–150,000 workers. However, the U.S. embassy report suggests that many of the workers only work a quarter of each year in the coca-cocaine industry.

Table 3.9 shows a summary of the most recent and most serious estimates, including those of Franks and Aguiló. The table assumes that the economically active population (EAP) was 1,718,000 in 1989 and 1,800,000 in 1990 (which does not include the population involved in the coca-cocaine production chain, as it is assumed most are registered as working in other sectors). If we ignore the Bolivian government's official estimate (which seems high), the table gives a range of between 120,000 and 243,000 for the years 1989/90, or a median figure of 181,500, equivalent to 10.1 percent of the 1990 EAP.

This last figure compares with the official employment figures from the INE (Instituto Nacional de Estadísticas) for 1989 of 781,000 workers in agriculture (36.0 percent), 34,000 in mining (1.6 percent), 8,000 in petroleum (0.4 percent), 212,000 in manufacturing (9.8 percent), and 94,000 in construction (4.3 percent).[19] However, this range of figures does not take into account the effects of the prolonged drop in coca prices from October 1989 to February 1991 and the accompanying eradication of nearly 8,000 hectares in 1990, which are assumed to have caused between 10,000 and 22,000 families to leave the Chapare[20] (see p. 57). Official government calculations suggest that U.S. $256 million was lost as a result of the coca price crash, equivalent to 5 percent of GDP or more than the private sector investment for the year.[21]

Bolivia, Peru, and Colombia

Table 3.10 summarizes the value of the Bolivian coca-cocaine economy in 1990 and compares it to the situation in Colombia and Peru (for the most part, 1990 has been taken as the year of reference for Bolivia and 1988 for Colombia and Peru). Lines 4, 6, and 8 of Table 3.10 clearly show the far greater relative weight of the coca-cocaine industry in Bolivia's formal economy than in the Peruvian and Colombian economies. Even though Bolivian figures for "Value Added" and "Income Remaining" in the country fall below those of Peru and Colombia in absolute terms, the smaller size of the Bolivian economy increases the importance of the coca-cocaine economy as a provider of jobs, income, and foreign exchange. It would be hard to find a country anywhere in the world that is so economically dependent on the production of a drug in these three areas.

This is hardly a new finding, but it is worth stressing the degree to which the Bolivian economy remains "narco-addicted" despite the recent fall in U.S. cocaine consumption, the long-term trend of falling coca prices, and the millions of U.S. dollars poured into alternative development and interdiction over the last fifteen years.

Indeed, it is a salutary reminder of what an effective supply-side approach—or "winning the war on drugs"—could eventually do to the Bolivian economy without adequate compensation or pickup in the rest of the economy. Even Gonzalo Torrico, the then junior minister for social defense and the government official in charge of coca and cocaine suppression, warned in late 1991 of a possible social explosion if Bolivia were to eradicate its 50,000 hectares of coca. It would, he said, cause "a loss in GDP of U.S. $4 billion, a loss of U.S. $200 million in foreign exchange, and reduce employment by 175,000."[22]

It is also worth stressing just how well the rest of the economy or alternative crops have to perform to counteract the benefits offered by the coca-cocaine circuit. Soya, for example, has boomed in the late 1980s to reach an output of 320,000 mt from 150,000 hectares in the 1990/91 harvest (compared to coca's 116,000 tonnes from 48,000 hectares). Yet the value of soya production, much of which is mechanized, was only U.S. $45 million in export revenue, roughly a fifth of the revenue from the coca-cocaine circuit.[23]

Samuel Doria Medina has compared the importance of narco-dollars to Bolivia's economy and to the United States economy, where he says it represents only one percent of GDP: "For the U.S. it's like cutting off a finger because it has gangrene. For Bolivia, it's like having a tumor in your head, which you cannot simply cure by an amputation."[24]

Table 3.1   Coca Production in Bolivia, 1963–1991 (in metric tonnes)

	SUBDESAL	U.S. State Department
1963	4,822	
1965	4,976	
1970	8,481	
1971	11,078	
1972	12,959	
1973	15,622	
1974	17,623	
1975	26,961	
1976	28,120	
1977	28,363	
1978	42,996	
1979	46,131	
1980	48,579	
1981	66,130	
1982	75,326	
1983	85,152	
1984	95,607	
1985	106,693	47,558
1986	118,408	51,520
1987	151,547	56,500
1988	143,979	68,500
1989	137,657	78,300
1990	116,605	74,400
1991[a]		66,500

Sources: SUBDESAL and U.S. Department of State, Bureau of International Narcotics Matters, *International Narcotics Control Strategy Report,* March 1992 (for 1987–
1991), and March 1989 (for 1985–1986).

Note: The SUBDESAL figures assume a yield rate of between 0.81 and 0.94 tonnes/
hectare in the Yungas, and between 2.65 and 2.76 tonnes/hectare in the Chapare.
U.S. figures assume between 1.0 and 1.6 tonnes/hectare. Both sets of figures include
coca for licit consumption.

a. Projected estimate.

Table 3.2 Paste, Base, and Cocaine Production, 1986–1990 (I)

	1986	1987	1988	1989	1990
Coca: (mt)					
1. Produced	51,520	100,900	121,823	131,721	123,235
2. Licit	(10,000)	(10,000)	(10,000)	(10,000)	(10,000)
3. Seized/lost	(4,152)	(9,105)	(11,199)	(12,214)	(11,336)
4. Available for conversion (1–2–3)	37,368	81,795	100,624	109,507	101,899
Paste: (mt)					
5. Potential	656	1,435	1,899	2,190	2,038
6. Available for refining	656	1,431	1,890	2,180	2,038
Base: (mt)					
7. Potential	174	406	576	717	728
HCL: (mt)					
8. Produced	159	370	524	652	662
9. Converted in Bolivia	11	52	110	183	232
Conversion Factors:					
a. Coca yield (mt/ha)	2.45	2.50	2.49	2.49	2.45
b. Coca to Paste	57.0	57.0	53.0	50.0	50.0
c. Paste to Base	3.76	3.52	3.28	3.04	2.80
d. Base to HCL	1.10	1.10	1.10	1.10	1.10

Source: Adapted from Jeffrey Franks, "¿La economía de la coca en Bolivia: Plaga o salvación?" Muller Associates, *Informe confidencial,* no. 64 (La Paz: June 1991), 19.

1. Using conversion factor a.
2. Assumption of U.S. State Department.
3. Figures from U.S. State Department.
5. Using conversion factor b.
7. Using conversion factor c.
8. Using conversion factor d.
9. Assuming that from 1986 there was a growing amount of cocaine actually manufactured in Bolivia, reaching 35 percent in 1990.

a. SUBDESAL assumptions.
b. SUBDESAL assumptions.
c. Supposition of State Department.
d. Supposition of State Department.

Table 3.3 Paste, Base, and Cocaine Production, 1986–1990 (II)

	1986	1987	1988	1989	1990
Coca: (mt)					
1. Produced	51,520	56,500	68,500	78,300	74,400
2. Licit	(10,000)	(10,000)	(10,000)	(10,000)	(10,000)
3. Seized/Lost	(5,152)	—	—	—	—
4. Available for conversion	36,368	46,500	58,500	68,300	64,400
Paste: (mt)					
5. Potential	331	368	498	740	588
6. Available for refining	325	364	490	731	575
Base: (mt)					
7. Potential	81	91	123	261	205
HCL: (mt)					
8. Produced	73	83	110	261	205
9. Converted in Bolivia	—	29	39	91	72
Conversion Factors:					
a. Coca yield (mt/ha)	1.40	1.36	1.36	1.41	1.27
b. Coca to Paste	110	126	117	92	110
c. Paste to Base	4.00	4.00	3.98	2.80	2.80
d. Base to HCL	1.10	1.10	1.10	1.00	1.00

Source: U.S. Department of State, Bureau of International Narcotics Matters, *International Narcotics Control Strategy Report* (March 1991), statistical tables on Bolivia.

1. Using conversion factor a.
2. Assumption of U.S. State Department.
5. Using conversion factor b.
7. Using conversion factor c.
8. Using conversion factor d.
9. Assuming that from 1986 there was a growing amount of cocaine actually manufactured in Bolivia, reaching 35 percent in 1990.

a. U.S. State Department assumes 1 Chapare hectare yields 1.6 mt of dry coca leaf annually, and 1 Yungas hectare yields 1.2 mt annually.
b. U.S. State Department assumes 75–110 kg of dry coca leaf yields 1 kg of coca paste.
c. Supposition of State Department.
d. Supposition of State Department.

Table 3.4   Value of Coca-Cocaine Production in 1990

	USAID	Franks
Coca:		
Has under coca cultivation	50,300	50,300
Yield used (mt/ha)	1.6	2.45
Production (mt)	70,480	123,235
1. Production available (mt)	66,956	101,899
2. Price per kilo (U.S. $)	0.53	0.52
3. Value (U.S. $million) (1 x 2)	35	64
Paste:		
Conversion rate	51.00	50.00
4. Available for refining (mt)	1,313	2,038
5. Price per kilo (U.S. $)	55–72	75
6. Value (U.S. $million) (4 x 5)	72–95	153
Base:		
Conversion rate	3.25	2.80
7. Available for refining (mt)	364	728
8. Price per kilo (U.S. $)	530–800	500
9. Value (U.S. $million) (8 x 9)	193–291	364
HCL:		
Conversion rate	1.125	1.10
10. Available for refining in Bolivia (mt)	162	232
11. Price per kilo	1,800–2,350	1,425
12. Value produced and exported (U.S. $million) (10 x 11)	291–380	330
Total Value (3+6+9+12) (U.S. $million)	591–801	911

Sources: Adapted from Jeffrey Franks, "La economía de la coca," 19; USAID Update, "Estimates of the Economic Impact of Coca and Derivatives in 1990," Mimeo, La Paz, April 1991.

Note: USAID uses its own sources for prices, while Franks relies on UDAPE/DIRECO figures. It is worth pointing out that if Franks's figures for yields are used, and USAID figures for prices, the total value of coca-cocaine production would be around U.S. $1.3 billion.

Table 3.5 Coca-Cocaine and Legal Exports, 1986–1990

	1986	1987	1988	1989	1990
Coca-cocaine (U.S. $million)	246	536	674	632	694
percentage of total	27.8	48.5	52.9	43.5	43.0
Minerals (U.S. $million)	197	207	273	403	401
percentage of total	22.7	25.2	30.0	36.9	33.5
Hydrocarbons (U.S. $million)	333	256	219	214	227
percentage of total	38.3	31.1	24.1	19.6	18.9
Nontraditionals (U.S. $million)	109	106	108	204	292
percentage of total	12.5	12.9	11.9	18.7	24.4
Total (without coca) (U.S. $million)	638	570	600	822	921
Total (with coca) (U.S. $million)	884	1,105	1,275	1,454	1,615

Source: Adapted from Jeffrey Franks, "La economía de la coca," 20.

Table 3.6 Income from Coca-Cocaine Economy Staying in Bolivia in 1990 (in millions of U.S.$)

	USAID	Franks
Coca:		
1. Total[a]	35	64
2. Left in country[b]	35	64
Paste:		
3. Total[c]	72–95	153
4. Value added[d]	37–59	89
5. Left in country[e]	37–59	71
Base:		
6. Total[f]	193–291	364
7. Value added[g]	120–196	265
8. Left in country[h]	48–79	53
HCL:		
9. Total[i]	291–380	330
10. Value added[j]	195–234	277
11. Left in country[k]	29–35	28
Total Income Staying in Bolivia (2+5+8+11)	150–208	216

Sources: Adapted from Franks, "La economía de la coca," p. 22; USAID Update, "Estimates."

Notes: a. Taken from Table 3.4, line 3.

b. It is assumed all the income from coca leaf production stays within Bolivia.

c. Taken from Table 3.4, line 6.

d. Table 3.4, line 3 less the value of coca leaf production.

e. USAID assumes 100 percent of value of paste remains within Bolivia; Franks assumes 80 percent.

f. Taken from Table 3.4, line 9.

g. For USAID, this is line 6 above less coca paste production value (line 3). For Franks, this is line 6 less value of paste used in exported base.

h. USAID assumes 40 percent of coca base remains in the country; Frank assumes 20 percent.

i. Taken from Table 3.4, line 12.

j. For USAID, this is line 9 above less base production destined to HCL manufacture. For Franks, this is line 9 less paste production used in exported HCL.

k. USAID assumes 15 percent of value of cocaine stays within the country; Franks 10 percent.

Table 3.7   Income from the Coca-Cocaine Economy Staying in Bolivia, 1986–1990 (in millions of U.S.$)

	1986	1987	1988	1989	1990
Lower estimate	160.0	157.6	169.0	198.3	105.8
Upper estimate	162.8	302.0	320.4	372.9	215.7

Source: Adapted from Jeffrey Franks, "La Economía de la Coca," 21–22.

Table 3.8   Number of Workers Employed in the Coca-Cocaine Industry by Sector in 1990

	Franks	Percent	Aguiló	Percent
Growers	122,000	58.9	300,000	65.7
Buyers	6,725	3.2	74,250	16.3
Carriers	45,000	21.7	40,000	8.8
Paste refiners	9,000	4.3	20,000	4.4
Stompers	22,500	10.9	22,500	4.9
Traffickers	2,000	1.0	—	—
Total	207,225	100.0	456,750	100.0

Sources: Franks, "La economía de la coca," 23 (Table 6); and Federico Aguiló, "Movilidad espacial y movilidad social generada por el narcotráfico," in Efectos del narcotráfico, Baldivia et al., eds. (La Paz: ILDIS, 1988), 68.

Table 3.9   Estimates of the Number of Workers Employed in the Coca-Cocaine Industry

Study	Year for Estimate	Number Employed	Percentage of Economically Active Population
Franks[a]	1989	207,000	12.0
Aguiló[b]	1987?	456,000	26.6
USAID[c]	1990	243,000	13.5
U.S. Embassy[d]	1989	138,000–143,000	8.2
	1990	145,000–150,000	8.2
Bolivian government[e]	1990	300,000	16.7
De Franco and Godoy[f]	1990	120,000	6.7

Sources: a. Franks, "La economía de la coca," 23 (Table 6). Franks's own figure for the percentage of EAP is 9.5 percent because he includes the 207,000 employed in the coca-cocaine industry.

b. Federico Aguiló, "Movilidad," 68. It is not clear from the study which year Aguiló is referring to. The Aguiló figure should more reasonably be taken as a percentage of the total Bolivian population (around seven million), which would give a percentage figure for EAP of 6.5 percent.

c. USAID Update, "Estimates of the Economic Impact."

d. U.S. Embassy, mimeo, La Paz, 1991.

e. UDAPE, Estrategia nacional de desarrollo alternativo, 31.

f. Mario De Franco and Ricardo Godoy, "The Economic Consequences," 13.

Table 3.10   The Coca-Cocaine Economies in Bolivia, Peru, and Colombia

	Bolivia	Peru	Colombia
Hectares under cultivation (1990)[a]	50,300	121,300	40,100
Production of coca (1990 mt)[b]	116,000	138,000	32,000
Total value added (U.S. $millions)[c]	695–911	498–1,219	1,127
Value added as percentage of GDP[d]	15.6–20.5	1.5–3.7	2.9
Income remaining in country (U.S. $millions)[e]	179–216	382–942	645
Income (5) as percentage of legal exports[f]	19.4–23.5	14.3–35.4	16.8
Workers employed in coca-cocaine[g]	207,000	165,000–279,000	40,000
Workers as percentage of EAP[h]	6.7–12.0	2.7–4.5	0.4

Notes: a. Source is U.S. State Department, Bureau of International Narcotics Matters, *INCSR,* 21.

b. Source for Peru and Colombia is U.S. State Department, *INCSR,* for Bolivia Table 3.1.

c. The Bolivian figure is for 1990; the Colombian and Peruvian figures for 1988. The source for Bolivia is Table 3.4; for Peru, from Elena Alvarez, "The Illegal Coca Production in Peru: A Preliminary Assessment of Its Economic Impact," paper presented at the Project Hemispheric Cooperation for the Prevention of Drug Abuse and Traffic at the Institute of the Americas and University of California (April 19–21, 1990), 21. It should be noted that these are Alvarez's lower estimates of the range. Source for Colombia is from Hernando Gómez, "*El impacto del narcotráfico en el desarrollo de la America Latina: Aspectos económicos*" (La Paz, CERID, 1991), 7. Other authors argue that Gómez's figures for value added and income staying in the country are low. See F. Thoumi, *The Political Economy of Colombia and the Growth of the Illegal Psychoactive Drugs Industry* (forthcoming, 1994, Lynne Rienner Publishers), chapter 6. Thoumi suggests as much as U.S. $2 billion for the amount staying in Colombia.

d. The Bolivian figure assumes a legal GDP for 1990 of U.S. $4,453 million. Source for Peru is Alvarez, "Illegal Coca Production," 21; and for Colombia, author's calculation assumes Colombian GDP in 1988 of U.S. $39,090 million.

e. The Bolivian figure is for 1990; the Colombian and Peruvian figures for 1988. The source for Bolivia is Table 3.6; for Peru, the source is Alvarez, "Illegal Coca Production," 20; for Colombia, Gómez, "El impacto," 13.

f. For Bolivia, assuming legal export figure (1990) of U.S. $921 million, and for Colombia (1988) of U.S. $3,841 million. The Peruvian figure is taken from Alvarez, "Illegal Coca Production," p. 20.

g. Source for Bolivia, chart 3.8; for Peru, Alvarez, "Illegal Coca Production," 21; and for Colombia, de Franco and Godoy, "Economic Consequences," table 1.

h. Source for Bolivia, Table 3.9; for Peru, Alvarez, "Illegal Coca Production," 21; for Colombia, *Statistical Yearbook for Latin America and the Caribbean* (ECLAC, Santiago, 1991), 712.

. . . 4 . . .

The Costs and Benefits

It is clear from the discussion in Chapter 3 that despite recent falls in value, the coca-cocaine economy continues to provide enormous benefits in the form of employment, local income for peasant farmers, and large infusions of coca-dollars into Bolivia's national economy. As one North American professor has summarized its attractions, the "drug industry is labor intensive, decentralized, growth-pole oriented, cottage-industry promoting and foreign exchange earning—desirable features of rural development in economically stagnating areas."[1]

The totality of benefits is unrivaled by any other sector of the formal economy (although by the early 1990s the booming informal economy, if taken as a whole, probably had overtaken the size and opportunities offered by the coca-cocaine economy).

But counterbalancing these benefits are a series of costs for the economy. They include an overvalued exchange rate, increasing imports (partly injuring local industry), a boom in financial speculation, and, according to some analysts, a decline in staple food crop output. Moreover, there is little evidence that the coca-cocaine economy enjoys close backward and forward linkages with the rest of the economy, except at a regional level (around Cochabamba). Nor do the Bolivian traffickers who garner most of the benefits from the drug trade invest much of their proceeds in productive industries. There are costs, too, for Bolivian society as a whole, with increasing ecological destruction (caused more by cocaine production than coca growing), more corruption of the body politic, and perhaps an increase in domestic drug addiction.

The Economic Effects

Many observers have argued that the degree of Bolivia's reliance on the coca-cocaine economy not only helped to avert a major social collapse (or explosion) in the early 1980s (there *was* a virtual economic and political collapse), but has, at the very least, facilitated the country's most radical restructuring of its economy this century.[2]

Bolivians will need few reminders of the depths of recession in the early 1980s (already outlined in Chapter 1). The coca-cocaine economy clearly acted as a huge social safety net, absorbing labor from the collapsed mining and industrial sectors and replacing large portions of the dollars previously generated by minerals, gas, and other exports. But coca and cocaine production also provided critical, and perhaps decisive, support for the success of the stabilization program initiated by the MNR (Movimiento Nacionalista Revolucionario) government in 1985, and maintained by the Acuerdo Patriótico (Patriotic Accord) under Paz Zamora from August 1989.

In 1985, Dr. Víctor Paz Estenssoro, previously best known as one of the main architects of Bolivia's nationalist revolution in 1952, embarked on a sharp break with his and the country's statist past and introduced a free-market experiment the like of which Bolivians had never experienced.[3] Within a fortnight of assuming the presidency in August, Paz Estenssoro passed a decree, no. 21060, which sought to stabilize the exchange rate, remove almost all price controls and state subsidies, drastically cut the public sector wage bill and public spending on health and education, and lift most restrictions on financial operations. These and later policies attempted to curb hyperinflation and a huge fiscal deficit as a prelude to the restoration of the goodwill of the International Monetary Fund and other financial institutions.[4]

Two of the key goals of the model were tight control of the money supply and a stable exchange rate, which would attract the local and foreign private investment the government felt was eventually needed to replace the state's dominant role with the neoliberal model. From 1972 to 1981, monetary emission, or M1, represented around 11 percent of GDP. By 1986, the first year the model was implemented, this had been slashed to around 5 percent, a level which by 1990 had fallen even further, to 3.4 percent (520 million bolivianos, compared to a GDP of 1,500 million bolivianos). Bolivia continues to register very low levels of money in circulation by regional standards. The underground coca economy gave the government and the Central Bank more flexibility in monetary policy because of the foreign exchange it generated.[5]

The ready availability of cocaine dollars also helped to finance imports at a level way beyond the country's formal capacity to import, which is generated by official exports and other capital flows. Export prices, primarily of tin and gas, slumped in the second half of the 1980s. From a positive trade balance of nearly U.S. $270 million in 1984, the country ran up a negative balance of between $30–$220 million over the next four years. Over the same period, the current account balance fell to between U.S. $180 million and $404 million, compared to a figure of $133 million in 1984.

It is of course difficult to assess how many of the cocaine dollars entered the formal economy through the Central Bank or private banking system. Decree no. 21060 of August 1985 set up a system of free trading in dollars through daily auctions at the *Bolsín* (currency market) of the Central Bank, which allowed the bank to compete with the free-market rate for dollars. The government also passed several measures designed to facilitate the repatriation of dollars, including a tax amnesty and a relaxation of the bank's disclosure requirements. Around twenty "open windows" were set up at private banks throughout the country; banks did not have to ask any questions as to the origin of any dollars deposited or traded.[6] Many economists and opposition politicians maintain that this policy was a deliberate attempt to capture legally the revenue from the cocaine economy, a charge denied by the government at the time.

The "Errors and Omissions" column of the Central Bank's current account show a positive contribution of U.S. $282 million in 1986, $220 million in 1987, and $65 million in 1988, before the column fell into the red for the following three years. Anibal Aguilar, the subsecretary for alternative development in the Paz Estenssoro administration, reckoned that the "Errors and Omissions" column represented around 40–45 percent of the total value of the coca-cocaine economy, although most experts are reluctant to hazard such a guess.[7] Other economists have argued that between 15 and 25 percent of the U.S. $1,489 million sold through the Central Bank's Bolsín from September 1985 to November 1988 could have come from coca-dollars (the rest coming from export earnings and donations). At its peak, as much as U.S. $20 million could have entered the private banking system every month, an amount sufficient to cause an economic collapse if the flow had been interrupted.[8]

However, the influx of coca-dollars also probably contributed to an overvaluation of the boliviano, a phenomenon known as "Dutch disease" (when one of a country's exports experiences a boom in production or a period of exceptionally good international prices).[9] De Franco and Godoy suggest that in 1987–1988 the parity exchange rate was 22 percent lower than the average rate during the 1970s.[10] The overvalued exchange rate contributed to making exports (and particularly nontraditional exports) uncompetitive, increasing imports, and thereby prejudicing local manufacturing industry. The participation of the industrial sector in GDP fell from 14.9 percent in 1979 to 12.1 percent in 1985 (although it recovered to 13.2 percent by 1990). The severity of the recession, the lowering of import tariffs to 20 percent, and high local interest rates caused the closure of many factories. But the overvalued exchange rate made it even more difficult for Bolivian light industries to compete with the flood of imports, particularly textiles and shoes from Brazil and Chile. The only sector to increase its participation in GDP was agriculture, which grew from 18.4 percent in 1980 to 22.4 percent in 1988, despite the drought and flooding during the period. Coca cultivation was the main reason for the increase.

De Franco and Godoy have run a computable general equilibrium (CGE) model to assess the direct and indirect effects of cocaine production on the rest of the economy.[11] Their main conclusion is that a 10 percent increase in cocaine production raises GDP by 2 percent and lowers unemployment by 6 percent. The CGE model also suggests that as cocaine exports expand, real incomes increase for nearly all social groups (and not just coca farmers), as the higher aggregate demand in the whole of the economy strengthens the commerce, construction, and service sectors.[12]

The results of the model show that main multiplier effect of coca-cocaine production derives from this increase in income and aggregate demand and not from close backward or forward linkages with the rest of the economy. The production of coca and cocaine needs mainly land and large amounts of cheap labor, but few other inputs except chemicals (most of which are imported).[13] They calculate that each dollar of cocaine exported only requires the purchase of U.S. $0.03 of goods and services from the noncocaine economy. This compares with the U.S. $0.23 required by the commercial agricultural, mining, manufacturing, and construction sectors.[14]

The backward and forward linkages may be as small as the model suggests, but at the regional level they are certainly more pronounced. In the department of Cochabamba, the boom in coca production was such that by 1987 it represented 63 percent of total agricultural production. The well-being of the local economy of the city of Cochabamba, which has a population of 300,000 and is the metropolis nearest to the main coca-growing district of the Chapare, is intricately tied to the fortunes of coca production. The effect of the boom period in the early 1980s on the regional economy has been clearly documented.[15] Much of the growth of the city was a direct result of its role as one of the main urban centers where narco-dollars were being invested, particularly in the development of urban real estate. The extra money stimulated the service economy, but also caused the local inflation rate to be higher than in the rest of the country.

There were sharp production increases in the few locally produced inputs into the cocaine trade, most notably toilet paper (used for filtering and drying paste), kerosene, and initially sulfuric acid (later mostly imported).[16] At least in the mid-1980s, 60 percent of the national toilet paper production was reported to have ended up in the Chapare, providing jobs for 2,000 people who transported and sold it.[17] The state oil and gas company, YPFB (Yacimientos Petrolíferos Fiscales Bolivianos), was said to be inadvertently providing 10,000 liters of kerosene daily for the local drug industry, and probably continues to do so, although at reduced volumes (particularly as kerosene is rapidly being replaced by gasoline in the paste-making stages).

When the coca price slumped in late 1989 and 1990, civic leaders in Cochabamba grew extremely concerned about the recessionary effects on the local economy. Construction work was slowing down, nightclubs were reported to have lost much of their clientele, and local markets reported a sharp drop in general sales. Within the Chapare, the slump caused not only a large exodus of partidarios and casual laborers but also a drastic fall in beer sales, demand for local transport, and the number of people eating at local restaurants.[18] The coca minirecession was even reported to have spread as far as La Paz, where one factory making plastic bags (used in the later stages of cocaine production) was said to have registered a 40 percent drop in output.[19]

Cochabamba's economy has come to revolve around the coca-cocaine economy, but there is little evidence that the cocaine industry in itself stimulates much increased production on a national scale. Only a small proportion of the coca-cocaine dollars are probably spent in Bolivia, and those that are probably do not promote much increased output of Bolivian goods or produce, except possibly food crops in some areas (see p. 63).

Coca farmers earn such a small proportion of the final value of their product that the meager increase in their earnings has not had a major impact on the national economy. Local evidence suggests that they put any extra income into short-term savings companies, small-scale land and housing investments outside the Chapare, and, in boom periods such as the early 1980s, into imported durable consumer goods such as electrical appliances, bicycles, watches, and motorcycles.[20] As described in Chapter 1, there is little evidence of much wealth being left in the Chapare, which remains a pocket of rural poverty similar to those found throughout Latin America.[21]

Drinking water, electricity, and basic health services have been remarkable for their absence until recently, when the UNDCP started some small-scale health and water schemes and a huge electrification program (see p. 130). This is partly because the local regional development corporations receive no tax revenue from coca or cocaine production. As described earlier, local coca sindicatos do recover a small amount of revenue from collecting and administering taxes on coca income. For example, a locally elected council in the town of Eterazama in the Chapare has used this money to dig wells and a sewage system and open a new secondary school. But even here, "insect-infested open sewers run along each side of the main dirt track; tuberculosis, yellow fever, parasites and hepatitis are rampant."[22] In general, the Chapare is a sorry story of bad sanitation, bad hygiene, and insufficient housing as well as high infant mortality, severe malnutrition, and numerous dropouts from junior and senior schools.

It is obviously difficult to ascertain with any accuracy where the few Bolivian "big fish" described in Chapter 2 put the proceeds of their businesses. But the little evidence that there is suggests that they prefer conspicuous but limited consumption of luxury imported goods, which has little or no impact on national production. Some authors have suggested that the close links between the cocaine barons and cotton, cattle, and sugar producers in the Beni and Santa Cruz departments in the late 1970s meant that some profits have been ploughed back into legal agricultural activities.[23]

However, a study carried out for the Subsecretariat of Alternative Development in 1988 suggests that between 55 and 60 percent of the money earned by local traffickers leaves the country, either to be deposited in private bank accounts (in Panama, Switzerland, or the Cayman Islands) or to finance the purchase of precursor chemicals from neighboring countries, Europe, and the United States. The remainder that stays, the study argues, is used to buy coca, acquire goods used for the manufacture of cocaine, pay off officials, and import luxury consumer goods.[24]

Roberto Suárez Gómez undoubtedly used his considerable wealth to boost his popularity in his hometown of Santa Ana de Yacuma in the north of the Beni.[25] Given that he was already a traditional latifundista and owner of extensive lands in the area, he may have used some of his illicit gains to extend his ranching activities. But there is overwhelming evidence that Suárez Gómez must have spent a sizable chunk of his fortune on influencing political developments. He was widely believed to have helped to finance the 1978 campaign of Gen. Juan Pereda, the official candidate of Gen. Hugo

Bánzer, the military ruler from 1971 to 1978 and currently the head of the right-wing ADN (*Accíon Democrática Nacionalista*) Suárez Gómez's favorite son, Robbie, was quoted as saying his father had "used a little of his money in favor of . . . Juan Pereda."[26]

There is also strong evidence to suggest Suárez Gómez helped to finance the coup of Gen. Luis García Meza two years later in July 1980, which is widely known as "the cocaine coup" (see p. 27). One version of events maintains that Suárez Gómez offered García Meza U.S. $1.3 million to launch the coup as traffickers felt more protected by military governments than by elected civilian leaders. His condition was apparently that Colonel Luis Arce Gómez, a relation of Suárez Gómez well known for his connections with the drug business, should be made minister of the interior responsible for antidrug operations.[27] After the collapse of the García Meza regime a year later, Suárez Gómez kept close links with leading political figures throughout the 1980s. The so-called "narco-video" and "narco-cassette" affairs of 1988–1989 showed that he was hardly a casual acquaintance of leading right-wing civilian politicians (see p. 73).

By the time of his arrest in December 1990 in Los Angeles, Suárez Gómez's nephew and reputed successor, Techo de Paja, had built up an impressive array of properties in Bolivia and the United States. He was arrested in a luxury nineteen-bedroom mansion in San Marino (valued at U.S. $11 million), and later discovered to have properties worth $9 million in the United States and $30 million in the Santa Cruz and Beni departments.[28] He also owned a restaurant, discotheque, and supermarket chain appropriately named "number one" in Santa Cruz. The contents of one of the mansions near Santa Cruz included fine carpets, expensive marble throughout, paintings, and swimming pools, which perhaps explain where much of his surplus cash was directed. Another major outlay must have been paying off a large number of officials.[29]

A close ally of Techo de Paja was said to be Carmelo "Meco" Domínguez, who was arrested in Santa Cruz in a large drug bust in September 1990 and sentenced in late 1991 to fifteen years' imprisonment. At the time of his arrest he was regarded as one of Bolivia's top three traffickers. Again the evidence suggests that real estate was his chosen investment area, as a number of properties (including an exclusive discotheque) were seized at the time of his capture.[30]

Local traffickers around Santa Ana de Yacuma (which the DEA in 1990 regarded as the key center of cocaine trafficking in the Beni), also invested a significant proportion of their income on conspicuous consumption. Journalists accompanying a DEA-organized raid on Santa Ana in June 1991 saw the luxury housing of a number of top traffickers, including Oscar Roca Suárez, Hugo Rivero Villavicencio, and Erwin Guzmán. The standard of their housing, swimming pools, and music systems far outshone anything their poorer neighbors could boast.

In summary, until traffickers publish their detailed biographies, it seems safe to assume that the "big bucks" were put back into the cocaine industry, directed towards real estate both at home and abroad or other forms of conspicuous consumption, or used to bribe politicians and local officials. In areas such as Santa Ana where the control of the state is weak and local patronage systems strong, traffickers could muster considerable local support by judicious small-scale investments in infrastructure, local TV and radio stations, and other forms of entertainment. But there is little evidence of traffickers making large-scale investments in other, more productive sectors of the legal economy. In short, in the 1980s the coca-cocaine industry provided a safety valve for the social cost of restructuring, significant increases in income for thousands of poor peasants and workers, and vast profits for a few traffickers at the top—but little long-term sustainable development.

Financial Speculation

Cocaine dollars have undoubtedly not only fueled isolated conspicuous consumption but also have stimulated the contraband economy and financial speculation, already given plenty of scope by the neoliberal economic model. A common form of legalizing or laundering cocaine dollars was to buy expensive electronic goods such as televisions, hi-fi systems, and video recorders in centers such as Panama City, import them, and then sell them at prices often below the purchase price. Stalls at markets such as Miamicito in La Paz and La Cancha in Cochabamba were, until recently, stacked high with such equipment.

Money could also be laundered (to a much lesser extent) by the importation of large volumes of cheaper items such as canned food, textiles, shoes, and plastic goods from Peru, Argentina, Chile, and Brazil, all of which have been readily available in local markets since 1985. Local chambers of commerce representing small and large industrial companies frequently complained of the negative impact of the flood of cheap goods onto the national market, which, they said, was often a way of legalizing money earned from coca-cocaine production.[31]

Increased financial speculation in the 1980s and early 1990s may also have been a by-product of the wash of cocaine dollars, although it is often difficult to distinguish the legitimate placing of dollars in high-yielding dollar bank accounts from the illicit laundering of narco-dollars. Government macroeconomic policies were designed to attract foreign capital back into the country by opening up the economy and liberalizing capital markets with few controls over the financial sector.

By mid-1991 deposits in the private banks had climbed to over U.S. $1 billion (of which around 85 percent were held in dollars rather than in bolivianos), a steady increase from a low of around $500 million in mid-1989. The main attraction of such accounts was the high annual interest rate of around 14 percent on dollars, a highly competitive rate by regional standards. Government ministers maintained that the money trickling back represented increased confidence from investors who had, according to World Bank estimates, removed U.S. $2 billion from Bolivia in the late 1970s and early 1980s. But cocaine dollars may have composed a significant part of it.[32]

However, perhaps the most startling—but least documented—indirect effect of the cocaine economy was the boom in financial speculation through small-scale *inmobiliarias* (building societies, or, in effect, savings societies), particularly in Cochabamba. By mid-1991, 40,000 depositors had entrusted between U.S. $100 million and $120 million to seven of these companies, which had emerged virtually from nowhere in the late 1980s.[33] The largest—and most notorious—of these was called Finsa (Firma Integral de Servicios Arévalo).[34]

Finsa first appeared in 1986 in the city of Oruro, as a radio-taxi company owned by the Arévalo family, who were reported to be small-time mechanics by profession. In 1989, Finsa began to expand (apparently with the help of a U.S. $30,000 inheritance from an uncle to the family) and could soon boast in Cochabamba alone not just a radio taxi service but a discotheque, a TV station, a hotel, a furniture factory, an air-taxi service, a travel agency, a construction company, and a financial interest in at least one major football club.

Perhaps not surprisingly, this attracted the attention of the antidrug police, who in February 1991 carried out a "narco-test" on two light aeroplane belonging to the family and discovered traces of cocaine aboard.[35] Two of the brothers, Nelson and Eddy, promptly disappeared but were later arrested near the border with Brazil. Finsa closed down its operations, leaving more than 20,000 depositors with little chance of recovering the U.S. $56 million they had entrusted to the company over the previous three years.[36] What had attracted such a rapid buildup of capital was a *monthly* interest rate of between 5 and 6 percent, which until its crash Finsa managed to meet. In fact, Finsa even paid depositors their first return a month in advance.

After (but not before) the fall of Finsa, antidrug officials and government ministers concurred that the only economic activity that could have generated such spectacular returns was cocaine trafficking. Some officials called Finsa a facade for laundering the cocaine dollars of two well-known local drugs barons, while press articles appeared that linked the pilot of the Arévalo planes with the same drug traffickers. Most commentators agreed that this type of rapid turnover of large amounts of dollars through Finsa fitted neatly the requirements of the cocaine business (which needs large amounts of ready dollars in cash at short notice). However, it was never actually proved that the Arévalo brothers were directly linked to cocaine trafficking.

Top police chiefs, senior politicians, at least one retired colonel, and members of the country's best-known folk music group (Kjarkas) were all known to have invested considerable sums of money in Finsa. At least one of the above had deposited more than half-a-million dollars. At the other end of the scale were thousands of small depositors—particularly resettled miners, sacked factory workers, and coca growers who had received some compensation for eradicating their coca—who had entrusted Finsa with their life savings of between 100 and 1,000 dollars. Some small-scale depositors even borrowed money from the formal banking system to receive a higher return from Finsa. When the crash came, hundreds of small depositors regularly organized angry demonstrations in Cochabamba's main square, demanding government intervention. On one occasion they even gave the Arévalos a hero's welcome back from Brazil, in the mistaken belief they were going to receive their money back.

In the early hours of September 30, the day the Arévalos had promised to start returning money to the small depositors, Nelson Arévalo, Finsa's president, was found shot dead in his car. The police version was that Arévalo paid one of his guards to shoot him (because he didn't have the courage to do it himself), while Nelson's surviving brother, Eddy, accused one of Finsa's creditors. At the time of writing, the depositors are still waiting for their money.[37]

The tragedy of Finsa—for the owners and small-time depositors at least—was principally a product of the supreme liquidity created by the coca-cocaine circuit. The government never pushed particularly hard to control the activities of Finsa and other companies like it until Finsa crashed. Indeed, there were allegations that the superintendent of banks had himself received large sums of money either to ignore or to legalize Finsa's operations.[38]

The ripple effects of Finsa's demise spread far and wide: One local candidate of the MNR had to stand down following accusations that he had acted as an intermediary in trying to legalize Finsa's activities. With the closure of the operations of Finsa and other inmobiliarias, Cochabamba's economy slumped. The local head of the chamber of commerce complained that at least U.S. $2 million a month and possibly as much as $5 million had been taken out of the economy as a result.[39] Some commentators even blamed Finsa's collapse for the slowdown in coca eradication in 1991. It was pointed out that U.S. $2,000 (the sum given to coca growers for eradicating 1 hectare of coca) deposited in Finsa had yielded a monthly stipend of around $115—not a bad salary by Bolivian standards—and an important compensation for the regular income from coca in better days.

Food Production

There is considerable debate whether the increase in coca and cocaine production has adversely affected the production of food crops. Those who maintain that it has, or that it will,[40] argue that coca's high demand for land and particularly labor either causes coca to replace other crops and reduces their output, or causes labor shortages by reducing the supply of highland laborers. UDAPE calculates that the hectares covered by all crops other than coca declined by 110,000 (or 8 percent) between 1985 and 1987, although it is not made clear whether this is entirely due to increased coca cultivation.[41] And Kevin Healy quotes reports of labor shortages for the production of potatoes and corn in the Cochabamba valley and sugar cane and rice in Santa Cruz during the 1985 coca-leaf harvests.[42]

The movement of large numbers of laborers into the coca-cocaine economy certainly has the potential to affect the production of other food crops, due to the peculiar structure of Bolivian agricultural society. The role of peasant small-plot agriculture is more important in national food production and commercial crop production than in other Latin American countries. Despite discriminatory credit and technical assistance policies, peasants still account for well over half the value of agricultural production.[43]

However, de Franco and Godoy maintain that expanding cocaine exports has not adversely affected food production.[44] They argue that although the growth of the cocaine industry attracts laborers from traditional agriculture, it also increases incomes and therefore demand for food. Moreover, they suggest that the number of laborers in traditional agriculture probably remained constant because of the vast reservoir of workers.

Official statistics throughout Latin America for the production of individual food crops are notoriously suspect, so the following figures should not be taken as gospel. But figures from INE[45] suggest that national production of maize and potatoes—the staple diet of low-income groups—did decline from 1980 to 1990. Potato production fell from nearly 800,000 tonnes to under 600,000 tonnes, and that of maize from around 400,000 tonnes to under 300,000. Wheat, which is regarded as being more for middle class consumption, held steady at around 60,000 tonnes. Rice, cassava, and bananas, though, have improved over the same period: rice from under 100,000 tonnes to over 200,000; cassava from 200,000 tonnes to over 300,000; and bananas from under 300,000 tonnes to over 400,000.

A downward tendency in the production of some crops is supported by recent studies by the World Bank and a Bolivian nongovernmental organization, CEDLA (Centro de Estudios para el Desarrollo Laboral y Agrario). The World Bank report shows that in the latter part of the decade the production of maize, wheat, potatoes, onions, sugar cane, and alfalfa remained considerably below the average for the period 1980–1985; and that total agricultural production fell by 17 percent from 1985 to 1988 and in 1988 remained 15 percent below the 1980–1985 average.[46] The CEDLA study found that if coca is removed from a list of twenty-two agricultural products, total agricultural production grew at an annual rate of only 1.4 percent from 1985 to 1988 (compared to a population growth rate of around 2.5 percent). If other export crops like soya and coffee were also excluded, then the aggregate fall for national food production was 4.1 percent over the same period.[47]

CEDLA's study also supports the INE figures that rice, cassava, and banana production increased over the same period. Healy points out that it is impossible to tell whether these increases have taken place actually in the Chapare or are a result of increased migration to lowland areas and a moving agricultural frontier.[48] Other figures from INE suggest that in the department of Cochabamba, the relative importance of production of staple crops such as cereals, fruit, and vegetables[49] dropped 50 percent between 1980 and 1987. Within the Chapare this drop was even more pronounced as coca increased its participation from 66 percent in 1980 to 92.5 percent in 1987; and the share of rice, cassava, oranges, and bananas dropped correspondingly. (What is missing from these data is whether the production of these crops declined in absolute terms.)

It is difficult to pinpoint to what extent increased coca cultivation contributed to the general stagnation of the rest of the agricultural sector in the latter half of 1980s and affected food production.

Declines in food crop production can be explained equally well by worsening environmental conditions, reduction in soil nutrients, lack of credit, high interest rates for credit, land distribution and pricing, low public expenditure in the agricultural sector, and a preference for increased agricultural imports and food aid over food self-sufficiency and self-reliance.

The neglect of the food sector did not begin with Paz Estenssoro's neoliberal model, although opponents of the model say it was probably exacerbated by it. They point out that trade liberalization (which reduced import tariffs), combined with expanded contraband trade (due both to the laundering of cocaine dollars and the general increase in unemployment), have resulted in a flood of imported agricultural goods with which peasants have been hard-pressed to compete.[50] The removal of fuel subsidies also made transport costs soar, worsening Bolivian peasants' historical problem of coping with mountainous and tropical terrain (where only 37 percent of the national road system is open all the year round). Bolivia's overvalued exchange rate, in part due to the influx of cocaine dollars, certainly did not help peasants to compete with imported food products.

The generally high level of population fluidity between the Chapare and the highland areas would seem to suggest that there never was a serious shortage of labor affecting food output in the altiplano. The main reason for wheat's stagnant performance over the last decade could have been the large donations of wheat through the PL-480 program from the U.S. government, rather than coca production. And disappointing potato and maize figures probably have more to do with competition from abroad (particularly, in the case of potatoes, from Peru) and seasonal factors than any scarcity of labor. Rice, cassava, and banana production did increase on a national level, but it is possible to argue that it would have increased more if it were not for coca production or that improved rural incomes (from coca) stimulated the demand.

The Impact on the Environment

The boom in coca cultivation—and more particularly, its processing into cocaine—is widely believed to have had a negative impact on the environment due to increased deforestation (and associated soil erosion), the dumping of precursor chemicals in streams and rivers, and the use of pesticides to improve production.[51] However, the absence of detailed studies on Bolivia, in part a product of the risks involved in collecting data, makes it difficult to have much more than an impressionistic view of the degree of ecological destruction.[52]

Coca in itself is not generally regarded as harmful to the land or to the environment. A recent study of the Chapare carried out by independent scientists working for USAID concluded, "*as a crop* [their emphasis] coca's effects on the environment seem average or even benign, especially in comparison with other crops that are grown in the region."[53] Similarly, a study of coca plots in the village of Rio Blanco, near Huancane in the zone of South Yungas, observed that coca there (where it is grown on steep terracing) actually helped to control serious land erosion, especially where there is a high percentage of stones or rocks in the soil.[54] The study also suggested that in the long term coca can contribute to recovering land fertility in this area, whereas other subtropical crops extract many more nutrients from the soil.

However, it should be pointed out that farmers in the Yungas tend to use well-tried, traditional methods of growing coca, whereas many of the farmers in the Chapare are recent arrivals who do not have much experience in tropical agriculture. They often apply large quantities of pesticides in an area that is more ecologically fragile than the Yungas. Surveys of the Chapare indicate that a very high number of farmers (89 percent) say they use pesticides to protect the coca plantations, and 15 percent say they use fertilizers.[55]

The search for land to grow coca creates a more serious problem: It extends the agricultural frontier at a rapid pace as farmers chop down or burn down forests to establish new coca fields.[56] As has already been observed, most of the increase in coca production has occurred because of more land being planted with coca and not because of increases in coca yields from already existing plots. In Peru, it is calculated that 700,000 hectares of forest—or 10 percent of all Peru's deforestation in the last fifty years—have been cleared to grow 200,000 hectares of coca.[57] Studies of the Chapare suggest that large areas of forest there, too, are being cleared to maintain relatively small areas of agricultural production.[58] Of particular concern, too, is the rapid increase in the number of colonists entering the Parque Isiboro-Secure, a national park that straddles the Chapare and the southern part of the Beni department. Environmental experts calculate that more than 15,000 hectares of virgin forest in the Isiboro-Secure have been cleared to grow coca.[59]

Farmers in the Chapare are estimated to clear between 2 and 6 hectares of land for every one in production.[60] Assuming a (low) peak figure of 52,000 hectares of coca under cultivation in the Chapare (see Table 1.1), and an average 2.5 hectares under cultivation with coca and other crops, this would mean that between 260,000 and 780,000 hectares have been cleared as a result of the boom in coca production. This would represent a significant chunk of the 250,000 hectares of forest estimated to be lost annually in recent years due to timber extraction, colonization, and cattle ranching.[61] However, it is perhaps worth comparing these figures to an agroexport project funded by the World Bank and known as *Tierras Bajas* (lowlands), which aims to clear land in the Santa Cruz department to grow soya and wheat. An estimated 300,000 hectares are likely to be affected.[62]

Before the arrival of the colonists and timber extractors, the Chapare was believed to contain some of Bolivia's tallest, densest, and most diverse forest with more than 1,000 species of trees.[63] These primary forests are apparently still intact on the steep upper slopes, but much of the rest of the lowland Chapare has been converted into secondary forests. Such has been the volume of new migrants to the area that some of the lower part of the upper slopes are now being cultivated, which is bound to cause greater soil erosion.

Perhaps the most damaging effect has resulted from the processing, rather than the growing, of coca. As already described, extracting cocaine from coca requires a mixture of precursor chemicals, including lime, sodium carbonate, sulfuric acid, and kerosene. Although only moderately toxic, kerosene has severe consequences for local flora and fauna, especially plankton, and therefore affects the oxygen supply. Sulfuric acid, acetone, and hydrochloric acid are extremely destructive to the environment. Even toilet paper used in vast quantities can be harmful.[64]

A 1990 study by the largest Bolivian environmental pressure group, LIDEMA (La Liga de Defensa del Medio Ambiente), suggests that in 1988 more than 30,000 metric tonnes of toxic chemicals could have been discarded that year, mostly into nearby rivers or streams, in order to turn 127,000 tonnes of coca into the final product (see Table 4.1). The authors of the study strangely assume all the paste in the country is converted within Bolivia to HCL (weighing 483 tonnes), so the damage may be less. But it must be remembered that another 127,000 tonnes of saturated coca leaves were left to rot.

Moreover, the magnitude of the damage is multiplied by the dumping of the chemicals into streams (processing laboratories need a lot of water, so they are normally situated close to a water supply), which often serve as irrigation systems. The ecological degradation is not helped by antidrug police regularly dumping confiscated chemicals into rivers, although this practice is reported to be on the decline. Again, it is worth stressing the lack of precision over the real extent of the problem, but some observers claim the Chapare is already an ecological disaster, and could eventually be turned into a desert.[65]

Consumption

At the time of this writing, there were no authoritative data available on the level of drug consumption in Bolivia, although there is a general consensus that consumption has probably increased in recent years. Even the U.S. State Department, in its 1991 *International Narcotic Control Strategy Report*, recognized the absence of reliable figures.[66] It is a little surprising that a U.S. government body should do this, as many U.S.-funded studies of drug consumption patterns have been dismissed, particularly by Bolivian experts, as trying to give the impression that Bolivia has a serious cocaine addiction problem, which would in some way justify the use of U.S.-imposed policies to eradicate coca.[67]

The true picture has been obfuscated by political interests. Bolivian governments are at pains not to portray the country as a nation of drug consumers, while foreign governments and institutions often issue dire warnings that producer countries usually end up as significant user countries. However, most government officials do believe that there has been an increase in consumption during the 1980s, particularly of tobacco cigarettes mixed with cocaine base (usually known as *pitillos*) and cocaine itself. For example, the government organization CONAPRE (Consejo Nacional de Prevención Integral del Uso Indebido de Drogas) said in 1988 that consumption had increased from 1980 to 1988 by nearly 54 percent, a larger increase than that for base and cocaine production over the same period.[68]

But the report took pains to stress that the incidence of Bolivians who had tried a coca derivative was still low and, in the worst of cases, 1.7 percent of the population. CONAPRE contrasted this figure, which it described as being about the norm for Latin American countries, with what it said was a much higher incidence in the United States and Europe. It concluded that the problem was "incipient, but not overwhelming." A similar type of claim was made by Health Minister Joaquín Arce in 1987, when he said only 0.5 percent of the Bolivian population was addicted to drugs and that a mere 2 percent had tried drugs, compared to the 60 percent of citizens of industrialized countries[69] who had tried drugs.

It is illustrative to compare the Bolivian government figures with those found in an unofficial 1991 U.S. embassy report, which estimated that twenty tonnes of cocaine base were consumed every year in Bolivia (mostly in pitillos), equivalent to between 4 and 9 percent of the total production of base in 1990. The report claimed that 6–7 percent of the urban population uses at least one pitillo every day, which is a *very conservative figure* [my emphasis].[70]

More neutral observers are virtually unanimous in saying that the studies carried out so far—which are many—fall short in some way of giving an accurate figure, whether it be due to the small size of the sample, the methodologies used, the type of people questioned, or the funding for the study. For example, a recent comprehensive study of the problem of drug abuse in Santa Cruz—regarded, along with La Paz and Cochabamba, as one of the main centers of consumption—concludes that all the available data on drug addiction in the city are "insufficient, sporadic, and untrustworthy."[71]

The studies that have been done give a range of between 5,000 and 240,000 Bolivians who are habitual users of cocaine or pitillos in the whole of the country for the late 1980s.[72] The upper estimate of 240,000 shows a higher percentage of users in La Paz, Santa Cruz, Cochabamba, and Trinidad, which is probably an accurate picture of which towns are most affected by drug abuse. Many observers accept a more conservative figure of around 100,000, which would be equivalent to 1.4 percent of the population (of 7 million). This compares with the 1991 estimate by the National Institute on Drug Abuse of 855,000 North Americans who used cocaine once a week—equivalent to 0.3 percent of the population.[73]

Part of the problem is that in other countries, a principal method of collecting data is by interviewing drug users in rehabilitation centers, but there are very few of these in Bolivia. Another method, one used for supporting the view that Bolivian consumption is on the increase, is to monitor the number of telephone calls made to rehabilitation centers. CESE (Campaña Educativa Sobre Estupefacientes) has registered a significant increase of calls to its helpline service. CESE's director, Laura Valdivieso, said towards the end of 1989 that calls had increased from twenty per month in April 1988 to 500 per month, although she, too, was reluctant to venture a guess on the number of addicts.[74] The increase in calls could, of course, have been due to the better publicity about CESE's work rather than any increase in consumption.

There is also no conclusive evidence that coca derivatives are the most popular drug among vulnerable groups. A study by the Red Cross of more than 1,500 people living in La Paz in 1986 showed that marijuana was the most popular, although cocaine was the best known.[75] The same survey found that 10.4 percent had once tried a drug (of which forty-two were listed), and that habitual consumption (of all drugs) had increased to 1.60 percent from 1.04 percent in 1979–1980.

The same Red Cross study found that men ages seventeen to twenty-two were the most affected group, a finding broadly supported by a study of 150 participants of drug rehabilitation centers in Santa Cruz.[76] A survey carried out by the same group of researchers based at the Gabriel René Moreno University of more than 500 street children ages five to eighteen showed that 18 percent had tried some drug, but pitillos (22.1 percent) came second to clefa (glue-sniffing; 47.7 percent) and only just ahead of petrol (21.3 percent) and finally thinners (7.6 percent).[77]

These sorts of figures do present an alarming picture of drug abuse among street children, who are particularly apparent on the streets of Santa Cruz, Cochabamba, and Trinidad—the three most important urban centers associated with cocaine production and trafficking. Personal testimonies show the ready availability of cocaine base and other drugs at cheap prices on the streets of these cities.[78] And it is hard to deny that the availability of coca derivatives, particularly in Cochabamba, has probably exacerbated consumption patterns, particularly among younger males.[79] But it is also the case that Bolivia would probably have a drug-user problem whether or not it was a producer country. Urban life for young people in economically marginal areas of Santa Cruz, La Paz, and Cochabamba is plagued by many of the social problems—lack of employment and poor housing, health care, and schools, to name the most obvious—that would make children vulnerable anywhere in the world. And it is worth remembering that marijuana—in some studies, the most popular drug among young users—is not known to be grown in Bolivia.

Corruption

There is less uncertainty over drug-related corruption. The bribing of police, government, and judicial officials features strongly as one of the major costs of Bolivia's drugs trade in virtually every U.S. official document ever published on narcotics. Although corruption does not lend itself to exact quantification, one of the U.S. government reports is sufficiently bold to claim that

> U.S. and host government officials agreed that drug corruption is the single most significant obstacle to U.S. counter-narcotic efforts. Allegations of corruption ranged from the U.S.-provided equipment

to transport drugs or precursor chemicals to production sites, to the re-sale of seized coca products to traffickers following a raid.[80]

A DEA report in December 1989 was also brazen enough to assert that corruption in Bolivia was "a major factor at all levels," and that "all elements of the military are involved in drug trafficking to some extent and police, prosecutors and courts have been subject to corruption and intimidation."[81] Similarly, the annual U.S. State Department reports regularly bemoan the widespread corruption that every year continues to seriously hamper more effective enforcement and prosecution. In 1989, it was the navy, UMOPAR, and the judiciary that were targeted for criticism.[82] In 1990, the corruption was "widespread,"[83] while the 1991 report pointed out that no less than five top government and antidrug officials were sacked during the year for "ineptitude and suspicion of being involved in narcotics-related corruption" and complained that, despite the changes, "one corrupt official often replaces another."[84]

Few observers in and outside Bolivia deny that the power of drug money penetrates into every social and professional class in the country, including top government officials, the judiciary, the police, the armed forces, the media, top football clubs, the political parties, and no doubt many more. This is hardly surprising when the same social groups in countries far richer than Bolivia are rarely completely free from accusations of some sort of corruption. In 1990, a Bolivian soldier earned as a normal salary around U.S. $50 a month (with a $50 bonus from UMOPAR for good behavior), an army lieutenant colonel $300, a judge $300, and a member of congress $800. These figures compare with the U.S. $15,000 and more a drug trafficker could offer a judge in cash for a certain decision in court, or a local UMOPAR commander for turning a blind eye while light planes landed and took off in his area of control.[85] Needless to say, such payments offer immediate benefits to the poor struggling to earn a living wage, and a form of life assurance for the professional classes in a country where pension schemes are not the norm.

Some of the more notorious cases of drug-related corruption have reached the pages of the international press. The García Meza regime (1980–1981), clearly the most important example of state power being abused to protect and expand the narcotics trade, has been widely discussed. But within Bolivia, the Huanchaca scandal has received more attention than any other since it first surfaced in September 1986, when the internationally renown Bolivian scientist Noel Kempff Mercado was killed along with two of his colleagues after stumbling on a major cocaine factory in the northern part of the

Santa Cruz department. Six years later, the Bolivian parliament was still trying to assess the degree of government—and possibly DEA—protection of the drug trade implied by investigations into the case.[86] Countless, too, are the cases of top traffickers set free by judges, or mysteriously allowed out of prison for medical checkups, never to return.[87] And it came as something of a surprise in April 1991, when the local head of UMOPAR in Oruro, Lt. Col. Alberto Rabaza, apparently hung himself after it was revealed that he was one of the main organizers of a trafficking organization ferrying precursor chemicals to the Chapare from Chile. The surprise for many Bolivians was not that Lieutenant Colonel Rabaza was supplying chemicals instead of seizing them, but that he should feel sufficiently ashamed of his crime to end his life.

The extent of the connections between drug money and political parties has probably not received the attention it deserves, in part due to the ability of Bolivia's political class to close ranks when threatened by too close a scrutiny. The suspicion that top politicians were on the take from drug traffickers was confirmed in many people's minds in March 1991, when Interior Minister Guillermo Capobianco resigned following allegations by unnamed U.S. officials published in the international edition of the *Miami Herald* that he had received money from cocaine trafficking organizations. Capobianco, who was a close friend of President Paz Zamora and number three in the ruling MIR (Movimiento Institucional Revolucionario), denied the allegations but said he was resigning to protect Bolivia's national dignity. Opposition politicians criticized the fierce pressure the U.S. government exerted to secure Capobianco's removal but commented that the resignation suggested some degree of culpability.[88] It was of note that Capobianco never seriously proceeded with his threat to bring a libel case against the *Miami Herald.*

Senior U.S. drug officials speculated that Capobianco was part of a wider network of corrupt officials deliberately placed in key anti-drug posts, which included the head of UMOPAR and the head of the police. Col. Faustino Rico Toro lasted only a few days as UMOPAR's head in March 1991 after the U.S. led a campaign to get him removed, in part because of his past involvement with the García Meza regime as head of the Bolivian army intelligence branch. U.S. ambassador Robert Gelbard was said to have been so annoyed by the appointment of Colonel Rico Toro that he personally orchestrated a threat to suspend all nonhumanitarian aid to Bolivia, worth U.S. $100 million a year. The head of the police and a MIR appointee, Felipe Carvajal, also resigned at around the same time after being named in the *Miami Herald* article.[89]

In total, the government was forced to sack five top officials in 1991, including Rico Toro's successor, Gen. Elías Gutiérrez; and Javier Dipps, the national director of the Precursor Control Agency. Indeed, the extent of the corruption seemed to confirm the State Department's worst fears about the Paz Zamora government. As an internal memo written by the program officer of the State Department's International Narcotics Matters warned in 1990, President Paz Zamora had appointed "a number of corrupt officials to key antinarcotic roles," and when questioned by the U.S. ambassador, replied that "since most police were corrupt it didn't matter anyway."[90] Worse, at the time of writing none of the five sacked in 1991 had been investigated, let alone prosecuted, despite adequate provisions found in law 1008 for pursuing charges of narcotics-related corruption.

But it would be unfair to focus too much attention on MIR to the exclusion of others. The so-called "narco-video" and the subsequent "narco-cassette" scandals principally affected the right-wing National Democratic Action (ADN) party, headed by Gen. Hugo Banzer, who has himself been unable to stop the questions about his precise role in the cocaine boom in the late 1970s. In April 1988 the country was first treated on national television to the sight of two senior members of the ADN and a businessman chatting amicably with Roberto Suárez Gómez, the then "king of cocaine," in Suárez Gómez's house in 1985. An investigation carried out by the Judicial Commission of the Chamber of Deputies apparently put the scandal to rest when it pronounced in June that the motive of the meeting had been to discuss archaeological discoveries on land belonging to the Suárez Gómez family.

The subsequent publishing of the content of tapes of the conversations in the London *Independent* and in the Spanish newspaper *El País* suggested that the meetings, held before and after the general elections of July 1985, were not so innocuous. The voices of two of the three who appeared on the narco-video were clearly identifiable as those belonging to Alfredo Arce Carpio, a leading ADN deputy and former minister of the interior in the Banzer military regime from 1971–1978, and retired general Mario Vargas Salinas, minister of labor under Banzer (but expelled from the ADN after the narco-video scandal broke). Much of the conversation centered on how an ADN government would legally launder narco-dollars, in part through local development corporations, to help stabilize the economy, which was then suffering from hyperinflation. Other parts of the conversation suggested Banzer's political leanings were far from democratic, while Suárez Gómez's lawyer, José Antonio Ayala, states at one point that Suárez Gómez had been approached by politicians and military officers "a thousand times."[91]

Arce Carpio was forced to resign from the ADN soon after the scandal broke, in part because his original explanation that he had visited Suárez Gómez in his capacity as a free-lance journalist (when no one could trace anything he had ever published) patently failed to carry any weight. But MIR, ADN, and MNR hurriedly agreed to reject a request from left-wing parties to carry out any further investigations. As many observers pointed out, the three main parties seemed to have reached an unwritten accord that any investigation would have to be buried as a matter of political expediency because each main party had too much evidence against the others.[92] Such unabashed closing of the ranks by the political elite has deprived the Bolivian public of a thorough investigation into any of the allegations. A further obstacle to proving any links between drug money and politicians is a legal stipulation that no party has to reveal the source of its funds—despite an estimated U.S. $15 million to $20 million spent on campaigning in the 1989 elections, equivalent to $10 a vote.[93]

The weight of evidence strongly suggests that drug money regularly finds its way into the pockets of senior politicians and antidrug officials and that this is yet one more obstacle to more effective interdiction. Corruption of all shapes and sizes is probably more pervasive as a result of the coca-cocaine trade than it would have been if the country had been left to its more traditional forms of kickbacks, payoffs, and *coimas* (bribes). But some of the more alarmist statements—particularly from U.S. government officials—of the corrupting power of the Bolivian drug mafia and the threat they offer to democracy sit uneasily with Bolivia's ten years of multiparty democracy since 1982 (after a long period of military rule), a decade that coincides with a period when the value of the drug trade has never been so important to the economy. It may be that Bolivia could be traveling down the path of violence and scarcely unfettered traffickers' power, as witnessed in Colombia. But for the moment such scenarios are only a possibility, not a reality.[94]

Table 4.1   Discarded Materials Used in the Manufacture of Paste and Cocaine in 1988 (in tonnes except where stated)

	Total Precursors Used	Discarded for paste	for HCL	Total Discarded
Coca leaves	127,050	127,050	0	127,050
Sulfuric acid	5,877	278	31	309
Calcium sulfate	0	7,726	0	7,726
Sodium sulfate	0	1,579	75	1,655
Kerosene*	29,213	11,685	0	11,685
Calcium carbine	1,310	0	0	0
Lime	7,244	4,057	0	4,057
Sodium carbonate	1,348	294	11	306
Lavatory paper	6,550	6,550	0	6,550
Acetone/ether*	1,932	0	386	386
Toluene*	1,449	0	169	169
Hydrochloric* acid	217	0	18	18

* In thousands of liters.

Source: Adapted from C. Curi and C. Arze, *Estudio del impacto de los precursores en la producción de cocaína sobre el medio ambiente en Bolivia* (La Paz: USAID/Lidema, July 1990), Table 9.

Notes: The authors assume 1,310 tonnes of paste and 483 tonnes of HCL were manufactured in 1988. The first column shows the quantity of precursors needed to manufacture that amount of HCL, including the intermediate stages of paste and base. Columns 2 and 3 show the amount of chemicals discarded after the first and second stage of processing respectively, and column 4 gives the final total amount of discarded chemicals.

Some of the chemicals are used and transformed during the processing stages. So, for example, sulfuric acid is mixed with lime and sodium carbonate to form sodium and calcium sulfate, although more is needed for the final stage.

. . . 5 . . .
Policies to
Curb the Drug Trade

Legislation

The extent of Bolivia's economic dependence on the coca-cocaine industry for export earnings and employment is such that any effective disruption of it would cause huge economic dislocation and widespread social unrest. Successive governments have been the first to grasp the political implications of this truism and have therefore tended to put a low priority on any aggressive crackdown on the country's drug trade. Most of the major departures from this norm—the use of U.S. troops in 1986, the establishment of annual eradication targets, the militarization of the drug war in 1991, the forced eradication and Operation Safe Haven in 1991—have come as a result of international (and usually North American) rather than domestic pressure. The internal costs to Bolivia of the cocaine trade described in Chapter 4 were not considered to be sufficiently harmful to prompt any sustained onslaught.

Bolivian leaders have repeatedly emphasized their desire to purge the world and their country of the drugs trade, but not if counternarcotic efforts weaken them economically. One of President Jaime Paz Zamora's favorite aphorisms was that Bolivia would join international efforts to combat cocaine production only if they did not make his country any poorer. Governments have therefore tended to follow the politically expedient path of doing the minimum necessary to appease the international community and thereby convince foreign governments of the wisdom of giving economic aid, while doing the least possible to disrupt the social peace of the country. There have been important differences of emphasis in the drug policies of the UDP (Unión Democrática y Popular) government (1982–1985), the MNR government (1985–1989), and the Acuerdo Patriótico (1989–1993), but all three followed a tripartite strategy of more efficient interdiction against traffickers, faster eradication of coca bushes, and more effective economic alternatives for coca farmers. In practice, all three have surrendered virtual control of interdiction efforts to the DEA, pursued eradication targets only when politically possible, and given voluble though largely ineffective support to the principle of alternative development to replace the country's coca and, latterly, the coca economy.

Drug-control programs have registered little success. Interdiction efforts have succeeded in seizing only 1 or 2 percent of the total coca paste, base, and cocaine produced in the country; more cocaine is now being processed within Bolivia; potential yields of coca are probably increasing; and eradication efforts failed every year until 1990 to register a net reduction in the total amount of coca grown in the country. The lack of political will prompted by economic necessity is not the only factor hindering efforts to stop drugs trafficking. Nationalist resistance to the perceived imposition of U.S. priorities, the strength of the coca unions' opposition to eradication, policy disagreements between and within official entities, the ability of traffickers to adapt to the changing exigencies of their trade, and the tortuously slow progress on releasing aid for alternative development and establishing markets for alternative crops have all proved to be huge obstacles.

There is however, a wide consensus that Bolivia has a solid legal framework for combating the drug trade (although some of the same obstacles prevent it from being implemented effectively). Since colonial times, controversy has flared up over whether to enforce coca's reduction legally, and if so, in what quantities. Although various laws designed to reduce coca cultivation were presented to the Bolivian parliament in the 1940s, it was only with Bolivia's ratification of the 1961 United Nations Convention on Drugs (which classified coca as a narcotic) that governments showed themselves willing to envisage any legal support to the concept of progressive coca eradication and substitution.[1]

In 1973 a decree was passed creating a national directorate to control dangerous substances, which classified coca as a narcotic and planned to replace coca with other agricultural products of equal profitability. A year later, the United States agreed to put an initial U.S. $8 million toward PRODES (Proyecto de Desarrollo Chapare-Yungas), aimed at reducing coca over the long term by promoting agricultural development in the Chapare and the Yungas.

In the 1980s virtually every government passed new legislation, often with the political aim of trying to show the outside world that Bolivia intended to reduce coca cultivation. A comprehensive new law in 1981, Decreto Ley 18714 de Control y Lucha contra Sustancias Peligrosas (Law Number 18714 for the Control and Fight Against

Dangerous Substances), enshrined the principle that coca reduction would proceed only as long as PRODES had the financial, technical, and organizational capacity to carry out an effective program of integrated development to substitute for coca. One of the last acts of the Siles Zuazo government was to pass a tough new law in May 1985, which introduced the concept of traditional, legal zones and other zones subject to voluntary and forced eradication.

The introduction of new legislation often accompanied ambitious plans launched with much fanfare but essentially designed to meet the obligations of international agreements and secure funds from overseas. A five-year plan launched in 1982 and aimed at reestablishing the goodwill of the United States after the fall of the García Meza regime was replaced in November 1986 by the Plan Trienal (Three-Year Plan), which had the ludicrously ambitious aim of attempting to eradicate 50,000 hectares of illicit coca by 1990, including half of the production in the Yungas.[2]

Law 1008 of July 1988 regulating coca and controlled substances was probably the most sensitive and difficult piece of legislation on coca ever passed, even though it was a distillation of many of the previous laws. It was finally approved by the Bolivian Congress only after extensive pressure from the U.S. embassy and months of debate within the coca growers' unions, the COB, the political parties, and many other sectors. Although it was immediately dubbed by its opponents a U.S.-imposed law,[3] the coca unions felt at the time that they had at least secured sufficient guarantees of the linkage between eradication and alternative development, particularly because the law formally included their participation in PIDYS (Plan Integral de Desarrollo y Sustitución) already agreed with the MNR government in February of the same year. Moreover, some members of the U.S. lobby, while particularly pleased by the inclusion of annual eradication targets and the classification of Chapare as a transitional zone, were noticeably aggrieved that the law specifically prohibited the use of herbicides in eradication.[4]

As promulgated on July 22, 1988, the law's 155 articles provided for the following:

- a traditional zone of coca production in two provinces of the Yungas (Article 9);
- the establishment of 12,000 hectares of licit cultivation as that required to meet traditional demands (Article 29);
- a transitional zone of excess production subject to annual reduction figures of 5,000 hectares initially, and up to 8,000 hectares ultimately, in the Chapare (Article 10);[5]

- that the meeting of these targets be conditional on the availability of financial resources from the national budget and on the disbursement of sufficient technical and financial cooperation from multilateral and bilateral sources, which must be directed to alternative development (Article 10);
- an illegal zone, in which coca cultivation is prohibited, comprising all territory outside the traditional and transitional areas. Existing cultivation will be subject to forced eradication without compensation (Article 11);
- a specific prohibition against the use of chemicals, herbicides, biological agents, and defoliants for the reduction or eradication of coca. Only manual and mechanical methods will be used (Article 18).
- that all substitution of coca will be planned in a gradual and progressive manner, at the same time as the execution of programs and plans of sustained socioeconomic development in the transitional and traditional zones (Article 22).

On December 29, 1988, President Víctor Paz Estenssoro signed regulations for implementing the law. They included a stipulation that SUBDESAL, which had been created in late 1987 as a dependency of MACA (Ministerio de Asuntos Campesinos y Agricultura), would be responsible for overseeing eradication and the alternative development programs in PIDYS. SUBDESAL would be responsible for organizing regional and local committees—later to be known as CONADAL, COREDALes (Comités Regional de Desarrollo Alternativo), and COLADALes (Consejos Local de Desarollo Alternativo)— to ensure growers' participation in the planning and execution of PIDYS. It was also decreed that all international antidrug aid would be coordinated by CONALID (El Consejo Nacional contra el Uso Indebido y Tráfico Ilícito de Drogas), which had been set up in 1987 (and consisted of no fewer than five ministers)[6] to oversee all of Bolivia's drug-control programs.

Interdiction

While SUBDESAL is responsible for coca substitution and alternative development, the 1,000-strong antidrug police unit, UMOPAR (also known as the Leopards) was set up in 1983 with U.S. funding and is nominally responsible for all interdiction efforts. These encompass destroying coca processing pits and laboratories; seizing paste, base, and cocaine; intercepting the flow of precursor chemicals; and arresting traffickers. UMOPAR falls under the aegis of Defensa Social, a branch of the Interior Ministry, and its director is usually a retired army officer (in part to appease the army's concern that their traditional rivals, the police, provide the recruits for one of the best-armed units in the country).

In practice it is U.S. officials, and particularly the DEA and military personnel in the U.S. embassy in La Paz, who control Bolivia's interdiction efforts. It is most often the DEA that plans operations, executes and usually leads drug raids, and coordinates and often monopolizes antinarcotics intelligence. DEA agents usually do not inform UMOPAR of potential targets until the last possible moment for fear the information will be passed on to drug traffickers. The Narcotics Affairs Unit (the NAU, later known as the NAS), which works out of the U.S. embassy in La Paz, sets the budgets for UMOPAR, including its bonuses and equipment allowances.

Between thirty and sixty DEA personnel are in Bolivia at any one time. In 1987 the U.S. Army Special Forces (Green Berets) began training UMOPAR at a base in Chimore in the Chapare, and some UMOPAR personnel are given instruction at Fort Benning, Georgia. The DEA also assigns some of its personnel to the Bolivian navy's antidrug river operations and to the air force unit supporting UMOPAR. A U.S. Border Patrol unit is based at the Chimore camp to help in providing training and advice at road checkpoints. In 1992 two airborne warning and control system (AWACS) radars were also monitoring air traffic in the Chapare.

DEA officials stress that they are merely helping the Bolivian government in its efforts, but it is quite clear that they call the shots.[7] Such domination has naturally caused plenty of nationalist opposition from Bolivian antinarcotics officials, who are exasperated by their country's loss of sovereignty.[8] Dr. Jorge Alderete, one of the heads of Defensa Social under the MNR government, resigned in March 1989. He blamed the DEA's domination of operations and its failure to share information.[9] In July 1991, the then commander-in-chief of the armed forces, Gen. Jorge Moreira, went further and called for the expulsion of DEA agents from the country, after allegations of abuses against navy personnel during an antidrug operation.[10] Moreira said the DEA had contravened a 1987 agreement between the two countries that the DEA could provide intelligence, planning, and assessment but not actively participate in antidrug raids. Government officials admitted that DEA officials not only accompanied operations but took an active role in them, often giving the orders.

Poor coordination between UMOPAR and the DEA is one reason the results of interdiction efforts are unimpressive. The DEA says that at times it does not want to share information for fear of it being passed on to traffickers, while UMOPAR officials complain of a lack of trust. In addition, lack of cooperation between the DEA, the U.S. Department of Defense, and the U.S. State Department has undermined the effectiveness of U.S. training operations.[11] U.S. Army special forces are not allowed to accompany UMOPAR troops on missions, but the DEA personnel (who do) have apparently ordered UMOPAR to carry out military tactics contrary to the way they were instructed by the special forces.

Official U.S. documents show that from 1988 to 1991, seizures never represented more than a tiny fraction of the total amount of coca paste, base, and cocaine produced in the country. In 1988 and 1989, they amounted to 0.5 percent of the base and HCL produced.[12] Even the 7,000 coca maceration pits said to have been destroyed in 1989 do not constitute a particularly notable achievement because the pits are easily replaceable, and their destruction does not decrease production noticeably. In 1990 the U.S. State Department reported a doubling of the number of HCL and paste laboratories destroyed, but only 200 kilograms of cocaine were seized out of an estimated production of 72 tonnes.[13] The number of HCL labs destroyed in 1991 shot up to 142 from 33 the previous year, but cocaine seizures were still tiny, at only 300 kilos. Seizures of base were slightly up in 1991 but still only represented less than 2 percent of the total base production in the country.[14]

To be fair to the DEA and UMOPAR, it needs to be stressed that interdiction efforts are designed not only to seize drugs but to keep the price of coca down (and thereby encourage eradication) by disrupting the processing and supplying of coca paste and base, so as to reduce coca-buying. During the 1980s, it was believed that this could be best achieved by constantly harassing small coca producers in the Chapare. This still continues, but DEA officials maintain that toward the end of the decade emphasis shifted sharply toward surgical raids against the big fish and, more precisely, their operations (chemists, buyers, pilots, labs, and aircraft). In probably the largest of these from March to June 1991 against the town of Santa Ana de Yacuma in the Beni, more than 600 antidrug police backed up by the DEA and forces from the U.S. Coast Guard and Border Patrol took part in Operation Safe Haven. The official verdict was that the operation succeeded in establishing control of the town of Santa Ana and severely disrupted trafficking organizations there, but it failed to capture any significant trafficker, probably because of a tip-off.[15]

Such operations, usually costing tens of thousands of dollars, have provoked considerable opposition from the local population, in part due to the participation of the DEA, in part due to the frequent abuses stemming from the heavy-handed manner in which the antidrug forces treat local people, and in part because of the perceived threat to the local economy.[16] As yet, they have never caused the type of bloodbath associated with similar operations carried out in Colombia.

Partly with the aim of keeping the country free of drug-related violence, the Paz Zamora government announced a plan in July 1991 that ended in the imprisonment of many of the traffickers the DEA had been trying to capture for some years. According to the "decree of repentance" passed on July 29, traffickers had 120 days to turn themselves in. In exchange, the government promised not to process any extradition request from any country.

The formula allowed for reduced prison sentences if traffickers confessed to their crimes and "made an efficient contribution" to the capture of other traffickers. The traffickers would be sentenced under law 1008, which stipulates a minimum five-year jail term for drug offenses. Government officials admitted that they had studied a similar deal offered to traffickers in Colombia (where extradition was banned by the Colombian constitution), but insisted that the main difference was that Bolivia wanted to avoid a bloodbath, whereas Colombia was trying to bring an end to one.[17]

As described in Chapter 2, by December 1991, seven top traffickers, most of whom were wanted in the United States,[18] eventually gave themselves up under the amnesty. Government officials claimed the mass surrender was the result of recent successful antidrug operations (particularly Safe Haven in Santa Ana) and their decision to accept U.S. training of the Bolivian army in the fight against drugs (see pp. 91–103). Other observers said the traffickers had close links with the Medellín and Cali cartels and could have been influenced by their colleagues. The constant rumors of a new extradition treaty with the United States probably played their part, too.

What the Bolivians could rightly boast was that the decree was probably the clearest example in recent Bolivian history of a Bolivian initiative having some success. The Roman Catholic church, the police, the army, and most opposition politicians supported it (those who opposed it argued the plan should be extended indefinitely). U.S. officials privately expressed their dismay at the decree, fearing that the traffickers, many of whom appeared on their unofficial list of extraditables, would receive much shorter sentences than they could expect in the United States. The main instigator of the plan, Interior Minister Carlos Saavedra, claimed that some of the traffickers were giving useful information about their links with the Colombian cartels. But the DEA was convinced that most of them, and particularly Erwin Guzmán, were not revealing anything, and that some of them continued to direct their operations from their prison cells.[19] Whatever the truth of this, it was clear that the traffickers' surrender had caused no more than a momentary interruption in the cocaine trade, because replacements, particularly Colombians, found new ways of maintaining their activities by reorganizing and reestablishing processing and production sites.[20]

The United States's worst fears were confirmed when three of the traffickers eventually received their sentences in May 1992. The *arrepentidos* (repentant ones) had been conducting a campaign for light sentences since their arrest, including a letter to President Paz Zamora in February asking for the application of the minimum sentence as a reward for their voluntary surrender and what they said was their collaboration with the authorities. On May 28 a court gave Erwin Guzmán a sentence of a mere five years, Antonio Naciff four years, and Hugo Rivero Villavicencio six years, all for *encubrimiento* (complicity) in the cocaine trade.

The obvious disquiet felt by U.S. officials over the short sentences prompted a renewal of calls for a new extradition treaty. In 1990 the government had been on the point of signing a new treaty several times but pulled back fearing a nationalist backlash. The United States had been arguing for some years that the last extradition treaty signed in 1900 (drawn up in an era when the U.S. outlaws Butch Cassidy and the Sundance Kid were hiding in Bolivia) needed to be updated because it did not include drug trafficking as an extraditable offence. The Bolivian government, for its part, maintained that the 1900 treaty and the 1988 United Nations Convention against Illicit Trafficking in Narcotics, which the Bolivian government had signed, were together sufficient to cover extradition of drug traffickers.

At the time of this writing, it was still the case that no Bolivian trafficker had ever been extradited to the United States. In December 1989, the Paz Zamora government expelled the former interior minister, Col. Luis Arce Gómez, to Miami to face trial on cocaine trafficking charges, but he was not technically extradited.[21] The government argued that the United States was right to fear that Arce Gómez would not stay long in a Bolivian prison. In June 1991, for the first time, the U.S. government formally asked the Bolivian government to extradite three suspected traffickers, namely the mother, brother, and sister of Jorge Roca Suárez (known as Techo de Paja). The U.S. embassy put forward the request as a test case for the possibility of using the 1900 treaty and the 1988 UN convention as a mechanism for extradition. Nine months later, the Bolivian Supreme

Court had still not ruled on the case, and the United States was pushing hard again for a new treaty.[22]

Eradication

Interdiction was always closely linked to coca eradication, not just because the former was intended to force the price down to facilitate the latter but because for many U.S. officials, highly visible coca bushes and leaves were an easier target than the low-bulk, high-value coca paste, base, and HCL. Indeed, for many supply-siders, success in the drug war depended more on the results of eradication than any other measurement.

Law 1008 provided the necessary legal framework; one of its principal aims was the rapid eradication of all the coca grown in illicit areas and also, eventually, in the so-called transitional areas. Annual eradication targets were set by the law, starting with 5,000 hectares a year and rising to 8,000 hectares, all within the context of PIDYS. The method of eradication could be mechanical or manual but could never involve the use of chemical agents, including herbicides and defoliants. In addition, it would be illegal to plant new coca in the illicit and transitional areas and to possess coca nurseries. The law also stipulated that eradication had to be voluntary (for already existing coca). The U.S. $2,000 per hectare compensation set in November 1986 was maintained, despite pressure from coca growers who argued for $6,000 per hectare—probably a more realistic reflection of coca's potential value, though not of the Bolivian state's capacity to pay. (Opponents of the higher compensation argued that U.S. $6,000 a hectare would also act as a greater incentive to plant new coca and cash it in.)

The ambitious objective of eventually eradicating all the country's excess coca was reiterated in CONALID's national executive directive in 1991. The directive set out a highly optimistic program of reduction for the years 1990–1995, which envisaged a dramatic drop in the total amount of coca from 55,753 hectares in 1989 (12,000 hectares in traditional areas, and 43,573 excess) to just 12,000 traditional hectares in 1995, by an annual reduction of 7,500 hectares (only 6,235 in 1995).[23] To meet the objective, CONALID estimated it needed between U.S. $1.2 billion and $1.8 billion, or between $200 million and $300 million annually.

Once law 1008 was passed, the U.S. government had the legal structure within which to offer aid, usually in the form of balance-of-payments support, as a reward for reaching agreed eradication targets. U.S. officials hoped the new law would help to avoid the impression that it was they who were imposing their will on Bolivia, because previous agreements had met with fierce opposition, not least for the secrecy surrounding them. As early as August 1983, the government had signed a confidential agreement with the United States to reduce production in the Chapare by 4,000 hectares by the end of 1985. When the agreement was finally revealed to the Bolivian public in early 1985, it provoked fierce opposition from deputies and coca growers on the grounds that it was unconstitutional. A later agreement signed in November 1985 stipulated that Bolivia had to eradicate only 1,000 hectares by the end of 1985 to receive full aid, but even this lower target was not met. However, the government did meet a 1,800-hectare target set in 1987 and to be reached by August 1988. The U.S. State Department expressed its satisfaction that eradication was at last beginning, but still complained that coca cultivation expanded by 20 percent in 1988.[24]

Significant eradication only really started in 1989 (see Table 5.1). The government reached a record eradication figure of 2,504 hectares (equal to the two previous years combined), but it was still less than the 5,000-hectare level specified under a new agreement with the United States, following the stipulations of law 1008. As a result, the Bolivian government lost the last tranche, worth U.S. $5.8 million, of a $11.8 million total ESF (Economic Support Fund) grant tied to meeting the 5,000-hectare target.

The peak year was 1990. Coca farmers eradicated 7,806 hectares —well over the 6,000-hectare target for the year, and the government duly received U.S. $23.9 million from the U.S. government in economic support funds. At times, dozens of coca growers queued up outside the local Chapare offices of the state eradication agency, DIRECO, in order to register to have their coca chopped down under the supervision of agency teams.[25] Previously, DIRECO had great difficulty in getting farmers to go to their offices. The reason for their change of heart was the sustained slump in the price of the 100–pound bag of coca (see Table 1.7). From a peak of U.S. $90 a carga in August 1989 prices fell below the break-even price of $30 in November, sometimes dropping as low as $5, and remained low until June 1990.

Bolivian government officials said the slump resulted from improved interdiction by UMOPAR and pointed to the reported arrest of more than fifty buyers of coca paste over a six-month period. Other observers said an overproduction of coca leaf had forced the price down, but the most convincing explanation was that the drive against cocaine traffickers launched by President Virgilio Barco in

Colombia in August 1989 had led to a dramatic drop in the demand for coca base and paste from Colombia.[26]

Also in 1990, for the first time ever, there was a net reduction in the amount of coca grown in the country. The official figure for total reduction was more than 7,800 hectares, but the 1991 U.S. State Department *International Narcotics Control Strategy Report* claimed that around 4,000 hectares of new coca had been planted during the year—and that the real reduction was from 53,900 hectares to 50,300 hectares, or 3,600 hectares total. The government strongly denied this supposition, but the UNDCP supported it. The 5 percent net reduction in 1990 apparently did not compensate for the 9 percent increase in new coca planted in 1989.[27]

Prices picked up again throughout 1991, and by October government officials admitted that it would be difficult to meet the 1991 target of 7,000 hectares due to the high prices compared to the 1990 slump. U.S. officials, for their part, warned that the government would lose the last tranche of U.S. $22 million out of a total grant of $66 million toward the balance-of-payments support if the target was not reached. In the end, coca farmers eradicated 5,486 hectares, including new and old coca, which represented 2,000 hectares less than the record 1990 figure. However, this was still regarded as an overall net reduction in coca cultivation for the second year running, this time of about 2,400 hectares. The U.S. State Department blamed higher coca prices for the reduced interest in the eradication program. Officials said traffickers had successfully reorganized and reestablished processing and marketing operations, which had served to keep the prices high. Officials also blamed the ineffective leadership of DIRECO, and their criticism led to the sacking of Mayor Javier Alvarez as DIRECO's head in October (U.S. officials regarded him as corrupt) and violent opposition to forced eradication by coca farmers.[28] After prolonged discussions, the U.S. embassy in La Paz announced in June 1992 that it was going to withhold U.S. $6.2 million in aid (not the whole $22 million) for the failure to the meet the 7,000–hectare target for the year.

There were strong hints, too, that Bolivia would not receive all of the 1992 allocation of U.S. $100 million, as it looked very unlikely in June that it would reach the 7,000-hectare target for the year.[29] And 1993 was an election year, traditionally a bad time for high eradication.

Forced eradication (with no compensation for farmers) started in earnest in 1991,[30] mainly as a result of fierce pressure from the U.S. government to stop new coca being planted in the Chapare (as stipulated by Article 31 of law 1008). The United States's determination to force the point was prompted by its disappointment that the record figures eradicated in 1990 would have represented more of an achievement but for the new coca being planted. Although U.S. officials denied it, there was strong evidence that the release of balance-of-payments support in 1991 was tied to the political will of the Bolivian government to make a determined effort to start forced eradication. The U.S. State Department's 1991 report clearly stated that "USAID will condition Economic Support Fund (ESF) balance of payments assistance to Bolivia for 1991 on Bolivian government . . . compulsory eradication of coca."[31]

As a result of U.S. pressure, some DIRECO eradication teams went out accompanied by UMOPAR forces, which led to some nasty clashes and a general rise in the level of tension in the Chapare. From January to August 1991, DIRECO forcibly eradicated over 500 hectares of "illegal coca" that they said had been planted since the passing of law 1008. The coca farmers often denied it, which further exacerbated the tension. In the worst incident, in August, one peasant was killed and several wounded after armed farmers confronted UMOPAR.

Coca union leaders had frequently warned that they had no alternative but to form self-defense committees to protect themselves from UMOPAR agents supporting DIRECO teams. Some coca union leaders admitted that the lack of alternative development had forced some of their members to plant new coca, perhaps as much as 1,500 hectares since the passing of law 1008.[32] But union leaders said this was because the government had failed to comply with law 1008, which stated that eradication had to be accompanied by new crops being found to replace coca.

Much to the dismay of U.S. drug officials, a three-month truce between DIRECO and the coca growers followed in September 1991 to allow tempers to cool. During that period, farmers agreed not to plant new coca, and DIRECO agreed not to use UMOPAR in forced eradication exercises. Tempers did cool, and farmers still continued to eradicate significant amounts of coca in late 1991 and the early months of 1992, despite prices on average above the U.S. $30 mark. However, government officials admitted it was unlikely that they would reach a target of 7,000 hectares for the year, and they expected to lose a sizable proportion of the U.S. $100 million in economic aid promised by the U.S. government on completion of the 1992 target.

In total, during a five-year period from 1987 to 1991, farmers had voluntarily eradicated more than 18,000 hectares of coca—at first sight, an impressive figure because it represented around one-third of Bolivia's coca. However, the U.S. State Department estimate of

47,900 hectares under coca cultivation in 1991 represented virtually no drop from the 1988 figure, and an 8,000-hectare increase over the 1987 figure, when eradication had started in earnest. In other words, new coca was being planted over that five-year period faster than it was being eradicated. Admittedly, there was probably a net reduction in 1990 and 1991, but U.S. officials calculated that 4,000 hectares of new coca were planted in 1990 and 3,000 in 1991. Indeed, some observers argued that even the 1990 and 1991 figures were a natural result of the market taking out the excess coca production because of oversupply and that Bolivia's total area under coca cultivation would probably stabilize at around 45,000 hectares. Others pointed out that any small net reductions in hectares were offset by the improved yields from coca bushes, which, by 1991, the U.S. State Department was also accepting.[33]

The new amounts of coca planted every year had for some time convinced some observers that the incentive of U.S. $2,000 paid in compensation for every hectare eradicated was misguided. They argued that the payment acted as incentive for farmers to grow more coca. Indeed, they said farmers often moved deeper into more remote areas (particularly the Parque Isiboro-Securé) after receiving their compensation, which often was paid out for older coca bushes whose productive life was coming to an end.

In June 1991, the Inter-American Commission on Drug Policy, made up of a distinguished panel of Latin American and U.S. experts, argued in a report that the policy of paying U.S. $2,000 a hectare in compensation "has actually had the effect of sustaining the income of coca growers and thereby keeping them in the coca-growing business, rather than moving them into licit pursuits. Bolivia and the U.S. are in effect wasting most of the U.S. $42 million of U.S. economic assistance provided to Bolivia in 1990."[34]

The report, which concluded by recommending that the policy should be discontinued, stated that in practice the U.S. $2,000 compensation had the effect of encouraging farmers to keep part of their land planted in coca and reduced the incentive for coca growers to look for other profitable activities outside the Chapare.[35]

One of the authors of the report was the former Bolivian agriculture minister from 1987–1989, Guillermo Justiniano, who was actually responsible for carrying out the policy. Justiniano argues that the compensation payment constitutes a type of minimum price, which prevents the farmer from having to absorb the full effects of the price reductions or fluctuations (which varied between U.S. $10 and $100 a carga between 1986 and 1990).[36] Curiously, he says, the policy goes against the dominant free-market model in the country, unfairly rewards farmers for growing coca, and effectively penalizes those who do not. Moreover, he argues that farmers know there is no sufficient administrative control over the planting of new coca and so take the calculated risk of "cashing in" their coca when they are short of money.

The payment scheme is also not supported by UNDCP officials in Bolivia, particularly because they feel it encourages farmers to grow new coca. But USAID and Bolivian government officials counter by saying that without the offer, coca growers would be even less likely to give up their coca in the absence of viable alternatives.

Some analysts argued that the U.S. $2,000 payment was made more attractive by the knowledge that the money could, until February 1991, be deposited in the financial companies, particularly in Cochabamba (described on pp. 61–63) and yield a decent living. Coca union leaders admitted that Finsa's closure, which included many coca farmers among their 20,000 small depositors, was a major factor behind the slowdown in eradication in 1991 compared to 1990.

The compensation was not the only policy to be criticized as an incentive for encouraging eradication. Other observers suggested that the eradication effort was too tied to interdiction. Price fluctuations, critics said, were caused by a combination of variables including the time of year; the prices of other local crops; and, above all, the price of cocaine, which was fixed miles away from the Chapare.[37]

DEA and UNDCP officials agree that effective interdiction is just one factor, although they concur it helps to bring the price down. One senior UNDCP official estimated that the price changes were not a result of the laws of supply and demand in the Chapare, but "90 percent a result of the cocaine cartels fixing the price for political as well as economic reasons."[38] Thus, he said, the buyers would raise the price at times when alternative development plans were bearing fruit, or when the buyers needed to be assured of the political support of the growers (particularly at times of antigovernment demonstrations).

That buyers mainly control the coca price is a view supported by the DEA. One DEA official said that until a series of antidrug operations in 1991 (particularly Safe Haven and Definite Notice), between thirty and forty buyers used to meet in Cochabamba twice a year to fix the broad parameters for coca prices.[39] The same official added that there were at least five other factors coming into play, but the buyers' control was the most important determinant.

It is almost impossible to ascertain the exact balance of factors in determining coca prices: whether the buyers do operate a cartel (given their numbers), whether they can maintain low prices, and what is the relationship between Colombian and Bolivian buyers. There is agreement among drug officials that forcing the price down through interdiction encourages farmers to eradicate. However, it is also accepted that probably just as many farmers process the coca into coca paste in crude maceration pits to absorb the price fall and maintain their income levels by adding value to their coca.

Military Options

Despite the low eradication figures and the poor interdiction efforts of UMOPAR, and given the desire for supply-side solutions from U.S. policymakers, it is surprising in hindsight that the use of U.S. troops and even Bolivian troops in antidrug operations was restricted to just two occasions throughout the 1980s. The first occurred in August 1984 when 500 Bolivian troops were sent by the Siles Zuazo government to destroy labs and arrest drug traffickers in the Chapare.[40] The other, widely publicized exception was in July 1986, when in an operation known as Blast Furnace 160 U.S. troops and six helicopters conducted a four-month campaign against trafficking operations in the Beni.[41]

Such moderation would change as a result of the increasing perception in U.S. policymaking circles at the end of the 1980s that the drug war was now more important than the Cold War in Latin America and that more manpower was necessary to improve interdiction results. Throughout 1989, a major new U.S. drug policy known as the Andean Strategy was developed by the U.S. Office of National Drug Control Policy (ONDCP) under the leadership of the then drugs czar, William Bennett.[42] A major objective of the initiative was to reduce the flow of cocaine to the United States by 60 percent over a ten-year period by improving crop eradication, interdiction, and enforcement in the Andean source countries.[43] While the initiative in many ways merely escalated past supply-side efforts, its major break with the past was the proposed incorporation of Andean countries' armed forces in the drug war, large increases in U.S. military assistance, and an expanded role for U.S. military forces in antinarcotics operations overseas.

The four presidents of the United States, Peru, Colombia, and Bolivia endorsed the essential components of the initiative at a special summit meeting in Cartagena, Colombia, in February 1990. The plan budgeted sizable increases in aid to the three Andean countries over the period from 1990 to 1992 and beyond. For fiscal year (FY) 1990 the sum was U.S. $265 million for military, security, and economic assistance, which was slated to rise to $370 million in 1991, and nearly $500 million in 1992. Over a five-year period, Bolivia was expected to receive U.S. $830 million in economic and military aid, the greatest share of assistance provided under the Andean Strategy. Indeed, Bolivia was always considered by U.S. officials to be pivotal to the success or failure of the initiative.[44]

Shortly after the Cartagena meeting, on May 9, 1990, presidents Jaime Paz Zamora and George Bush signed a separate bilateral agreement in Washington on joint efforts in the war on drugs. The agreement's most controversial section was Annex III, which dramatically expanded the participation of the Bolivian military, and particularly the army, in the antidrug fight in exchange for increased military aid from the United States. The annex stipulated that the U.S. government would provide U.S. $33.23 million for FY 1990 to the Bolivian armed forces in return for their participation in antidrug operations. Two infantry battalions were to be trained by U.S. instructors and equipped specifically for antidrug activities, while one engineering and one transportation battalion were to be trained and equipped for civic action schemes.

It was later revealed that U.S. $14.7 million of the total military aid package went to the army, of which $9.7 million was for the two engineering and transport battalions and $5 million for the two infantry battalions, the Jordán and Manchego. The remainder was earmarked for the navy and the air force, both of which had already been providing logistical support to the activities of UMOPAR since the mid-1980s.[45] The navy would receive eight new boats, while the air force would get six new helicopters and a fleet of new support planes. The agreement specifically did not mention any involvement of U.S. military forces in antidrug operations. The 112 U.S. army instructors to be sent to train the two battalions in 1991 were to return home soon after the training courses were completed.

Details of the May 9 agreement reached the Bolivian press from U.S. sources some days later and were published on May 26. The government was immediately put on the defensive by the widespread impression that it had something to hide. Ministers initially focused their defense on playing down the new role for the army and arguing that they were not "militarizing" the drug war, a phrase that those opposed to the policy employed with obvious political success. Officials argued that the army would merely have a logistical and supportive role in fighting drug traffickers, particularly to seal off suspected drug-producing towns; its role would resemble that of the Bolivian navy and air force.

But opposition politicians and analysts countered that the term "militarization" was indeed appropriate. They pointed out that for the first time, the U.S. government was offering military aid to the Bolivian army in exchange for a role in the drug fight. It was also the first time that the army was being trained by United States army advisers to enter the drugs war (although it was *not* the first time the army had carried out antidrug operations), which implied an expanded role for the U.S. army in the region. Finally, it was argued, the role of the navy and particularly the air force was essentially that of ferrying troops or equipment, whereas the army would be expected to enter into direct contact with drug traffickers.

Critics also pointed out that the U.S. government was making a fivefold increase in military aid to Bolivia, from U.S. $5.8 million in 1989 to more than $33 million in 1990 (with further increases to more than $40 million slated for FY 1991 and 1992). The final figure for 1990 was expected to reach nearly U.S. $45 million, which made the increase even more remarkable.[46] The aid represented no less than a 40 percent increase in the Bolivian army's total military budget (of around U.S. $110 million).

The government immediately came under fire for apparently bowing to U.S. pressure to introduce the army into the drug fight. Indeed, several ministers, top army officers,[47] and even the president privately admitted much later that the government had taken the decision against its better judgment because of fierce pressure from the U.S. government, and particularly from the U.S. ambassador to Bolivia, Robert Gelbard.[48] Senior officials in the U.S. embassy in La Paz described Gelbard as involved in a "personal crusade" to persuade the Bolivians to accept the policy. One minister explained that the Bolivian economy was so dependent on bilateral aid from the United States and on multilateral aid from the World Bank, the Inter-American Development Bank, and the International Monetary Fund (where the United States exerts a huge influence) that it was virtually impossible to resist the pressure.[49]

Despite any personal misgivings, in the months following the publication of the agreement, U.S. and Bolivian officials used various arguments to justify the policy. The one used most frequently by U.S. embassy staff was the need for "institutional balancing": that a major increase in U.S. antidrug aid to the army was necessary to appease the army's jealousy of the large amounts of money going to UMOPAR, a branch of the police and a force that had historically been at odds with the army. The police fought on the side of the rebels during Bolivia's 1952 national revolution, while the army supported the status quo.

A second common argument was that the 1,000–strong UMOPAR did not have sufficient resources to hit remote laboratories or patrol

Bolivia's 250,000 square miles of subtropical jungle and flatlands in the north and east of the country. (Critics pointed out that any need for greater manpower and resources could have been met by simply increasing the personnel, training, and equipment for UMOPAR. But this, it was countered, could have further exacerbated the army's resentment of UMOPAR's preferential treatment.)

One argument that ignored the army's new role was that Bolivia's sovereignty was being eroded by the increase in the number of Colombians and other foreigners arriving in the country to work in some branch of the drug trade.[50] U.S. ambassador Robert Gelbard also frequently asserted that because Bolivia was now the world's second-largest producer of cocaine after Colombia, this process could represent a serious danger to the country's young democracy. Gelbard added that there was evidence of an increase in the number of armed drug-trafficking groups within the country.[51]

An October 1991 audit report by the U.S. Office of Inspector General expressed concern that there was disagreement within the U.S. mission about the Bolivian army's precise role, its areas of operation, and the frequency of its operations.[52] DEA officials in particular were known not to be in full agreement with the policy; they argued that the type of antidrug operations in Bolivia called for only "limited and probably unnecessary" army support.[53] One official told a British journalist that the policy was born out of Washington's desperation to win the drug war and described it as the "biggest mistake we have ever made. You haven't seen corruption till you've seen the military involved in fighting drugs."[54]

DEA officials complained that "doing business with a whole new organization was very difficult" and that the army's capacity for intelligence and investigative work was low. One senior DEA official in La Paz added that there was genuine widespread opposition to the army's role within Bolivia (opposition that had not been financed by drug money), and he feared that the policy had been "rammed down the Bolivians' throats."[55]

Virtually all Bolivia's opposition parties (and some important deputies from the two governing parties), the Roman Catholic church, leading academics and commentators, most of the country's major newspapers (in their editorials), the trade union federation the Central Obrera Boliviana, and the five coca federations in a rare degree of unanimity all came out strongly against the policy. Various U.S.-based organizations, congressional reports, and individual U.S. specialists added their concerns.[56]

Different arguments were expounded, but probably the most insistent was the fear that the hand of the army could be strengthened in a historically weak democracy such as Bolivia. Since independence from Spain in 1825, the country had suffered more than 190 coups— by repute, a record for any country in the world. To be sure, the last coup had occurred over ten years ago, but critics argued that with such an unstable past, the government and the United States should not run the risk of boosting the army's strength and undermining civilian authority in a country where authoritarian tendencies were still not curbed.[57]

A second, equally insistent line of reasoning was the fear that the involvement of the military could "Colombianize" the war on drugs by creating more violence and human rights violations.[58] The doubters suggested a number of scenarios that could break the relative absence of drug-related violence: drug traffickers could violently resist the army's incursions, or could deliberately encourage such incidents to provoke political outrage. The proposed "sealing" of small towns in the Beni, Pando, and Santa Cruz by the army could provoke strong reactions from the local populations. However, the greatest fear was that coca growers in the Chapare could, in the absence of real economic alternatives, violently oppose any army presence. Some even speculated that the Chapare could witness a process similar to that of the upper Huallaga Valley in Peru, where Peruvian antinarcotics efforts provided the Sendero Luminoso (Shining Path) insurgents with a perfect opportunity to recruit peasant support.

Others also pointed out that the Bolivian army had a sorry record of past corruption. The last military government of Gen. Lucas García Meza (July 1980–August 1981) was internationally infamous for engineering a symbiotic relationship between the state and cocaine traffickers. As recently as December 1989, the regime's interior minister, Colonel Luis Arce Gómez, had been extradited from Bolivia to the United States and later received a thirty-year sentence from a Miami court for introducing cocaine into the United States.

The State Department's *International Narcotics Control Strategy Report* for 1990 and 1991 had both pinpointed widespread corruption as a major impediment to more effective drug control. Not only were UMOPAR forces deeply involved, but the two branches of the armed forces already taking part in antidrug operations, the navy and the air force, had been frequently fingered. It would be extremely likely, critics argued, that the army—with its already rich background of involvement in drug-related activities—would soon follow suit and be tempted by the rich bribes offered by drug traffickers.[59]

The Roman Catholic church and peasant federations came out strongly against the policy, partly on the grounds that it contradicted the government's successful promotion of alternative development (see Chapter 6). Ever since President Paz Zamora had expounded alternative development as the "Bolivian thesis" at the United Nations in September 1989, this policy was clearly the official one. So it was not immediately obvious, critics argued, why the government had decided on the introduction of the military, which could actually harm national and international efforts to promote alternative development.

The Bolivian Episcopal Conference issued a statement criticizing the decision on pacifist grounds and reasserting its view that the solution lay in promoting an "authentic alternative development."[60] Giovanni Quaglia, the UNDCP assessor, told the local press that repression in the Chapare would be "counterproductive" to the UNDCP's efforts to introduce alternative development. He said that the army should concentrate its activities in the Santa Cruz, Beni, and Pando departments, where the paste was transformed into base and cocaine, and not the Chapare, where four or five years were needed to work in peace on alternative development.[61]

The government and the U.S. position was not helped by statements from Gen. Felipe Carvajal, the head of the police, that the army would have to be prepared to take orders from the police in antidrug operations, an observation that, unsurprisingly, caused outrage in the army.[62] Indeed, U.S. officials admitted that who would give the orders between the police and the army and what sort of joint command would be in operation were their major concerns. It was hard to see which side would ever accept an order from the other, when, as one U.S. report described it, the tension between them amounted to an "outright refusal to cooperate."[63]

Such was the political sensitivity of the army's possible role in the drug fight and the strength of the opposition to it that for ten months (from May 1990 to March 1991, just days before the U.S. army instructors were due to enter the country), the government maintained its position that, despite the May agreement, the final decision had not yet been taken. President Paz Zamora himself reiterated that the army would only intervene if UMOPAR was overwhelmed by the drug traffickers, or if the security or sovereignty of Bolivia were threatened. For most of the intervening months, the arguments for and against dominated the political debate in the country.[64]

By November 1990, U.S. officials were getting increasingly concerned that the government was dragging its feet too far on a final decision. Polite threats were published that the army could lose its U.S. $14 million of aid and that the United States would not wait for years for a decision.[65] Part of the package of planes and boats (two C-130 planes and six patrol boats) was released to the air force and navy as a gentle reminder to the army of what it might have to forgo.[66]

Finally, in mid-March 1991, a press leak from a source in the United States (not an official announcement) revealed that fifty-six U.S. army instructors were due to arrive in early April to start a ten-week training course for 500 members of the Manchego battalion in Montero, 30 miles north of the eastern city of Santa Cruz, as part of an operation code-named "White Spear." Despite initial government denials, it was left to Samuel Doria Medina, then the chief economic adviser to the president, to confirm on March 19 that two U.S.-trained army battalions would soon carry out antidrug operations.

But the government was still concerned by threats from opposition parties in congress that they would start judicial proceedings against the government for its failure to get congressional approval for the May agreements. On April 4 the Bolivian congress, where the ruling ADN-MIR coalition had an unassailable majority, finally approved the sending of the U.S. instructors after a long and heated debate. All the opposition deputies walked out in protest before the vote. Just five hours after the Congressional approval, ninety tonnes of ammunition for the army were being unloaded from a U.S. C-5 Galaxy plane at the La Paz airport.

Journalists were allowed to visit the Montero base in June to watch the instructors from Fort Bragg, North Carolina, train young recruits in high mobility ground operations, such as patrolling and ambushing.[67] Each of the 500 recruits had been given brand-new M-16 A-2 submachine guns, one of the most modern weapons in the U.S. arsenal. According to the major in charge of the training, the recruits received the same basic course as a light infantry battalion in the United States would receive with no special emphasis on drug-related operations. Ironically, the last time the U.S. army had trained a Bolivian battalion was in 1967, when the same Manchego battalion had received instruction on fighting the followers of Che Guevara, the Argentine-Cuban guerrilla who was then operating in Bolivia.[68]

A second contingent of around fifty U.S. advisers arrived later in October of the same year (1990) to start training around 400 members of a second light infantry battalion, known as the Jordán, in Riberalta in the Beni on October 7. U.S. officials said that the twelve-week training course would be exactly the same as the one received by the Manchego battalion. But Defense Minister Alberto Saenz announced that the training would include instruction in "low-intensity conflicts," which implied training in combating not just drug traffickers but also left-wing insurgents.[69] The U.S. embassy issued a strong and immediate denial, but Saenz apparently never retracted his statement.

The arrival of the U.S. advisers had the effect of galvanizing the coca growers into stepping up their protests. The growers, who were highly organized and under threat of being most directly affected, were always going to offer the most powerful and sustained opposition to the entry of the army. Leaders of the country's umbrella peasant federation, the CSUTCB (Confederación Sindical Unica de Trabajadores Campesinos de Bolivia), argued that they did not necessarily oppose the strengthening of the army and the police, but bitter experience had shown them that they were usually the easiest targets and the only victims.

More worrisome for the government, coca growers announced as early as March 1990 that they would form *comités de autodefensa* (self-defense groups) as the best way of preventing any excesses by the military.[70] More radical leaders frequently announced that they would be prepared to defend their coca with their lives.[71]

At the first large protest held on November 17 in Chimoré, in the Chapare, the 10,000 attending threatened to march on La Paz if the government proceeded with its plans to send the army into the Chapare. They called on UMOPAR to help them expel any future army presence. Coca union leaders repeated their arguments that they grew coca as a means of economic survival, and if the government wanted to change this it should prioritize alternative development and not "militarization."

The government strategy was based on trying to reassure the coca growers that the army was going to operate only against drug traffickers and not coca growers, thus avoiding the army-peasant clashes that the coca unions had predicted. Interior Minister Carlos Saavedra warned, however, that the government could not meet the union demand that the army should not even enter coca-producing areas because acceding to this demand would create no-go areas where drug traffickers could freely operate. This last demand proved to be the sticking point in prolonged negotiations between the CSUTCB and the government.[72]

The CSUTCB called a two-day nationwide road and rail blockade for June 17 and 18, 1991, in part to protest the training of the two army battalions and their subsequent involvement in antidrug operations. The blockade met with little success, which the leadership of the CSUTCB put down to the deployment of around 20,000 members of the army and police throughout the country. A subsequent thirty-four-point agreement between the government and the CSUTCB included a promise to release around fifty peasants arrested during the blockade and a commitment to release peasants from a tax paid on rural properties, but made no mention of the entry of the military into coca-growing areas.

The failure of the blockade and the ongoing fears of the coca growers prompted the start, on June 24, of the "March for Sovereignty and National Dignity" from the town of Ivirgarzama in the Chapare. More than 200 coca producers set off with the intention of walking the 700 kilometers to La Paz to demand the cancellation of Annex III and greater peasant participation in alternative development projects. Each of the 300-odd sindicatos in the Chapare agreed to send two delegates and make an economic contribution to the march. By June 30, the number of marchers had increased to more than 600. On the same day, at a town called Paracti, 85 kilometers from Cochabamba, and only 100 kilometers from Ivirgarzama, several hundred members of the army and police stopped the march and transported the marchers back to the Chapare. Two of the coca growers' leaders, Evo Morales and Germán Portanda, were detained and taken to Cochabamba but later released.[73]

On July 11 representatives of four of the five coca federations met again with the government and signed another agreement, which included the same commitment that the army would only operate against cocaine traffickers and not coca growers but again made no mention of any guarantees that the army would not enter the Chapare. The government also reiterated its promise to implement new alternative development programs, and agreed to form a special commission, made up of growers, journalists, church leaders, and government officials, to investigate future cases of alleged abuses by UMOPAR.

As it turned out, the coca growers had little to fear from the army's first incursion into the drug fight. Its first operation, code-named "Green Berets" (later named Definite Notice), took place a year and five months after the signing of Annex III. On the night of October 2, 1991, around 130 troops from the Manchego infantry battalion, previously trained by the U.S. instructors, set out from their base to carry out search-and-destroy missions against cocaine laboratories and drug traffickers in a 200-square-kilometer area in the eastern part of the Santa Cruz department. The target area was the province of Angel Sandoval and part of Chiquitos, Busch, and Velasco, one of the most remote and underpopulated regions of Bolivia.

It was not an auspicious start when some of seventeen civilian trucks used to transport the troops got bogged down on the way to the target area and arrived late at their base of Las Petas, just 10 kilometers away from the border with Brazil. For eight days a total of 300 men from UMOPAR and the Manchego battalion, backed up by six DEA agents, carried out patrols.

Ministers were quick to describe the operation as a success, pointing to the three cocaine laboratories found, one secret airstrip destroyed, and the small amount of radio equipment confiscated. But the head of the armed forces, Gen. Victor Guzmán described the results as "nothing out of the ordinary."[74] Indeed, local press reports generally questioned the official verdict, pointing out that no drugs were found and no major arrests were made in an operation that must have cost tens of thousands of dollars.[75] Army officials privately blamed the disappointing results on the bad weather and the fact that the public announcement of the operation was made (by the Defense Minister Alberto Saenz) even before the troops had arrived at their target area.

Ministers also stressed that the operation had taken place in a underpopulated area and not in areas of possible conflict, such as the Chapare, as promised to the coca growers. Indeed, Interior Minister Carlos Saavedra, in his first official report to congress, said that the army would not enter either the Chapare or the Yungas, apparently changing his earlier position.

Saavedra also denied that UMOPAR was overextended, which had previously been the rationale for use of the army. Instead, he justified the army's participation by repeating his argument that the 1,000 men in UMOPAR could not cover the whole of the vast Amazonian region and, second, that the army had established Bolivian sovereignty in the area. This, he said, was part of a general strategy whereby the army would "seize drugs, carry out operations, arrest traffickers, and dismantle cocaine laboratories in areas where UMOPAR cannot have access," partly with the objective of ensuring Bolivia did not become a producer of cocaine hydrochloride.

In a second report to congress, Saavedra admitted that the entry of the army was due to pressure from the U.S. government, although he stressed that the final decision was Bolivia's. He added that "there was no need for the army to enter into the war on drugs, but we believed it was important because drugs trafficking had declined in Bolivia, and was half-disbanded."[76]

In seventeen months, the Bolivian government had come full circle in its logic. One of the original justifications was that drug trafficking had increased and, therefore, army participation was necessary. But political priorities now predominated. The U.S. government was stepping up the pressure, the army wanted its aid and new weapons, and the government wanted the politically safest operation, with no violent clashes and the least amount of controversy. As Saavedra admitted, "it was the precise moment to demystify the entry of the army."[77]

The timing of the army's first foray was unfortunate because politicians from both government and opposition parties had been arguing that it was unnecessary, given the recent surrender of a number of top suspected traffickers under the terms of the recently passed decree of repentance. The church repeated its fears that the army's next operation could be directed against coca growers. The CSUTCB declared a state of emergency, while the coca growers said their self-defense groups were ready to combat the army. And every opposition political party in congress (and some leading members of the ruling MIR and ADN parties) repeated their by-now-familiar objections. Even Gastón Encinas, president of the Chamber of Deputies and a leading member of the MIR party, condemned the government action by arguing that the policy did not respond to the will of the government, but was a product of outside pressure.

One new element was that the country's main left-wing party, the MBL (Movimiento de Bolivia Libre), started legal proceedings against three ministers for violating the constitution by not securing the approval of congress before signing the May 1990 agreement with the United States. Only the U.S. embassy and the private sector organization CEPB (Confederación de Empresarios Privados de Bolivia) came out enthusiastically in favor of the army's incursion.[78] Nevertheless, the political and psychological barrier had been broken. Soon after the operation, U.S. officials announced that training and equipment would continue and was slated to rise to U.S. $40 million in FY 1992. Fifty more U.S. instructors were due to arrive in April to train another 500 recruits from the Manchego battalion.

But as the early months of 1992 passed without any further army actions, it soon became apparent that both the United States and the Paz Zamora governments were revising the policy. Indeed, one year after Definite Notice, it remained—and looked likely to remain, in the short-term at least—the only antidrug operation to be carried out by the army.

Rumors from the San Antonio presidential summit in Texas in February—which was a follow-up to the Cartagena summit—suggested that the Bush administration was revising its policy of offering military aid tied to antidrug operations to the Bolivian army. Newspaper reports suggested that the aid would be reallocated from the army to the other branches of the armed forces, particularly the navy and air force, which had much more experience in support operations.

It seemed that U.S. officials were fed up with the political costs of the policy, with the reluctance of the army to carry out operations, and with the lack of results. In short, they had made a bad investment. As an embassy official expressed it in June 1992, "The U.S. at this point has no plans to provide further counter-narcotics training to the Bolivian army. It cannot be justified to the U.S. Congress to continue counter-narcotics expenditure for the army if they're not going to be used in counter-narcotic actions."[79] Also in June, Bernard Aronson, the U.S. assistant secretary of state, wrote in a letter that Bolivia's "civilian leadership was uneasy about army participation. The army participated in only one counter-narcotics operation after two anti-narcotics infantry battalions completed U.S.-funded training in 1991. In view of this, we will shift future U.S. assistance to more effective programs."[80]

The decision appeared to be mutual. In the early months of 1992, both Saavedra and President Paz Zamora went on the record saying that the army would not be sent on antidrug operations, as it was no longer necessary. And in July, Saavedra went further during a visit to Washington D.C., stating that Bolivia would be the first Andean nation to delink the army from the antidrug fight.[81] A new bilateral aid agreement was signed in August, which virtually tolled the death knell for antidrug aid to the army. Out of U.S. $200 million package, $66 million of balance-of-payments support was tied to eradication, more than $100 million allocated to alternative development, and $25 million of military aid for all the armed forces provided for FY 1992 (a reduction from the $40 million originally agreed to by the U.S. Congress). The exact allocation of the money within the various branches was not spelled out, but press reports suggested that only U.S. $2 million was earmarked for the army. More important, the agreement stipulated that the army's role would be restricted to one battalion being equipped and trained and a service unit also being equipped. Direct army participation appeared a policy of the past—only two years after the idea was enshrined in the infamous Annex III.[82]

Some analysts pointed out that the drastic reduction in the army's role and in the amount of antidrug aid it was to receive did not represent a change in the U.S. government's emphasis on the enforcement option.[83] They argued that the money was merely reallocated to other branches of the armed forces. But at least in Bolivia, it did appear that the sustained opposition to the policy has succeeded in restricting the army's participation in the antidrug war to the one, benign, Operation Definite Notice in October 1991. It must have become obvious that not only was the policy a deeply unpopular and divisive one, but also that it would be ineffectual unless enacted with a degree of enthusiasm.

But despite the apparent reversal of the policy, analysts believed the damage to the government's image had already been done. Few in Bolivia believed the official assurances that the original adoption of the policy was a sovereign decision by the Bolivian government. To be fair, it is doubtful that any Bolivian government could have resisted the U.S. pressure to accept the policy, given the country's degree of economic dependence on the goodwill of the U.S. government. The pressure was also fierce from some sectors of the army, which were keen to secure increased military aid.

The Paz Zamora government was, in essence, caught between the desire to maintain the goodwill of its major benefactor and to keep the lid on political opposition to the policy. But the government's handling of the issue was a sorry sequence of denials, then admissions, contradictions, and evasions, and then changes in its reasoning, which undoubtedly increased opposition to the policy. It also probably increased anti–United States sentiment as the government struggled not to appear to be bowing to U.S. pressure in implementing an unpopular measure. But perhaps the lasting legacy was the undermining of the government's sensible attempts to portray Bolivia's coca-cocaine problem as essentially economic, which required large infusions of economic aid, new markets, and new crops to wean the country from its economic dependence on the coca-cocaine industry. It was difficult to argue that alternative development was still the government's priority when it had accepted significant amounts of military aid in the face of concerted opposition from virtually every political force in the country.

Table 5.1 Coca Eradication, 1985–1992

	1985	1986	1987	1988	1989	1990[a]	1991[a]	1992[b]
January				52.0	91.7	668.1	712.6	523
February				120.5	92.3	797.7	445.2	359
March				18.5	94.8	801.3	217.1	359
April				32.1	336.7	1,093.4	187.9	355
May				314.1	156.8	512.5	313.6	
June				415.3	271.9	505.5	319.5	
July				0.0	272.6	698.9	747.0	
August				108.5	50.6	705.4	704.0	
September				10.8	85.7	503.5	401.0	
October				229.9	196.2	402.9	401.0	
November				108.3	256.3	435.1	438.0	
December				65.6	598.7	681.9	445.0	
Total:	30	200	1,040	1,475.6	2,504.3	7,806.2	5,331.9	1,596

Sources: For 1985–1987, U.S. Department of State, Bureau of International Narcotics Matters, *INCSR*, 1986, 1987, 1988. For 1988 through June 1991 (SUBDESAL), La Paz, handout. For July 1991–1992, U.S. embassy, La Paz, Bolivia, handout.

Note: a. In 1990, 281 hectares of new or illegal coca were eradicated without compensation, and in 1991 the figure was about 800 hectares.
b. The 1992 figures are provisional, and include both old and new coca.

... 6 ...

Alternative Development

Alternative development—in all its guises—was and remains the cornerstone of the strategy pursued by successive Bolivian governments to curb the cocaine trade. Nowhere is the concept more clearly enshrined than in law 1008 of July 1988, which dedicates ten of its first thirty-one articles to alternative development and coca substitution. It is worth reiterating that Article 10 of the law clearly stipulates that the meeting of eradication targets is conditional on the disbursement of technical and financial cooperation from multilateral and bilateral sources for alternative development. Article 22 backs this up by stating that coca substitution "will be planned in a gradual, progressive form and be simultaneous to the execution of sustained programs and plans of socioeconomic development *in zones (a) and (b) defined above* [in effect, the Yungas and the Chapare]" (author's emphasis and translation). And PIDYS was established to ensure, among other things, that coca producers eradicating their coca would receive adequate compensation, financial facilities, and the necessary technical assistance (Article 25). Few pieces of legislation could be clearer, and yet the levels of eradication achieved by farmers particularly since 1988 are all the more impressive because they have taken place despite, and not because of, government and international efforts to provide alternative sources of income.

The policy of alternative development is an explicit recognition that for Bolivia, the coca-cocaine industry is essentially an economic or development issue, or as one recent report has described it, "mainly a problem of failed rural development."[1] This perception has shaped the desire of many Bolivian officials to convince overseas observers and donors that their country's contribution to suppressing the cocaine trade is dependent on the willingness of foreign countries to channel funds to pursue essentially economic—and not repressive—solutions to the drug trade.

That at least has been the stated desire, although governments have been forced by outside pressures to put as much, and usually much more, emphasis on other types of approaches. Indeed, by the early 1990s both U.S. and Bolivian government officials were unanimous that alternative development could not work in isolation but only in tandem with interdiction. If interdiction was the stick to encourage farmers to eradicate, then alternative development was the carrot. In the face of the economic benefits from coca, effective interdiction was perceived to be the only way to keep the coca price below the break-even point of U.S. $30 a carga, thus encouraging peasants to accept the $2,000 per hectare offered in compensation and making other crops and economic possibilities more attractive. Even if interdiction could not make the price fall below U.S. $30 all the time, price fluctuations (often sharp) could create enough uncertainty in the farmers' minds for them to question the advisability of growing coca.

Indeed, senior USAID officials interviewed in late 1991 often prefaced any conversation about alternative development with stark commentaries that good interdiction is the sine qua non of effective alternative development. This policy is clearly stated in USAID's public documents.[2] One official even went as far as saying that "the way to get rid of coca is not by offering alternative crops, but by good interdiction, which forces the price down."[3] It is a view echoed by senior Bolivian officials. As former planning minister Samuel Doria Medina has said, "Alternative development will not work on its own, as no other product gives the returns coca does. You need interdiction to keep the price down."[4]

This coupling of alternative development with interdiction may seem innocuous and rational, but to some Bolivian observers it masks important contradictions. Despite official protestations that alternative development is the priority, they say, interdiction both logically and in practice predominates over development, making it a form of *desarrollo interdictivo* (repressive development).[5] Moreover, most of the rewards of development (credit, public works, crop schemes) are conditional on achieving eradication targets, when many argue farmers should be asked to eradicate only when alternative development—and particularly other productive activities—is firmly in place.[6] Indeed, Article 10 of law 1008 would seem to endorse that order of priority.

The linking of interdiction and development has also brought contradictions in policy priorities. As mentioned in Chapter 1, the provision of lime would considerably aid the search for effective alternative development because it could help to neutralize the acid in the soils, but lime is banned from the Chapare as a precursor chemical. Similarly, in 1986 USAID stopped building roads in the Chapare because it thought this aided the drugs traffickers.[7] But the lack of proper infrastructure and transport is a major impediment to getting alternative crops to markets, whereas coca is easily carried by farmers on bicycles along poor roads. In fact, the policy was changed in 1988 because USAID perceived that drug traffickers would find a way to carry out their activities whether or not there were roads, whereas the absence of roads was a huge obstacle to alternative development. Now, coca growers frequently complain that the DEA blows up minor farm-to-market access roads in the Chapare—sometimes funded by USAID money—on the grounds that they are used as landing strips for planes ferrying out paste, or as coca union leaders often express it, "USAID pays for what the DEA destroys."

Similar concern was expressed that supplying electricity to the Chapare would undoubtedly help the drug trade. U.S. ambassador Edwin Corr said electricity would "allow narcos to work at night" (although they already did).[8] In the early 1990s, however, USAID decided to reverse the policy and partly fund a large electrification program, arguing that without electricity it was very difficult to process or industrialize alternative crops (and thus add value), and that electricity was normally required only for the later stages of cocaine manufacture (principally drying), most of which takes place outside the Chapare.

Both Bolivian government and USAID officials have gone through several definitions of what alternative development is and what it should be. It may be an oversimplification to say that early thinking was dominated by the view that alternative development meant coca substitution, or at least the gradual substitution of coca with other economically viable crops, mainly in the Chapare. But it was soon only too obvious that no crop could compete on a one-hectare-to-one-hectare basis with coca's returns, for the reasons outlined in Chapter 1. So the concept was broadened from an emphasis on crop substitution to include support for alternative development in areas outside the Chapare, particularly where it was thought large numbers of potential or actual migrant laborers to the Chapare lived. The Associated High Valleys project (AHV) was conceived in 1987 as a reflection of this change (see pp. 119–122).

More recently, the thinking has moved even further away from the idea of crop substitution to include any economic activity that assists in weaning the Bolivian economy from its dependence on coca-cocaine production to a diversified, sustainable, legal, and growing economy that does not depend on it. Within that framework, USAID now believes it is supporting alternative development by replacing foreign exchange earnings generated by the coca-cocaine industry, providing funds to help economic stabilization and reactivation, and generating income and employment for anyone actually or potentially involved in coca cultivation or its processing.[9]

Official USAID thinking at present mirrors that of the former government of President Jaime Paz Zamora. The chief architect of the shift in government thinking, Samuel Doria Medina, argued that previous alternative development strategies stumbled on the same block of the irreplaceability of coca on a one-to-one basis. Instead of finding alternative crops like coffee or citrus fruits to substitute for coca, his and the government's new plan of *coca por desarrollo* (coca for development) was not to replace each hectare of coca with one hectare of something else but rather to find substitutes for the jobs, income, and exports created by the coca-cocaine industry—in short, to replace the cocaine economy.[10] To that end, the government sought funding for a special social emergency fund to provide short-term employment for farmers giving up their coca, balance-of-payments support to replace the dollars earned from cocaine, and foreign investment and aid to help boost and diversify the formal sectors of the economy. Particular support was given for projects promoting export capacity or agricultural growth (provided that Bolivia did not incur any more debt in the process).[11]

Aid for Alternative Development

The money to fund the policy of alternative development comes from three main sources: USAID, the Bolivian government, and the UNDCP, previously known as UNFDAC (the United Nations Fund for Drug Abuse Control), whose funds come mainly from European governments. Funds from the Bolivian government are negligible compared to the large amounts earmarked by USAID. Indeed, USAID provides virtually all the funding for the nominally Bolivian organizations in charge of the eradication and alternative development effort, namely SUBDESAL, PDAR (Programa de Desarrollo Alternativo Regional—formerly known as PDAC), IBTA-Chapare (Instituto Boliviano de Tecnología Agropecuario), and DIRECO. When the U.S. food aid program PL-480, which administers the credit scheme, is added to the list, it is perhaps not surprising that Bolivian observers complain that USAID has created a "superstructure of alternative development" in which the Bolivian state has little control and little capacity to decide its own development priorities or projects.[12]

It is a difficult task to find accurate figures for how much money the Bolivian government and USAID have actually spent on alternative development in recent years. There are as many figures as there are offices working on alternative development—in itself, an indication of where much of the money has been allocated. In addition, at least five kinds of reports of U.S. government aid figures exist for Bolivia, ranging from requests by the executive branch, approval by the U.S. Congress, allocations to projects in Bolivia, disbursements by USAID to Bolivian organizations, and, finally, funds actually spent by these organizations.

Yet another obstacle is that USAID has changed its criteria in recent years for what is included under the rubric of aid for alternative development. In 1990 aid for alternative development was redefined to include virtually anything USAID was doing to help economic reactivation and diversification (as part of the process of easing Bolivia away from its dependence on coca-cocaine production), which in effect amounted to virtually all USAID's budget. As a result, USAID has published figures like those found in Table 6.1, for the amount of aid classified as "aid for alternative development" for the years 1988 to 1992. The figures include virtually all the economic support funds (which admittedly were tied to meeting eradication targets), PL-480 food aid (some of which was being used for credit programs), and most of USAID's development assistance.

Such tables give the impression that USAID gives large amounts of money to help alternative development. But once the figures are disentangled, it emerges that the actual amount of money spent on alternative development that directly aids or reaches coca producers since 1983 has been remarkably small; the amount spent in the Chapare even smaller; and the amount spent on concrete, productive, income-generating activities there even smaller still.

Virtually all the USAID money invested in the Chapare has been channeled through CRDP (the Chapare Regional Development Project), which was established in 1983 under an agreement with the Bolivian government. Within the CRDP, the main recipient of aid has been IBTA-Chapare, an agricultural research and extension center, followed by PDAC/PDAR, the SNC (Servicio Nacional de Caminos), and more recently the AHV project (which falls within PDAR).

Official figures from the USAID office in La Paz show that between 1983 (when the CRDP started) and 1990 USAID spent a total of U.S. $33.8 million on the CRDP (see Table 6.2), which does not include the PL-480 credit program. The figure of $33.8 million is not dissimilar to one given by Charles Hash, the head of USAID's rural development program in Bolivia, who said in an interview in September

1991 that USAID had actually spent $30.4 million on alternative development since 1983. Of this figure, he estimated 60 percent had been spent on the Associated High Valleys project and only 40 percent (i.e., about U.S. $12 million) had gone to the Chapare, specifically IBTA-Chapare, road construction, and "high impact" public works projects.[13]

A senior USAID official in Cochabamba gave a higher figure of U.S. $74 million spent on the CRDP since 1983, which included the 1991 budgeted figure of $18 million, $14.8 million for operational costs (mostly salaries and rent), and $5.6 million for the credit program. If these three items are deducted, then the final figure for monies actually spent would be U.S. $35.6 million, in line with Hash's estimate and the USAID's official figures. The official also reiterated the point that, of the U.S. $35.6 million, around 40 percent had been spent on the Chapare (i.e, $14.2 million), which was "almost exclusively spent on IBTA-Chapare and high-impact projects."[14]

It would therefore seem reasonable to conclude that USAID spent between U.S. $30 and $35 million on the CRDP between 1983 and 1990, which would work out to an average of about $4.6 million for each year between 1983 and 1990. It would also seem safe to assume that no more than 40 percent was spent in the Chapare, equivalent to around U.S. $14 million, or around $1.86 million a year. If USAID's estimate is assumed to be correct—that IBTA's budget has absorbed between U.S. $1 million and $2 million every year between 1983 and 1990[15]—IBTA must have accounted for at least $7 million and possibly as much as $14 million of the total CRDP budget, which leaves very little money for other projects.

Those other investments have consisted mainly of a small program of road construction (which was suspended between 1986 and 1988), and a program initiated in 1990 of high-impact public works (health posts, community centers, and schools, in the main) for communities eradicating 30 percent of their coca. By June 1991, thirty-four of these projects had been completed at a maximum cost of U.S. $20,000 each, amounting to a maximum possible expenditure of $680,000.

All this suggests that the proportion of the alternative development budget left over for investing in supporting the production, processing, and marketing of other crops—in short, the activities that would be most likely to generate an income for farmers eradicating their coca—has been very small. Although the official figures are closely guarded, the president of the Civic Committee in Cochabamba, Alvaro Moscoso, calculated in December 1991 that the figure for total investment in productive units in 1991 was a mere

U.S. $667,000.[16] This huge gap has at least been recognized by USAID officials as one that has to be filled in the near future.

The low level of investment in alternative development in the Chapare is confirmed by official figures from PDAR in its 1990 annual report. The report states that PDAR spent just U.S. $13.3 million from 1984 to 1990 (inclusive), of which $11.5 million came from USAID, $1.4 million from PL-480, and just $0.4 million from the Bolivian treasury.[17] Of the money from USAID, U.S. $4.56 million was for technical assistance, $1.51 million for training in social communication, $1.3 million for construction work, $0.53 million for material and equipment, $2.7 million for operating costs, and the remainder for other contingencies. SUBDESAL's official budget figures for 1990 suggest similarly small amounts actually earmarked for the Chapare, namely U.S. $2.41 million for PDAR (for its work in the Chapare), $3.1 million for IBTA, and $1.16 million for the SNC for road building.[18] And yet another set of calculations from Samuel Doria Medina gives a figure of U.S. $90 million programmed (not spent) for alternative development (defined broadly) for the years from 1988 to 1990, of which $62 million was to be spent on construction works, $13 million on electricity and water supplies, and nearly $10 million on agricultural investments.[19]

The range of figures given for expenditures on alternative development by USAID and the government pale in significance against the value of the coca-cocaine economy and against the amount of money the Bolivian government and coca growers estimate they need. In its expenditure forecast for 1990–1995, the government calculated it would require between U.S. $1.2 and $1.8 billion, or between $200 and $300 million per year, for alternative development (broadly defined).[20] The coca unions estimate they need at least U.S. $300 million a year of investment and compensation for every 6,000 hectares of coca they eradicate.[21] And the UNDCP calculates, perhaps most realistically, that U.S. $100 million would be needed every year for the next eight years to eliminate excess coca production, compared to the total figure of $30 million (estimated to be $20 million from USAID and $10 million from UNDCP) available for 1991.[22]

But perhaps the most telling comparison is between the U.S. $30–35 million USAID spent on alternative development over a seven-year period between 1983 and 1990, and the $44 million the U.S. government gave the Bolivian armed forces for its role in the drug war for just one year (1990). As Samuel Doria Medina has bemoaned, "The United States shows remarkable efficiency in disbursing money for the military, but not for alternative development."[23]

It is hard to disagree with the view of both coca growers and their union leaders (and many independent observers and USAID officials) that USAID made virtually no significant investment in the Chapare until 1991, with the possible exception of IBTA-Chapare. And even at IBTA, as many argue, the impact has been very limited (see pp. 116–118). In short, for eight years, one of the key components of both Bolivian and United States government policy to combat the cocaine trade has failed almost completely to bring tangible benefits to coca growers. This failure has caused extensive disenchantment to thousands of potential beneficiaries and jeopardized the chance of strong support from coca growers for new alternative development projects.

The Chapare Regional Development Project (CRDP)

To be fair to USAID and the Bolivian government, since its inception in 1983 the CRDP—the main vehicle for implementing alternative development programs—has been dogged by policy changes; government corruption; interorganizational rivalry; lack of clear strategy; bureaucratic obstacles; and, according to many, an unwillingness on the part of USAID to put its money, people, and expertise permanently into the Chapare.

In its early days, the project was a nonstarter in part due to the inability of the Bolivian state to exercise any sort of control over the Chapare. Its initial primary focus was to substitute other cash crops for coca and stimulate agro-industrial processing of tropical products. Its results were, to put it kindly, meager, in part due to heavy-handed repression from the antidrug police, which alienated any support the farmers may have had for U.S.-funded projects, and in part due to the absence of any cropping system that could substitute for coca's short-run profitability.[24]

After a sweeping policy review in late 1986, the CRDP underwent a major change of emphasis, from trying to tempt farmers to grow other crops to attempting to reverse or at least stem the flow of migrant farmers and workers into the Chapare from their highland communities. This transformation, formally embodied in Amendment 7 of the CRDP, which was signed in November 1987, meant a reallocation of over half the budget away from the Chapare into the AHV project (see pp. 122–126).

The signing of the amendment caused a major conflict between USAID and SUBDESAL, the Bolivian organization created a few months earlier in July 1987 to oversee all alternative development plans. While USAID was redirecting much of its time, money, and effort into the highland valleys of Cochabamba, SUBDESAL was still attempting to persuade coca growers in the Chapare to reduce their coca plantings with the carrot of alternative crops and community works such as water, roads, and other buildings. The conflict was exacerbated by the perception, common among Bolivian officials, that USAID's condition (in place until December 1988)—that a community had to eradicate 70 percent of its coca before qualifying for any development assistance—was hopelessly ambitious.

The main organization responsible for implementing alternative development projects, the PDAC (later PDAR) found itself caught between two sets of "external masters with two different sets of priorities and goals."[25] A review of USAID's work carried out in 1990 described the AHV project as "victimized by a combination of administrative ineptitude, personal ambitions displacing development goals, and venal national and international political interests."[26] The same report called SUBDESAL's decisions (using a charitable characterization) "whimsical" and described relationships between PDAC and SUBDESAL as so bad that at the end of 1988, almost the entire staff of PDAC were fired, mainly because they were trying to implement the AHV project. The report also revealed that the CRDP only survived as an institution because of the appointment of a new technical chief for PDAC in mid-1989, the arrival of a new government, and an agreed commitment to the AHV project.

Against this sort of political and institutional infighting, it is no wonder that so little money has been invested in alternative development. As an internal USAID evaluation wrote in September 1991, "Although in bureaucratic terms, the [CRDP] is more than five years old, CRDP actually began implementation in earnest one year ago [September 1990]."[27] Indeed, one senior USAID official put the effective date even later. He said in an interview in September 1991 that "USAID wasn't really doing anything in the Chapare until six months ago."[28]

By the end of 1991, the mood had changed sufficiently within USAID and PDAR (which had replaced PDAC, in part to give it a new image) for the organizations to start publishing their lists of achievements. Prior to that date, it is hard to see what they would have published. As listed by USAID in September 1991, the "specific accomplishments in the Chapare" were

- by the end of 1991, planting material with a potential for over 5,000 hectares of improved crops distributed by IBTA-Chapare, and the potential for an additional 5,000 hectares distributed by farmers and other nurseries;
- nine road-improvement projects in the former red zone (so-called, as it was the center of coca paste production in the Chapare);

- the planning of fresh fruit packing and cooling facilities;
- forty-seven community high-impact projects;
- stone paving of the road from Villa Tunari to Chipiriri;
- a credit program worth U.S. $6 million to farmers; and
- the first export of alternative crops (turmeric, pineapples, and bananas) worth as much as U.S. $800,000 in 1991.

These achievements were perhaps something to be lauded, given the sorry state of the whole alternative development project in late 1988. But the list is also a reflection of just how little had been achieved in almost eight years of trying and more than U.S. $30 million spent.

IBTA-Chapare

There is universal agreement among officials that IBTA-Chapare is the success story of the whole CRDP project, if perhaps the only one. It is USAID's largest project in the Chapare and consists of two research and extension centers at La Jota and Chipiriri. Official USAID documents warmly describe La Jota as "the most technologically advanced agricultural research station in the entire Andean tropics."[29] Many point out that IBTA-Chapare's work was able to benefit from a degree of continuity not available to other institutions, because it was maintained throughout the difficult period of the mid-to-late 1980s (although it was hampered by the contradictory messages coming from SUBDESAL and USAID).

By 1991 IBTA claimed it had identified numerous crops or, more accurately, "production systems," as viable alternatives to coca. It said it had also increased agricultural productivity by promoting such concepts as ground-cover plants to reduce weeds and produce nitrogen in the soils, thus eliminating the need for fertilizers. The center's research showed that out of the dozens of crops tested, macadamia nuts, coconuts, peanuts, spices, black pepper, dyes, hearts of palm, and various tropical fruits such as maracuya and passion fruit could be successfully grown in the Chapare. Subsistence crops such as maize, beans, and rice, and improved strands of bananas, pineapples and citrus fruits have also been developed. To get away from the idea of swapping one hectare of coca for one hectare of one of these crops, IBTA recommended crop diversification: intermingling annual crops with higher-value, long-term, or perennial crops so that farmers could generate a steady income until the higher-value crops were ready to sell.

By 1991 IBTA also claimed considerable success in the appeal of its agricultural fairs and training programs. In 1990 over 17,000 farmers were reported to have attended educational tours or fairs at the stations, compared to 250 the year before. Similarly, in 1990, 681 farmers took part in training offered in communities, more than triple the 170 participating in 1989.[30] However, many observers pointed out that this increase in interest in IBTA stemmed more from external factors (low coca prices) than initiatives taken by the institution to address particular problems facing farmers.[31] Others stressed that the training programs had only reached a very small percentage of the households involved in coca growing.[32]

Indeed, IBTA has been widely criticized, particularly by coca farmers and their union leaders, for being far too concerned with on-site research to establish the theoretical levels of productivity and the suitability of crops, and for not doing enough to work with coca growers on their farms to identify constraints and problems there. It is not uncommon to find coca farmers familiar with IBTA dismissing IBTA's work as "a bunch of scientists running around in a station." It is a criticism accepted by USAID officials (who point to the political obstacles, most notably the opposition from the unions to alternative development), who say that the number of extension workers has now been markedly increased. Of the 100-odd staff members at IBTA in 1991, about sixteen were now said to be extension workers, compared to only about five in 1988.[33]

It was also far from clear how many farmers participating in IBTA technical courses had actually planted IBTA crops at their farms. Again, the official figure is that by the end of 1991, as many as 7,000 farmers had actually planted IBTA-supplied seeds in 3,000 hectares of land. It is a figure highly disputed by other observers, who believe the figure is more like 1,000 hectares of land formerly given over to coca and now being grown with new crops.[34] Some USAID officials accept that this may be a more realistic figure, because it is not known how many of the 3,000 hectares planted with IBTA seeds have actually replaced coca. Certainly, the coca unions complained that only about one in ten of the 12,000 hectares eradicated by coca farmers had been planted with other crops.[35]

Coca farmers also frequently complain that they have to pay IBTA for the plants or seeds, which in the case of macadamia nuts can cost as much as U.S. $13 per plant—a heavy investment (or disincentive) for farmers calculating whether they can wait seven years for any return from it. The cost of macadamia plants has apparently achieved some notoriety, forming the basis for some farmers' criticism of the cost of all IBTA's plants. Coconut plants and pepper seeds were also expensive, costing, respectively, U.S. $5.00 per plant and $1.50 per seed in 1990.[36] Farmers also reported that they sometimes had to pay higher prices for some plants than those in nearby markets, and often questioned whether the seeds were the right ones for the distinct microregions in the Chapare.

But perhaps the most telling criticism of IBTA is that it has been production-driven rather than market-driven, again a criticism accepted by USAID but not altogether by IBTA officials (because they say markets were not their area of expertise). That is to say, the focus of IBTA's work has been

> validating the technical feasibility of producing certain crops in the Chapare that, presumably, are potential alternatives to coca leaf, and defining the combinations of physical conditions and input packages under which production can be maximized. It has done little to define where and under what conditions these products might be sold, or under what sorts of organizational and financial arrangements processing and commercialization might be handled.[37]

With hindsight, it seems scarcely credible that so much effort has been put into the perfection and promotion of new crops (many of them unknown to the Chapare), and so little attention paid to the identification of markets and selling prices. One of the most infamous disasters caused by the lack of proper market analysis was the growing of ginger, for a time one of the favored alternative crops. In the early 1990s, several tonnes of ginger grown in the Chapare swamped Bolivian markets, causing the price to slump to U.S. $1 per kilo, when the farmers were told they could anticipate a price of between $3 and $4 per kilo. Moreover, the farmers were paid only after a considerable delay.[38]

It took years of experimentation before USAID hired two market analysts (in 1991), finally marking the shift of emphasis away from what can be grown to the identification of crops that can be sold. Again, with hindsight, it is remarkable that private businessmen were expected to invest in the Chapare, which must rank as having one of the most risky investment climates in the world, given its close links to the cocaine trade, its general state of lawlessness, and its high potential for violence. As one USAID official ruefully remarked in 1991, "Marketing was regarded as someone else's concern. Under [President] Reagan, we assumed the private sector would do all these things, but they never showed up."[39]

Alternative Crops

The failure to study and identify markets for alternative crops was one of the main reasons why it took eight years of IBTA experimentation before any alternative crop could be exported from the Chapare. In that period, a vast array of crops, perennial and annual, subsistence and cash, many of them alien to the Chapare, were tried and tested.[40] Only in late 1991 could USAID proudly announce that the very first exports from the Chapare—of turmeric, pineapples, and bananas—were expected to be sold, mainly in Argentina and Chile, for the sum of U.S. $800,000. A very senior USAID official in La Paz commented in an interview in September 1991 that the marketing of two of these crops—pineapples to Argentina and bananas to Chile—was "much more serendipitous than planned." Indeed, he said that none of the highly paid consultants contracted by USAID over the years had recommended the two crops, and IBTA had not carried out a great deal of research into varieties of bananas and pineapples which could be marketed, even though they grew in abundance in the Chapare.[41]

Government and USAID officials were quietly optimistic in late 1991 that bananas and pineapples would turn out to be the success stories of the Chapare, although they agreed there were a number of problems to be overcome before these crops could benefit more than a handful of farmers. Official figures from SUBDESAL estimated that more than 7,000 boxes of bananas (weighing 22 kilos a box) of the Cavendish variety had been exported to Chile in 1991, and that the potential existed to export up to 6,000 boxes a month in 1992. Exports of pineapples to Argentina also started in 1991, although in smaller quantities (officially, about 1,800 boxes weighing 12 kilos a box), and 11 tonnes of turmeric were also sold, some to Venezuela. USAID officials admitted that these were still only early days, estimating that at most fifty farmers had benefited from the export of pineapples and up to 500 from the export of bananas (although other observers doubted the figures). But they said there were simply not enough bananas and pineapples to meet the huge potential demand from the two markets.

However, they were the first to point to a number of obstacles: The most common pineapples grown in the Chapare are considered too bulky and perishable for export, and only a very small percentage of the Chapare's bananas are export quality, so the marketable varieties have to be slowly introduced; the bad weather and roads out of the Chapare plus the lack of proper cooling, washing, and packing facilities for the fruit made it difficult to supply a regular amount of exportable crops;[42] and a "chicken and egg" scenario had developed because of the reluctance of wholesale purchasers to make large orders unless they were sure they could receive the goods at a decent price and in good quality, and the reluctance of farmers to grow the crops unless the markets were assured.

The coca unions also criticized the two "wonder crops." One leader complained that farmers participating in the banana export scheme could only supply twenty boxes each, worth only U.S. $30 per month, due to the small scale of the scheme.[43] He said only twenty hectares were given over to growing export bananas, while another observer said the figure was only seven hectares, compared to the 13,000 hectares of other types of bananas in the whole of the Chapare.[44]

Two of the most general—and justified—concerns of farmers thinking of substituting their coca are the absence of markets for other crops and the long wait for any income from them. At least it could be said that bananas and pineapples start generating an income relatively quickly after seeding, compared to other crops. USAID studies show that bananas begin producing in the second year after planting, while pineapples begin in the first year and enter full production in the second year. This compares favorably with nine other crops touted in 1991 by USAID as potential alternatives, one of which—macadamia nuts—needs nine or ten years for full production (see Table 6.3). Of the nine listed, only corn can compete for time delay, but its expected income is low (see Table 1.9).

Ginger, maracuya, black pepper, and hearts of palm were being promoted as crops with potential for the Bolivian market. Of these, ginger, as described above, left dozens of farmers disappointed when the price slumped; maracuya was being supplied to a small ice cream outlet in La Paz, but in very small quantities; "the jury was still out" on black pepper, which is known to grow well in the Chapare, and to have at least a potential local market because Bolivia imports all its pepper from Brazil and Peru; and the future of hearts of palm depended on finding a local cannery in Cochabamba or Santa Cruz. Much hope was placed in macadamia nuts for its low-weight, high-volume characteristics (like coca), but very few peasants had showed much interest due to the long wait before any return.

Visitors to the Chapare are always amazed to see hundreds of rotting citrus fruits lying on the ground at seasonal picking times and to question why these could not be processed into juice. At present, Bolivia's fruit juice companies import concentrates from Brazil and Chile, when there are an estimated twenty-five million oranges alone in the Chapare. Apparently, the poor quality of the fruit and difficult transport out of the Chapare are the explanation, although efforts were being made in late 1991 to persuade a large Bolivian company, Frutal, to buy 10 percent of its needs (or 600,000 oranges) from the Chapare on an experimental basis.[45]

Associated High Valleys (AHV) Project

It was always hoped that the shortcomings of the CRDP's program in the Chapare would have been partly compensated for by a success with the AHV project, the focus of official alternative development efforts after 1987. As mentioned earlier, a team of mostly North American experts carried out extensive research in 1986–1987 and concluded first, that migration to the Chapare stemmed from a long-standing problem facing a large portion of smallholding farmers in the central valleys, namely their inability to support themselves through agricultural production; second, that the Chapare was merely the latest addition to the number of migratory destinations attracting poor rural Bolivians; and finally, that migration had become a self-perpetuating dynamic, driven by interrelated processes of economic stagnation and environmental destruction.[46]

The growing of coca was now perceived to be not just a localized problem in the Chapare, but an economy-wide phenomenon of migration.[47] The shift in thinking resulted in a change of emphasis, away from a focus on trying to persuade coca farmers to grow other commercial, more acceptable crops to putting a brake on migration to the Chapare, or, as one official described it, "getting people to stay put in immediately adjacent areas."[48]

In budgetary and geographical terms, this meant a major redirection of resources away from the Chapare and to the high valleys of Cochabamba. The project had two main objectives: to improve income and employment in the area so that the portion of the population in the high valleys that moves to and from the Chapare and provides the narcotics industry with cheap, seasonal labor would decline: and to stimulate a process of economic growth that would allow the area to become an alternative source of employment for people migrating to the Chapare from other areas. A third, more political, objective was to create a "political space" in which people and institutions could contribute to reducing participation in the cocaine industry (by focusing on development problems) without seeming to endorse U.S.-funded repressive actions in the Chapare.[49] This major shift of emphasis away from the Chapare seemed to go against Article 22 (supported by Articles 8, 9, and 10) of law 1008, which states that coca substitution should be accompanied by investment in the Yungas and the Chapare, particularly the provinces of Chapare, Carrasco, Tiraque, and Arani (all in Cochabamba), but makes no mention of Mizque and Campero.

USAID officials drew on previous studies of the high valleys by CORDECO (Corporación de Desarrollo de Cochabamba) to select the *distrito sur,* consisting of the provinces of Campero and Mizque and centering on the town of Aiquile, as having the potential economic growth to allow it to become a secondary center of development or population attraction.

Despite the general aim of stemming migration underpinning the whole shift to the AHV, the area was obviously not chosen because it was a major provider of migrants to the Chapare. As Table 1.4 shows, the two provinces of Mizque and Campero only supply around 2.7 percent of those migrating to the Chapare from within the department of Cochabamba. Only the provinces of Jordán and Bolívar supply less. Rather, it was thought Mizque and Campero offered the best chance of a higher return on investment, compared to other areas like Potosí. The aim was to create a development center based on the area's perceived agricultural potential (particularly through irrigation) and geographical position between the three departments of Santa Cruz, Cochabamba, and Chuquisaca. Other areas such as Punata, Jordán, and Esteban Arze were not selected on the grounds that they were too linked to the regional economy of the city of Cochabamba.[50]

The AHV project got off to a bad start. According to a November 1990 evaluation of USAID's work on alternative development:

> Although officially approved, Amendment 7 [which created the AHV project] was opposed by key functionaries in La Paz of both the Bolivian and U.S. governments. Together they sabotaged the Project, removing PDAR, the Bolivian agency responsible for implementing the project, almost entirely and diverting support funds from the newly arrived AHV Advisory Team.[51]

Of the U.S. $4 million initially allocated to the AHV, only $140,000 was actually disbursed because USAID officials reassigned the money to IBTA-Chapare to produce more seeds and plants for coca farmers. Work did not start until 1989, over a year after Amendment 7 had been signed.[52]

By 1991, the mood had changed and between 60 and 70 percent of the whole CRDP budget was being earmarked for the AHV project, mostly for road and infrastructure improvements, natural resource management, and improved agricultural and animal husbandry techniques. By the end of year, USAID said it had upgraded over 300 kilometers of roads, completed four major bridges, and created salaried employment for more than 1,000 people. Official documents also said it had completed a large number of "immediate impact" community works such as nurseries and mothers' clubs, forty-two irrigation systems, several potable water systems, and the upgrading of the electricity supply to Aiquile and Mizque.[53]

However, it was very much open to question whether the AHV project had gone any way to meeting its two original objectives of slowing migration and creating a development center. A senior USAID official in Cochabamba said in an interview in September 1991 that the project had been a success in installing roads and irrigation systems and in "stopping a small number of people migrating to the Chapare, possibly a couple of hundred."[54] But other USAID and Bolivian officials admitted that even if it had done these things, the project would have had an insignificant impact on the overall flow of migrants to and from the Chapare. One senior USAID official said it was an impossible task to stop migration, because labor was so mobile within the country that even if the AHV project was successful in the years to come in Mizque and Campero, other departments like Santa Cruz could easily take up the slack. In November 1990 some members of a team of evaluators echoed these doubts:

> Most residents in the Chapare are there to stay. Even if development efforts in the AHV reduce migration from the AHV to the Chapare, or increase migration from the Chapare back to the AHV, labor will become available from other regions in Bolivia. In any event, AHV economic development will not contribute to the reduction of coca production in the Chapare.[55]

Representatives of Bolivian nongovernmental organizations (NGOs) with a long history of working in the Mizque-Campero area reported in late 1991 no signs of any reduction in migration to the Chapare, or indeed, any sign of the area becoming a development center by attracting workers to it. (The 1991 USAID statement of objectives actually makes no mention of the development center idea, suggesting that it had been dropped in favor of the more general purpose of "improving living conditions to order to generate employment and income to stem migration to the Chapare.") One observer made the point that people preferred to migrate to the cities of Cochabamba and Santa Cruz or the Argentine frontier to find work and that the whole AHV project failed to address the real problem of the area, namely the small size of landholdings.[56]

The NGOs also pointed out that the PDAR/USAID team usually decided on projects because of the enormous political pressure they were under to produce immediate results, particularly public works. The lack of an overall, regional, ecologically sustainable policy made serious long-term planning for development of the area virtually impossible.

They also expressed concern that few if any socioeconomic studies had been carried out in the area before the "rush to build." Some did say that the water, health, and home improvement projects had met with some success, but others harshly criticized the emphasis on road construction (which absorbed around 60 percent of the budget) rather than on long-term food security measures. It was not clear, they said, how the roads were going to be maintained in an area of high erosion. They also pointed out that stressing the importance of market-oriented crops was risky because, if the markets failed, then the farmers' solution would be to migrate to the Chapare. A better emphasis, they maintained, would be on improving food production for local consumption.

USAID officials also admitted that some of the community works had hardly been used or soon abandoned for lack of community participation, because villages or farmers had not felt they were theirs. Again, NGO representatives complained that the impact of these projects, far from benefiting the communities, had actually been at times divisive, because they often favored small groups of peasants willing to collaborate at the expense of the local unions.[57] More cynical observers suggested that the main "development" they had observed in the distrito sur had been a boom in the sales of Ford and Toyota jeeps for officials visiting the area and increased income for roadside restaurant owners servicing them and the increased traffic resulting from the road improvements.

To be fair to the AHV project, it could of course be claimed that it was still too early to tell in late 1991 and that perhaps more time was needed before passing judgment on what is, at the time of this writing, the major thrust of U.S. policy on alternative development. But at the very least, there was room for considerable doubt as to whether the main aim of the AHV project—to stem migration to the Chapare—could ever be achieved given the huge reservoir of cheap labor available near the Chapare, let alone in more distant parts. There were many observers who argued that for this reason alone, the shift of emphasis from the Chapare had been miscalculated and that alternative development money should be redirected as soon as possible back to the coca farmers there. Of course, critics believed that work in the Chapare remained both politically and physically more difficult.

Credit Policy

The provision of agricultural credit by USAID both to farmers in the AHV and the Chapare was always regarded as a central component of the alternative development strategy. The policy had the political objective of trying to demonstrate good faith with farmers prepared to eradicate some of their coca, and the development objective of offering a financial bridge between the time of eradication and the expected income from alternative crops.

There is a remarkable degree of agreement between USAID and UNDCP officials, independent analysts, and the coca growers themselves over the failure of the credit program since its inception in 1987. One senior USAID official was honest enough to describe it in September 1991 as USAID's "biggest flop," while a former USAID director for Bolivia in the same month admitted it was "a disaster." Specialists differ as to the reasons for its failure, but it is hard to find anyone who will defend the scheme's record of low numbers of farmers participating in the scheme and the high level of debt arrears for the few that have. At worst, the scheme might have actually encouraged farmers to return to growing coca as the only solution to debt arrears incurred as a result of taking on loans.

An initial sum of U.S. $17.51 million was earmarked for a revolving credit fund in November 1987. But in nearly three years, from December 1988 to September 1991, a total of 1,017 loans worth only U.S. $5,739,000 were committed in principle to farmers in the Chapare (around $5 million was actually disbursed), and a further fifty-six loans worth $203,000 were earmarked for farmers in the AHV project. The average loan was U.S. $6,500, with around half the loans granted for planting agricultural crops (mostly perennials, particularly citrus fruits) and the remainder for buying livestock and equipment. Around 85 percent of the money was for improving production and livestock on land in the Chapare and 15 percent for the area around Yapacani. About 3,500 hectares were covered by the loans, the majority new areas to be brought under cultivation.[58] Initially, it was envisaged that farmers had to eradicate 70 percent of their coca before qualifying for any credit, as it was felt a strong link had to be made between the "stick" of eradication and the "carrot" of credit. However, the policy was harshly criticized both within and outside USAID for the totally unrealistic assumption that farmers, in effect, had to surrender 70 percent of their income at a stroke. Indeed, the 70 percent stipulation—also in effect for communities—was so tough that no community qualified for any of the public works projects. A policy review carried out by a USAID team from September to October 1988 argued that the conditions were too stiff to encourage farmers to give up their coca and inhibited the farmers' "natural desire to diversify" at a time when other crops were becoming available through IBTA-Chapare, and when coca prices were beginning to fall.[59]

Accordingly, the team's recommendations resulted in a change of the conditionality of the loans to three basic requirements: (1) the possession of a certificate from DIRECO for the eradication of a minimum of 10 percent of land under coca; (2) the possession of a certificate of attendance at an IBTA course, and an approved farm plan; and (3) the possession of some sort of evidence of ownership of the land. Communities now had to eradicate 30 percent, and not 70 percent, of their coca to take advantage of the public works projects. Loans for a minimum of U.S. $2,000 were to be awarded to farmers with 0.5 hectares who eradicated 10–20 percent of their coca, and loans for a maximum of $20,000 went to those with 4.5 hectares who eradicated 90–100 percent.

The terms of the loans were normally a twelve-year period of repayment with six years of grace on the principal, with interest fixed at an annual 13 percent rate in dollars, which effectively amounted to a rate of between 20 and 30 percent because of the steady devaluation of the boliviano against the dollar—a high rate in times of low inflation for farmers often contemplating a four-year wait for any income from the new crops. Moreover, in most cases a farmer had to start repaying the interest on the loan within twelve months and sometimes as little as six, even though most of the crops being offered to replace coca did not yield any sort of income for at least two years and sometimes as many as seven years. Officials involved in the scheme justified the harsh conditions on the grounds it would make the farmers "used to the idea of repaying a loan from an early stage."[60] Or, they said, farmers had a mixed-crop system and coca to allow them to start repaying.

Perhaps not surprisingly, few farmers of those eligible for credit applied for it, and of those who did, a large majority soon fell into arrears. The October 1991 report by the U.S. Office of Inspector General estimated that of the 15,001 farmers who had eradicated coca between 1987 and 1991, only 2,398 (16 percent) had actually received the coca eradication certificates they needed to apply for the program, and of these only 842 (6 percent) had received a loan.[61] The same report gives a figure of 40 percent for those in arrears, whereas some senior USAID and UNDCP officials put the real figure at between 80 and 90 percent. Indeed, in November 1991 the coca growers announced that they could not pay back the U.S. $7 million they owed to PL-480 and asked for forgiveness of the interest on the credit.[62]

The coca farmers blamed their inability to keep up payments on the harsh repayment conditions, the lack of markets for other crops, and the practice of receiving part of the loan in seeds or plants. Often, these later died or at least did not give proper yields, partly because of the lack of appropriate technical advice and backup for crops with which the coca farmers (many of them recent migrants) were not familiar. In the few villages like Nueva Canaan where villagers had been prepared to experiment with new crops like coffee, tea, and coconuts, farmers complained bitterly of the six-month period before repayments had to start, compared to the four years' wait for an income from coffee.[63] Worse still, when the U.S. lending agency handling the credit scheme, PL-480, started issuing legal writs in 1991 against farmers in default, the coca union federations warned their only recourse would be to revert to growing coca as the only means of maintaining payments.[64]

Senior USAID officials privately admitted that the terms of the loans were so stiff that growing more coca was, indeed, the principal way farmers were actually meeting payments. It was generally agreed that no farmer in the world could afford to repay loans at an interest rate of between 20 and 30 percent[65] (when inflation was low) and that perhaps coca—when prices were high—was the only crop capable of giving the necessary regular, high returns. Other problems were manifest: DIRECO regularly fell behind in its payments to farmers and in issuing its certificates[66]; obtaining proof of ownership of land in the Chapare was even more difficult than in other parts of the country, usually necessitating a trip to La Paz and often a bribe to an official of the Ministry of Agriculture to secure a land title. Moreover, the few land titles that have been issued have often been given not to individual farmers but to community or colony leaders.

USAID officials also recognized that credit had been granted to farmers on the wrong criteria. Loans had been advanced to farmers who had eradicated coca, rather than to "dynamic, business-orientated" farmers capable of successfully implementing a mixed-crop farm plan. Others pointed out that no credit program in Bolivia had ever worked, partly because farmers did not believe in "paying back money to the gringos."[67]

Compounding all the obstacles above was the absence of a proper lending institution in place in the Chapare for managing the credit program. PL-480 only stepped in as a stopgap lender of last resort when both state and private Bolivian banks were unwilling to do so, and at a time when in 1988–1989 coca farmers in large numbers were beginning to eradicate their coca in large numbers.[68] As an internal November 1990 USAID evaluation pointed out, PL-480 was not a licensed bank under Bolivian law, could not take deposits, and therefore could have no significant impact on the mobilization of savings or the development of a full credit system.[69] Furthermore, PL-480 ran the risk of severe decapitalization because rates of nonpayment and default increased.[70]

A similar credit scheme was set in motion for the AHV project, but with the different aim of facilitating credit to farmers to allow farm development, including better irrigation, improved soil and water management, and more technical support, all within the framework of trying to reduce migration to the Chapare. In September 1990, an agreement was reached with the state bank, Banco Agrícola, to operate the scheme, but by mid-1991 only six loans worth a total of U.S. $21,000 had been approved. Unfortunately, the Banco Agrícola went virtually bankrupt in mid-1991, with "pretty disastrous results" for the credit scheme, as one USAID official described it. A new credit intermediary was under discussion, particularly because it was thought local credit cooperatives in the areas had a good repayment record.[71]

Throughout 1991 PDAR and USAID officials aired a number of new ideas to make the credit policy more effective. These included changing the conditionality to only a certificate of entitlement from PDAR and a technical plan issued by IBTA-Chapare (and no DIRECO certificate), although this was yet to be approved[72]; simply giving farmers a start-up grant instead of credit; asking farmers to pay in kind rather than in cash; and moving from a "credit mentality" to a "financial systems mentality," by which farmers would be assessed more by criteria such as cashflow and small business skills. It had been virtually approved that farmers not growing coca would be included in the scheme (because the current credit scheme seemed to penalize them). But perhaps the most promising proposal was to make the loans to credit cooperatives, so that a community and not an individual would be responsible for repayments, a system that had some success in the city of El Alto.[73] Or, perhaps (see pp. 130, 132), the best hope lay in asking farmers to pay back loans in kind, for example, with milk, cassava, or mint, and not in cash (as the UNDCP was planning to do in its huge milk project in the Chapare).

The abundance of new options under discussion only served to confirm the almost universal acceptance that the credit system in its first three years of operation had been almost a complete failure. The intensity of the search for different approaches also implied there were no simple solutions available to make it more effective. But perhaps the most important legacy of the credit program was to exacerbate the lack of appeal of alternative crops and packages and lend weight to the coca growers' assertion that they could not be expected to chop down their coca bushes until there were realistic, alternative sources of income.

The United Nations Projects

The United Nations Fund for Drug Abuse Control (UNFDAC, later UNDCP) began its first alternative development program in the Yungas in 1985, known as the Agro-Yungas project, with the two objectives of lessening the economic dependence of the farmers there on coca and attempting to contain any increase in the amount of coca grown in colonization areas.[74] The chosen means was to offer farmers production and income alternatives and a package of services. New crops, new technologies, agro-industrial processing, and a soft credit scheme were all to be introduced and a support infrastructure built throughout the region to improve access to markets. To benefit from the scheme, farmers had to sign an agreement not to expand their coca.

Five years and U.S. $21 million later in December 1990, when project no. UN AD/BOL/84/405 was officially brought.to an end,[75] both UNFDAC and outside assessors concluded that the results had been on balance positive, especially when the project was faced with two external variables beyond UNFDAC's control—an abrupt decline in international coffee prices and the introduction of law 1008 in July 1988, which defined most of the Yungas as a "traditional zone," thereby legalizing the growing of coca. An official UNFDAC document stated that the project had concluded successfully because any potential social conflicts had been peacefully controlled; the economy of those farmers who joined the project had been diversified (mostly through the introduction of new varieties of coffee); and it had prevented coca expansion in the fifty-six communities that had participated in the project.[76]

The same document added that around 2,200 hectares had been planted with improved coffee, which increased the production potential yield from 800 kg/ha attained by the traditional varieties of coffee grown in the Yungas to 2,500 kg/ha from the new varieties, most commonly *caturra* (which requires more attention but produces sooner). However, a major obstacle to farmers actually achieving this potential yield was the need to adopt a new technology package, which included the regular applications of fertilizers. Around 70 percent of the 2,400 families estimated to have planted the new coffee were reported not to have fulfilled the technical requirements, due in part to high levels of illiteracy and the shortage of trained outreach workers.[77] In spite of this, it was generally held that farmers were beginning to depend less on coca than before the introduction of the new coffee, which now represented more than 6 percent of the total coffee grown in the region, and 22 percent of the total area grown with coca.[78]

The delicacy of the new varieties of coffee meant that they required much more attention than farmers were used to and that the new varieties were more prone to disease. These problems were compounded by the drastic drop in international coffee prices from U.S. $50 a quintal (= 100 kg) in 1986, when the project was just starting, to $20 in 1990. Not without justification, many of the coffee producer associations complained bitterly that the income returns were much lower than UNFDAC had anticipated and asked for a total forgiveness of debts they had incurred from receiving soft credits to finance the switch to coffee.[79]

But despite these complaints, independent analysts concluded that farmers taking part in the coffee scheme and other agro-industrial projects probably were able to maintain their income levels at 1985–1986 levels, whereas those who did not saw them drop by 34 percent.[80] Moreover, it was calculated that by 1992 a coffee farmer using the whole technology package correctly could expect U.S. $850 more income per year than a farmer staying with traditional coffee— a considerable sum of money in an area where average annual per capita income is $313. It was also estimated that the farmer prepared to experiment could achieve a profit of U.S. $6,860 after a twelve-year period, compared to a profit of $1,998 for the farmer who did not.

Overall, it was expected that by 1992 at least 83,000 quintals of the new coffee would be available for the export market which represents an income of U.S. $2.2 million, equivalent to 17 percent of the 1989 figure for Bolivia's total coffee exports. UNFDAC officials hoped that by 1993 the new coffee would represent 40 percent of all the coffee grown in the Yungas and earn at least U.S. $3 million a year. A new emphasis was to be put on keeping more of the added value for the farmers by processing the coffee in the Yungas and bypassing the intermediaries who transported the coffee to exporters in La Paz.

After 1988, when law 1008 was passed, UNFDAC began to reorient its projects toward the transitional areas of La Asunta in South Yungas and Caranavi in North Yungas. Here too, it was never the intention simply to swap coca for coffee, but to offer a package of income opportunities, including the rearing of pigs, chicken, fish, and bees. Reports from journalists visiting La Asunta suggested some initial success.[81] Also, eight new centers known as *mayachasitas* were set up, mostly in the transitional zones, as a form of peasant enterprise designed to expand local participation in alternative development projects through animal husbandry and the production or processing of a variety of crops. An additional 1,500 families were estimated to have participated in the centers.[82]

UNFDAC's shift to transitional areas produced more protests from critics that, after encouraging farmers to switch to coffee and other crops, UNFDAC was now abandoning them to their fate without resolving their debt problems. Some of these protests seemed partly justified, and reinforced the opposition to the Agro-Yungas project from some of the 400 union and 120 cooperatives in the Yungas (and some NGOs working with them), who were vehemently opposed to the project, partly on the grounds it had been politically divisive by setting up new producer associations or working with some farmer groups to the exclusion of others.[83] Indeed, many observers felt that UNFDAC faced an almost impossible political task in trying to balance the pressures from their funders (mostly the Italian government), which wanted to see results in coca eradication; the Bolivian government, which also wanted to see even more immediate results and benefit politically from the project; and the farmers themselves, who wanted the maximum number of beneficiaries or resources directed to their local union or organization.[84] At times, tensions ran very high; the Agro-Yungas offices were occasionally attacked and, on one occasion, thousands of new coffee plants destroyed.

Official figures from SUBDESAL show that coca production in the Yungas probably increased in 1986 and 1987 to reach 8,900 hectares, but then dropped to 8,200 in 1990 (see Table 1.1). It may be that UNFDAC's work in some areas of the Yungas contributed to the decline after 1987. However, the real test of the efficacy of any alternative development plan was always going to be in the Chapare, where coca yields were better; the terrain and access much more suitable for coca production, processing, and transport; and the power and influence of drug traffickers much stronger.

UNFDAC had for some time wanted to work in the Chapare but apparently only received the tacit permission of USAID in 1988. Some USAID officials saw the Chapare as their area of operation and were concerned that UNFDAC's presence presented what some called a "wild card" in the area.[85] Although there is better coordination between USAID and UNFDAC now, officials of both organizations remain privately critical of each other, which some government officials see as healthy rivalry, others as unhealthy competition.[86]

UNFDAC had similar aims in the Chapare to those in the Yungas, namely to reduce the farmers' economic dependence on coca by offering a package of income-earning opportunities that would diversify the local peasant economy and eventually offer incomes similar to those generated by coca growing.[87] Again, the idea was not simply to swap one hectare of coca for one hectare of something else. More specifically, UNFDAC proposed to add value to the already existing agricultural production by setting up agro-industrial units locally; improving roads to help marketing and providing an electricity supply to enhance local living conditions and agro-industrial opportunities; and, finally, to promote the participation of (resident) farmers, and particularly women, in alternative development projects.[88]

Between late 1988, when UNFDAC started work in the Chapare, and late 1991, the official achievements were listed as follows:

• forty-five communities benefited from small-scale water schemes;

• two hundred fifty kilometers of road were constructed or improved, benefiting an estimated 4,000 families;

• an agreement was made to install a large electricity generating and distribution system, which would benefit 13,000 families and 200 small industries by the year 2002;

• six small agro-industrial plants were either built or improved, including one for drying yucca and bananas for animal feed; a small tea processing facility; and others for extracting glucose (from bananas), mint essence, and flavoring (from lemon grass). (All the final processed products were designed to be sold locally in competition with imported products. For example, it was estimated that the animal feed plant could produce one tonne per day and provide a sizable portion of the national demand for 550 tonnes/month. The tea and lemon grass facilities existed before UNFDAC started work, but were barely functioning);

• two small programs helped farmers to improve standards of rubber and coffee production before processing;

• a large milk processing plant was constructed at Ivirgarzama, covering 1,500 square meters of industrial plant, with an eventual capacity to produce 50,000 liters of milk a day; and various related community schemes to benefit 3,000 families.

From late 1988 to the end of 1992, UNDCP estimated it would spend U.S. $23 million[89] in the Chapare, a figure that compares favorably with the $13 million estimated to have been spent there by USAID over a longer period. To be sure, UNDCP officials knew that their projects were still very much in an experimental phase, suffered from the same lack of market studies that had bedeviled USAID programs, and needed at least five more years for a final judgment to be made. The official estimate was that around 350 families organized into ten producer associations had benefited from the agro-industrial projects and that around 500 hectares had been planted with new crops.[90] A study carried out for COREDAL in 1991 concluded that the agro-industrial projects had reached fewer families (276, or 0.6 percent of the 45,000 families in the Chapare) than the official estimate; that the projects had suffered so much from limitations of soils, crops, credit, and machinery that they were little more than experimental; and that some of the projects (tea, mint, and fruit processing) faced serious organizational problems and limited capacity for expansion.[91]

Nevertheless, UNDCP officials were confident that the degree of receptivity toward alternative development among the Chapare's five federations had improved significantly during the UNDCP's three years of work. Officials ascribed this change of attitude in part to their "capacity to deliver" and their policy of establishing contact and goodwill through the public works programs (to show alternative work can provide what the coca economy does not, and to get the coca farmer on our side, as one official described it), although they recognized that farmers were increasingly willing to diversify in the face of declining or highly fluctuating coca prices. The strategy of concentrating on what Chapare farmers already knew how to produce in abundance—bananas, yucca, citrus fruits—seemed to have met with more immediate acceptance than IBTA's long search for new crops.

UNDCP detected a revolution in attitude from the coca unions when in March 1991 for the first time, all the five federations agreed to participate in its alternative development schemes, apparently after pressure from rank-and-file members in the leadership. In 1991 UNDCP finally gained access to the "Red Zone," which was an area under the strong influence of the FETCTC and was previously out of bounds. Indeed, interviews with individual coca growers and some of their leaders and observations from others did seem to suggest that the Chapare farmers both knew more about UNDCP projects and were more favorably disposed toward them than toward USAID-funded projects.[92] In the second meeting of the five coca federations in Chimore on June 6 and 7, 1992, coca growers recognized that UNDCP projects had been accepted in the communities because of their greater efficiency and lack of conditioning, whereas USAID, PDAR, and IBTA projects were sharply criticized.[93]

However, the UNDCP was the first to accept that it faced a series of problems over the next two to three years, which would be the real test of the viability of its program. Successful public works projects had certainly improved the appalling lack of services in the region and had made a favorable political impact. As many coca farmers pointed out, however, these by themselves could not replace the regular income that coca provided.

UNDCP officials and many other observers still doubted that the small agro-industrial projects could be expanded significantly to replace some of that income and grow beyond the present "showpieces" on offer. Some analysts criticized the one large project at Ivirgarzama, arguing that the supply of milk would not be sufficient to meet the capacity; that it would be difficult to ensure a regular, reliable supply from the four planned milk collection centers; that the relationship between the project and the producer associations and the project was too hierarchical; and that the market for that amount of milk and milk products was far from assured. However, at least it could be said that the UNDCP was making a serious effort to bring development to the Chapare, that coca farmers were showing more interest in other income-generation activities, and that there were some limited but visible projects actually in operation in the area.

Further Observations

Most officials of the Bolivian government, UNDCP, and USAID do share one view, that alternative development, still "in its early stages" after eight years of trying, can eventually work. They differ as to how much money is needed over what sort of period and where to invest it, but they have the common vision that even though there is never likely to be one low-volume, high-value, easily transportable crop to compete with coca, nevertheless a package of services, credit, and other crops will over time be able to approach the levels of income generated by coca. The main justification for their optimism is a belief that coca prices will continue to fluctuate but will inexorably fall over the medium to long term.

They also point to signs that more coca farmers and their union leaders are willing to experiment with alternative development packages without surrendering all of their coca, despite the poor record of such packages and the very small number of farmers who have benefited. It was rightly regarded as highly significant that in January 1991, for the first time, five NGOs based in Cochabamba and all the federations in the Chapare presented a 200-page proposal to the government and international organizations on alternative development called the PACP (Plan de Acción a Corto Plazo). The PACP was an attempt to avoid the so-called "militarization" of the Chapare (see pp. 91–103), but it also clearly confirmed the coca unions' belief in effective alternative development, and particularly in income-generating agro-industrial projects, as the most appropriate response to the coca-cocaine industry.

One of the main recommendations of the PACP was to achieve a much more effective participation of the coca growers in alternative development policies, in order to reverse their more customary status as passive recipients of the projects. The coca federations and their advisers pointed out that the whole concept of alternative development enshrined in the PIDYS program in 1989 had been mostly at their instigation, and yet the government had been unable to put much flesh on it and, worse, had paid virtually no attention to the efficient functioning of the national, regional, and local committees set up within the PIDYS program to ensure regular consultation with peasant farmers. Indeed, it was pointed out that in the two years since its formation in 1989, CONADAL, the national committee on alternative development, had not held a proper meeting.[94]

CONADAL, which is composed of six representatives of government ministries and five from peasant unions, monitors foreign-aid funds earmarked for the Chapare and gives coca farmers some input into state planning of new investments in rural development. If it had functioned as planned, it could have enabled peasant unions to serve as watchdogs over the alternative development program.[95] The coca unions bitterly criticized the formation of FONADAL (Fondo Nacional de Desarrollo Alternativo) in July 1991, which was designed to capture funds from international lenders in order to channel money into areas where farmers were eradicating their coca and to provide immediate compensation in terms of a job and income.[96] Union leaders, disheartened by their experience with CONADAL, dismissed FONADAL as yet another bureaucratic, vertical organization that would supposedly be working in their interests without their participation.[97]

In their PACP, the coca farmers proposed to replace the state with NGOs and USAID with other potential funders. This proposal was a little unrealistic, given that some union leaders were talking about the need for at least U.S. $300 million per year for the next five years to eradicate their coca. But the sentiment was prompted by their bad experiences with PDAC programs, including IBTA and the credit scheme. IBTA in particular was criticized in the PACP for concentrating only on production and not on processing and marketing; for defining packages that demanded far too much capital input; and for being too closed an operation, thereby impeding fuller peasant participation. As the farmers and many other critics pointed out, the government had not complied with the priorities of law 1008, which clearly stated in Article 22 that coca substitution would be carried out simultaneously with development programs in the Chapare.

Coca farmers in the Chapare knew better than anyone how little money had been invested there and how poor their participation (particularly that of women farmers) had been in the planning and enactment of virtually every alternative development project—arguably, the most important cause of these projects' failure.[98] Worse still, the farmers were not the only ones to point out that from 1987, at least 15,000 coca farmers had actually eradicated over 18,000 hectares of coca, but probably no more than 2,000 hectares of that had been planted with new crops. These figures gave strong support to those who argued that there was only really coca eradication and not coca substitution in the Chapare. In a stinging attack in late 1990, Evo Morales, probably the best-known coca union leader and one of the most vocal critics of the failure of alternative development plans, complained that 9 out of 10 hectares eradicated were covered with weed and undergrowth because of the failure of IBTA to hand out new species to replace the coca.[99]

The government defense is often that it could do much more if bilateral and multilateral agencies would give them more money. It points out that it has often sought this money, only to have it turned down or granted in much smaller amounts. For example, in 1990 SUBDESAL drew up a list of 132 projects costing U.S. $961 million, which it presented to the Paris Club group of donor countries, UNFDAC, and the European Community (EC). The government complained that few of these projects could be implemented because the request was either rejected or still under consideration.[100]

In part to meet the criticism of insufficient funds, the U.S. government signed a new agreement in July 1991 with the Bolivian government worth U.S. $120 million, which they said was destined for alternative development programs over the next five years. All the money was earmarked for the Cochabamba department and its area of influence, with the aim of generating employment and income there to stem the flow of migration to the Chapare. In effect, USAID was now broadening the AHV to include the whole of Cochabamba and parts of the departments of Santa Cruz, Potosí, and Chuquisaca (a further movement away from the Chapare).

Of course, the key question was not how much money USAID or any other donor agency was prepared to earmark for alternative development but where, on what sort of projects, and under what conditions it would be spent. The signing of the U.S. $120 million agreement indicated that the U.S. government would put even more emphasis on areas outside the Chapare, because it believed in the proven success of the AHV in creating viable economic alternatives for marginal farmers there.[101] Official USAID documents even stated that the new program was "a successor activity to the current Chapare Regional Development Project."[102] The rationale was the same, namely that concentrating on the low-income groups of this geographical area may help to stop the flow of labor to the Chapare. Such a major injection of capital would perhaps have been justified if strong evidence had suggested that the AHV project had met its original objectives of constructing a development center and stopping migration. But USAID seemed determined to concentrate its efforts away from the Chapare, with the optimistic aim of stopping only a small percentage of the migrants to the Chapare, who, in the unlikely event of success, could easily be replaced by the thousands of peasant farmers and laborers who every year travel in search of a higher income.

Moreover, coca unions were not alone in suspecting that a sizable proportion of the new money allocated would continue to be spent on maintaining a large bureaucracy of middle-class professionals, often appointed for reasons of political loyalty rather than technical proficiency. Even a senior leader of the governing MIR party admitted in late 1991 that there was already a great danger that PDAR had become a "white elephant" because of its large, inefficient workforce. He complained that the 400 personnel in PDAR, DIRECO, and IBTA (of whom 120 were agronomists) absorbed up to 50 percent of the total budget for alternative development in the Chapare. He said the number of employees and quantity of resources were "out of all proportion" to the level of investment.[103]

It was also left unclear whether the conditionality element in much of USAID's alternative development program would remain in place. In 1991 USAID was still working to enforce the condition that coca farming communities had to eradicate 30 percent of their coca before they qualified for any of the high-impact public works projects on offer. UNDCP was nominally working on the same condition, although in practice officials said communities only had to show some willingness to eradicate, even to the point of starting eradication at the same time as a new project; UNDCP thought it was initially more important to get peasants involved in the schemes than to get them to reduce their coca.

The USAID conditionality was coming under increasing criticism because it effectively allocated the infrastructure improvements in response to coca reduction and not a coherent regional economic development plan for the Chapare. Many argued that some minimal conditionality was necessary (otherwise there would be no incentive for a community to even think of eradicating), but that coca eradication should not be the only criterion.[104] They believed that the goals of the USAID program in the Chapare should shift fundamentally toward general economic development objectives and not just the replacement of coca. Within this conceptual framework, more money and investment should be spent, not on rewarding eradication, but on identifying and supporting the development and marketing of profitable crops and business activities.[105]

A slow shift toward income-generating activities in the Chapare and away from public works seemed to be a wise strategy, although not one that was spoken of except by UNDCP officials. As already pointed out, the high-impact community projects had enjoyed some success in generating trust, but in the long run they were not going to provide the only incentive that would get farmers to reduce their coca—the profitability and reasonable certainty of being able to market other crops. In this context, it is worth mentioning a point made frequently by Bolivian ministers, that Bolivia could produce up to 300,000 tonnes of soya a year, which could serve as a useful alternative to coca and employ a large number of seasonal workers. But the U.S. Department of Agriculture blocked a crop-assistance program on the grounds that it could harm the competitiveness of U.S. soya exports.[106]

Table 6.1 U.S. Government Development Aid to Bolivia, 1984–1992

	1984	1985	1986	1987	1988	1989	1990	1991	1992[d]
Development aid[a]	52.3	18.4	24.9	20.5	21.4	21.1	24.2	23.5	31.0
Food aid[b]	22.1	29.5	29.9	31.6	31.5	30.2	33.2	32.1	33.0
Economic support fund[c]	—	—	7.2	7.2	7.8	11.8	33.4	77.0	125.0
Total	74.4	47.9	62.0	59.3	60.7	63.0	90.8	132.6	188.0
Total classified as aid for alternative development	—	—	—	—	59.0	49.0	82.0	121.0	130.0

Sources: WOLA, *WOLA Brief, November, 1989,* for 1984 and 1985 data; USAID/Bolivia Actual and Projected Obligations FY 1986–1989, FY 1990 Projected, and FY 1991 Requested, U.S. Embassy, La Paz, mimeo, La Paz 1990 (for 1986–1991); 1992 figure from U.S. Embassy official, La Paz.

Notes: a. Development aid includes projects in finance, exports, agriculture, agro-industry, policy reform, housing, education, small enterprise development, and coca substitution.

b. Food aid includes both PL-480 Title II, which grants food aid to private voluntary organizations, and PL-480 Title III, which grants imports of U.S.-supplied wheat at subsidized prices, which the Bolivian government can sell on Bolivian markets and use the revenue as counterpart funds for development projects.

c. Economic support funds are mainly funds for balance-of-payments support. They attempt to compensate the government for income and foreign exchange earnings lost because of coca eradication. The funds are used to finance government payment of U.S. and multilateral debt and U.S. exports to the Bolivian private sector.

d. Projected.

Table 6.2   USAID Alternative Development Aid to Bolivia Actually Disbursed, 1983–1990 (in millions of U.S.$)

	1983–1987	1988	1989	1990	Total
Chapare regional development (CRDP)	16.5	5.3	3.6	8.3	33.8
Economic recovery[a]	—	8.0	12.0	33.0	53.0
Export promotion	—	—	1.3	1.5	2.8
Small enterprise development	—	1.5	1.1	0.1	2.7
Private voluntary organizations	1.8	1.2	0.9	0.7	4.6
Community and child health	—	2.6	1.0	1.7	5.3
Household survey	—	—	—	0.4	0.4
Total	18.3	18.6	20.0	45.7	102.6

Source: USAID/Bolivia, "Assistance for Alternative Development," Mimeo (La Paz, October 1991).
Note: a. This is balance-of-payments support tied to the successful meeting of eradication targets.

Table 6.3   Number of Years Before Commercial and Full Production After Seeding for Crops in the Chapare

	Years Before Commercial Production	Years Before Full Production
Macadamia nuts	7	9–10
Black pepper	4	5
Rubber	10	15
Cacao	4	8
Corn	1	—
Coffee	4	6
Annatto	3	5
Bananas	2	—
Hearts of palm	4	5
Pineapples	1	2
Oranges	4	7
Coca	1	2–3

Source: Extrapolated from C. Joel, "At What Price of Coca Is Our Compensation and Credit Program Effective in Inducing Eradication? And What Is the Relative Profitability of Alternative Crops?" Mimeo, U.S. Embassy, La Paz (May 1990), Table A.

. . . 7 . . .

Conclusions

The Bolivian experience of the coca-cocaine industry is distinct from those evident elsewhere in Latin America. First and foremost, as argued in Chapter 1, the production of coca and cocaine in Bolivia is essentially an economic or development problem. It is inextricably linked to the country's long-term structural poverty and underdevelopment, which has made it the second-poorest country (after Haiti) in the Western Hemisphere, with social statistics more similar to those of sub-Saharan Africa. Thousands of landless and land-hungry farmers migrated to the Chapare in the early 1980s to take advantage of the improved incomes offered by coca, at a time when Bolivia was suffering from the social costs, first, of a prolonged economic recession, and then, after 1985, a radical economic restructuring designed to escape from it.

Coca's economic rewards helped to cushion the worst extremes of poverty but did not bring sustained development in terms of improved housing, education, or health (see Chapter 2). The nature of Bolivia's entry into the international cocaine trade was such that the thousands of poor farmers—though clearly better off by growing coca—received less than 2 percent of the final multimillion-dollar profits. As such, Bolivia has repeated its historical role of supplying world markets with a raw material, now coca (previously silver and tin), without being the major beneficiary. The small group of rich traffickers to benefit showed patterns of consumption shaped by U.S. tastes and fashion but little inclination to invest their narco-dollars into productive activities to support the formal economy. The traffickers remain capitalists par excellence and only invest when they perceive good profits to be made.

Chapter 3 described the economic benefits of the coca-cocaine industry to such a battered economy as Bolivia's, particularly the improvement in rural incomes, employment, and inflow of foreign exchange. The total value of the industry in 1990—a bad year because of the fall in prices for coca and coca paste—was probably in the range of U.S. $700 million to $900 million, of which around $200 million, or 20 percent of the value of legal exports, stayed in the country. More may have been laundered back into the country through contraband and other economic activities financed by narco-dollars.

Before the price fall, about 180,000 Bolivians were employed in the various branches of the industry, equivalent to 10 percent of the economically active population (EAP). While the overall value of the industry has probably declined from its height in the mid-1980s (to around 12 percent of GDP in 1989), a major attack on it would still cause severe social, political, and economic disruption.

The small size of the Bolivian economy compared to those of other Latin American countries (particularly Colombia and Peru) has exaggerated the incidence of the coca-cocaine economy in relation to the size of the formal economy, and made the economic narco-addiction correspondingly more pronounced. Although the income staying in the country is less than in Colombia or Peru, as a percentage of GDP or legal exports it is probably higher. Similarly, more workers are employed in the industry in Peru, but the Bolivian figures are the highest in the region as a percentage of the EAP. Although reliable figures are notoriously hard to find, in the late 1980s Bolivia may have been the country in the world with the highest degree of dependence on the revenue and jobs from the production and trafficking of a narcotic.

The benefits of the coca-cocaine trade helped to ensure the "success" of the stabilization plan initiated in 1985, by providing narco-dollars that gave the government more flexibility in exchange rate and monetary policy and helped to finance imports (see Chapter 4). The major drawbacks were—initially at least—an overvalued exchange rate, which weakened local industry and lowered the value of nontraditional exports; and a boom in financial speculation that occurred when a number of saving companies collapsed in the early 1990s, and affected thousands of poor Bolivians. The costs associated with coca and cocaine production, such as youth addiction, ecological degradation, and widespread corruption, have so far been considered insufficient in domestic public opinion to justify endangering the overall economic benefits of the coca-cocaine industry by launching a crusade against it.

The weakness of the Bolivian economy and its dependence on the goodwill and aid of the U.S. government and multilateral agencies has made Bolivia particularly vulnerable to the demands of outside (usually U.S.) governments to follow their prescriptions for combating the drugs trade. Nowhere was this more apparent than in the U.S. insistence on a role for the Bolivian army in antidrug operations in 1991, which put undue emphasis on repressive solutions to coca and cocaine production, caused widespread opposition to the policy, and probably undermined support for U.S. antidrug efforts in general (see Chapter 5).

The policy also threatened to alter Bolivia's poor but peaceful status, a characteristic not shared by Colombia and Peru, where social and political drug-linked violence has exacted a heavy toll on national political life. With some notable exceptions, particularly the massacre at Villa Tunari in June 1988, drug-related death counts are not the Bolivian statistics that attract the attention of the world. More attention is focused on the figures for eradication, the amounts of U.S. aid, and the value of the trade to the economy. The violence that does exist is perceived more as stemming from repression, the state, and the United States and not from any isolated or sustained challenge to the Bolivian state from local traffickers. Still less is the violence seen as originating from the coca growers, who have drawn on the Bolivian popular movement's long history of passive resistance to pursue their demands, particularly through the use of road blockades. They have channeled these demands through well-organized federations, whose leaders have often negotiated successfully with governments.

The threat of a significant break with Bolivia's relatively quiescent past still exists, but it stems less from traffickers' armed resistance than from the attempts of U.S. governments to improve interdiction results. Washington will certainly deem it necessary to step up forced eradication in the Chapare to build on the small net eradications achieved in 1990 and 1991. Insensitive treatment of coca growers reluctant to eradicate in the absence of other alternatives could deprive Bolivia of its other peculiarity among drug-producing countries—the absence of any guerrilla or significant paramilitary forces with close links to the cocaine trade.

Much has been made of the possible galvanizing effect the militarization policy had on the appearance of two new, small left-wing guerrilla groups, the CNPZ (Comisión Nestor Paz Zamora), and the EGTK (Ejército Guerrillero Tupac Katari), in 1990 and 1991.[1] It may be that there are some links between such groups (particularly the EGTK) and some coca growers in the Chapare (the Bolivian government certainly believes it), but such reports should be treated with caution because they clearly serve the interests of other sectors than the coca growers. Like all left-wing groups throughout Latin America, the CNPZ and the EGTK's ideology includes a strong anti-U.S.

position, but there are a myriad of possible justifications for such a stance in the Bolivian context other than the U.S.-inspired policy of militarizing the drug war. However, the possibility of an armed group—right- or left-wing—exploiting the genuine grievances of coca growers to gain considerable support should never be underestimated, especially as the Chapare remains a political powderkeg.

Assuming that the United States will not provide any more money for militarization, then the Bolivian armed forces were rewarded with more U.S. aid in one year than coca growers received for eight years (1983 to 1990). This imbalance between money for interdiction and money for alternative development (actually disbursed) will come as no surprise to many observers despairing of U.S. priorities for "producer countries."[2] It is worth reiterating, however, that such an emphasis fails to address the essential manner in which the coca-cocaine trade manifests itself in Bolivia—as a development problem that affects thousands of poor farmers and needs development-orientated solutions.

The imbalance is also important to register for those who, expounding variations on the theme of "nothing can compete with coca," are keen to dismiss alternative development out of hand; or who think that growers should be simply left to the vagaries of Bolivia's latest commodity boom and bust. Of course, the search for alternative sources of income remains an arduous one—infrastructure and transport are still very underdeveloped, storage and packing are difficult, and profit returns are long in coming. This search may prove fruitless, but there is a strong case for arguing that alternative development has not really had its chance, because the amounts of money actually reaching coca growers in the Chapare for those alternatives have been so pitiful. In 1990, when coca growers chopped down around 8,000 hectares of coca, worth at least U.S. $30 million in future revenue according to the growers,[3] USAID probably invested no more than U.S. $3 million in the Chapare. Peasant farmers had clearly kept their side of the eradication bargain enshrined in law 1008, whereas the compliance of the government and the United States was more questionable. While growers were eradicating their coca in the absence of the other options promised by law 1008, USAID was pouring most of its money into the high valleys of Cochabamba, an area *outside* the Chapare (contravening the spirit of Article 22) for the probably unrealizable aim of curbing migration.

If coca prices do remain lower than the peaks common in the early part of the 1980s, then more farmers will be interested in alternatives. It was very poignant to visit the Chapare during the time of the price slump at the end of 1989 and talk to coca farmers queuing up to eradicate their coca and eager for more information about alternative development opportunities. Such a window of opportunity was probably lost to thousands of them for the sort of reasons outlined in Chapter 6—insufficient funds, institutional infighting, bureaucratic bungling, inefficient allocation of resources in the wrong area, a usurious credit policy, and the lack of farmer participation in the planning and execution of alternative development programs.

The argument of this book is not that the experience of alternative development has been so poor that it should be dismissed as an option. Rather, it could be made to work better, and should be given a chance to do so over the next five years, particularly as the long-term downward trend in coca prices would seem to offer favorable conditions for doing so. More coca farmers appear increasingly concerned about price instability and the downward trend and more prepared to diversify away from coca, if not give it up completely. The Bolivian and U.S. governments seem to have backed off from the militarization policy, which would have made such diversification more difficult to implement.

Large-scale electrification of the Chapare, mostly funded by the UNDCP, will have an impact by improving the possibility of creating income-generating agro-industrial projects. The UNDCP has provoked strong opposition in some sectors for its work in the Yungas, but at least it seems to have placed more emphasis on concentrating on farmer participation in the Chapare. The UNDCP can also point to greater receptivity in two years' work than USAID/PDAR has had in eight, a sentiment that was clearly expressed in the second meeting of all five coca federations in Chimore in June 1992.

Effective farmer participation will be the key test for any successful alternative development program, and therefore far greater emphasis should be put on contacts and discussions with coca union representatives for joint elaboration and execution of projects. The political climate for such an approach seems more favorable because the coca unions' 1991 PACP, while perhaps a little ambitious in terms of the amount of money being requested, was an important indication of their willingness to take part in serious joint discussions on alternative development. The resolutions of the June 1992 meeting of coca federations also strongly supported the principle of alternative development and stressed the need for their active participation, particularly through the national, regional, and local committees for alternative development (CONADAL, COREDAL, and COLADAL).[4]

As argued by the 1990 team of USAID evaluators, more emphasis should be put on identifying and supporting the development of income-generating activities through the marketing of profitable crops rather than ones that can simply be grown in the Chapare, within a context of the general economic development of the Chapare. To that end, it would seem appropriate to reverse President Paz Zamora's slogan of *coca por desarrollo* (coca for development) to *desarrollo por coca*, thereby shifting the priorities.

Some authors rightly stress that in the past alternative development policies have been implemented within the context of a free-market economic model, which appears to work at cross-purposes with U.S.-Bolivian drug policy.[5] The new economic policy introduced in 1985 has probably exacerbated the national and regional agricultural decline by stimulating increased agricultural imports and more labor migration to the Chapare. It may be a little unrealistic to expect any radical reversal in Bolivia's economic model in the next five years, but a greater emphasis on economic growth with more social spending and more income redistribution would undoubtedly strengthen alternative development efforts. This may be a unlikely prospect in the present economic climate, and even more so in Bolivia where there is little money to redistribute. But it is an aim that could be pursued much more vigorously through thoughtful tax reforms to raise government revenue, less defense spending and more on health and education, a second agrarian reform to reduce landlessness, and a national agrarian credit and investment policy to stimulate food self-sufficiency and security for land-poor small-plot producers.

Undoubtedly, more money will be needed from Western governments. As mentioned in Chapter 6, the UNDCP talks of U.S. $100 million a year needed for eight years, while the coca growers and Bolivian government say they need U.S. $300 million a year for the next five.[6] Whatever the figure, it will have to be significantly more than the U.S. $30 million available for 1991, and much more of it will have to be directed to the Chapare. To those flinching at such a prospect in an era of tight fiscal spending and demands of aid for former Soviet-bloc countries, famine-afflicted countries in Africa, or economic reconstruction in Cambodia and Vietnam, it is perhaps worth pointing out that U.S. $100 million would represent just over 1 percent of the U.S. $9 billion total U.S. drug-control budget for 1990, or nearly the equivalent of two years of U.S. military aid earmarked for the Bolivian army for 1991 and 1992.[7]

Perhaps, too, targets analogous to those for eradication could be set for the effective disbursement of economic aid for alternative development efforts in the Chapare. Thus eradication targets would become more into line with the state's financial and productive capacity to provide alternatives, as envisaged by law 1008. This would also help to correct the current unhealthy relationship of unequals between Bolivia and the United States—at present the United States can and does withhold aid when Bolivia fails to meet eradication targets, but Bolivia has little recourse if the United States fails to reduce the number of cocaine users.

It may be the case that whatever reduction in coca Bolivia achieves, it will have little effect on the availability, price, and therefore consumption of cocaine in the United States. Many have argued convincingly that successful eradication or interdiction in one area or country will almost certainly shift it to another—a process that was clearly taking place even within Bolivia. Bolivia could make headway, but the general cocaine supply would not be affected if Colombia and Peru continue producing it and the demand remains high. Moreover, widely known research by Dr. Peter Reuter of the RAND Corporation has suggested that, because the price of the coca leaf accounts for less than 1 percent of the final retail price (and even at the point of export, the price of processed cocaine is still only 3 to 5 percent of the consumer price in the United States), even an enormously successful crop eradication program able to triple the costs of production for farmers would raise cocaine prices in the United States by 1 percent, if at all.[8] The same RAND study suggests that even if interdiction programs were able to seize an unlikely 50 percent of all the cocaine arriving from Colombia, this would add less than 3 percent to the retail price of cocaine in the United States. The realities behind these figures are that traffickers are so adaptable and the costs of labor in the final product are so low.[9]

If true, the logical conclusion of such analysis is that only demand-side solutions, or the legalization or decriminalization of cocaine to take out the huge profits at the retail and distribution end, will work to reduce the cocaine trade. It is not the place here to discuss the efficacy of demand-side solutions or review the well-rehearsed arguments in favor of and against decriminalization or legalization.[10] However, it may be worth pointing out that Bolivia could not take the decriminalization or legalization option on its own without running the risk of becoming the destination of the more unsavory members of Latin America's "most successful multinational." Such an initiative would have to come from the United States but seems unlikely while there is little public acceptance for it, and while supply-side solutions are politically more popular and easier to explain.

Tackling underlying problems of poverty could help to stem cocaine use and coca production. Federal spending on alleviating the misery of unemployment, poor health care, and housing in North American urban marginal populations, where cocaine use is high, has been widely advocated. An overwhelmingly clear option for a more effective alternative development policy in Bolivia could place the same sort of emphasis on alleviating misery and have the added bonus of reducing the possibility of violence. Bolivian observers are not alone in noting the relatively few number of deaths as a result of cocaine use worldwide, compared to the potential number of Bolivians who could die as a result of an ill-conceived policy to contain cocaine's production and distribution.[11] Even if it proved impossible to find economic alternatives to coca, even if coca production were to move elsewhere, and even if a successful policy did little to stop the availability of cocaine in the Unites States, at least policymakers favoring alternative development could be left with the honorable objective of contributing to Bolivia's efforts to escape underdevelopment and helping poor farmers in their efforts to escape poverty—which was, after all, why most of them started growing coca in the first place.

Notes

. . .

Notes for Chapter 1

1. Antonil, *Mama coca* (London: Antonil Publications, 1978), 17.

2. Amado Canelas and Juan Carlos Canelas, *Bolivia: Coca cocaína* (La Paz, Bolivia: Los Amigos del Libro, 1982), 29–97.

3. It is almost impossible to have an accurate estimate of the number of regular users. Many Bolivian experts say the figure of one million is conservative, but most accept that the number is probably dwindling due to increased urbanization.

4. See for example the study by CEEDI-LIDEMA, *Evaluación ecológica de los cultivos de coca* (La Paz: CEEDI-LIDEMA, 1990).

5. For a discussion of Coca-Cola and attempts by a Cochabamba-based family firm, Coincoca, to market a wide range of medicinal coca-based products, see James Painter, "Bolivians Prospect New Niche for Coca," *Christian Science Monitor,* 17 May 1991.

6. José Antonio Quiroga, *Coca/cocaína: Una visión boliviana* (La Paz, Bolivia: AIPE/PROCOM-CEDLA-CID, 1990), 13.

7. José Antonio Quiroga, *Coca/cocaína,* 55.

8. See Guillermo Bedregal and Ruddy Viscarra *La lucha Boliviana contra la agresión del narcotráfico* (La Paz, Bolivia: Los Amigos del Libro, 1989), 477. Article 14 (pp. 550–551) states in its second paragraph, "The measures to be adopted must respect fundamental human rights and must take into account traditional legal uses, where there is the appropriate historical evidence, and the protection of the environment."

9. Amado Canelas and Juan Carlos Canelas, *Bolivia,* 108. The Chapare usually refers to three provinces of the Cochabamba department, Carrasco, Chapare, and Tiraque. It covers an area of 24,800 square kilometers at a height of between 20 and 1,200 meters above sea level, although most of the coca farms lie between 200 and 300 meters. There are important differences between the five microregions of the Chapare, particularly the agro-ecological conditions (there are at least ten distinct life zones) and the mean landholding size.

10. Figures taken from Chart 1b, SUBDESAL (Subsecretaria de Desarrollo Alternativo), *Superficie y Producción de Coca en el Chapare y Yungas,* Mimeo (La Paz, Bolivia: SUBDESAL, 1991).

11. Bolivia lost 15 million hectares of its tropical rain forest to Brazil after the Acre War from 1899–1903. The loss was in part attributed to the lack of investment and population in the tropics.

12. José Blanes and Gonzalo Flores, ¿Dónde va el Chapare? (Cochabamba, Bolivia: CERES, 1984), 48–50.

13. Mario de Franco and Ricardo Godoy, "The Economic Consequences of Cocaine Production in Bolivia: Historical, Local and Macroeconomic Perspectives," mimeo (Cambridge, Massachusetts: Harvard University Institute for International Development, June 1990), 9; and Kevin Healy, "The Boom Within the Crisis: Some Recent Effects of Foreign Cocaine Markets on Bolivian Rural Society and Economy," in Deborah Pacini and Christine Franquemont, eds., Coca and Cocaine, Effects on People and Policy in Latin America (Boston: Cultural Survival, 1986), 102.

14. As Carlos Pérez-Crespo points out in Why Do People Migrate? Internal Migration and the Pattern of Capital Accumulation in Bolivia (Binghamton, NY: Institute for Development Anthropology [IDA], January 1991, 1), there is virtually no data available on the effect of fertilizers on coca production, even though farmers in the Chapare use fertilizers extensively.

15. Cited in Mario de Franco and E. Godoy, "The Economic Consequnces," 11.

16. Carlos Pérez-Crespo, Why Do People Migrate? 17.

17. M. Painter and E. Bedoya Garland, Socioeconomic Issues in Agricultural Settlement and Production in Bolivia's Chapare Region (Binghamton, NY: IDA, 1991), 9.

18. J. Tolisano et al., Environmental Assessment of the Chapare Regional Development Project, Bolivia (Washington, D.C.: Development Alternatives Inc., September 1989), 27.

19. J. Tolisano et al., Environmental Assessment, 26.

20. See A. Rivera, "El Chapare actual," in Debate regional: El Chapare actual; sindicatos y ONGs en la región (Cochabamba, Bolivia: ILDIS/CERES, 1990). Rivera doubts many of the previous calculations of the population, as they tend to simply multiply the number of families registered in union lists by the number of family members. He says often a colonist does not live with all his family in the Chapare, and the union lists include all the farms in the Chapare (which may or may not be occupied).

21. It should be stressed that the DIRECO survey does show bias because only farmers willing to approach DIRECO (with at least a potential interest in voluntary eradication) are included. But Painter and Bedoya argue the sample is sufficiently large to be a useful preliminary profile of the Chapare. See M. Painter and E. Bedoya Garland, Socioeconomic Issues, 1–4.

22. José Blanes and Gonzalo Flores, ¿Dónde? 99.

23. M. Painter and E. Bedoya Garland, Socioeconomic Issues, 24, quoting CERES survey.

24. M. Painter and E. Bedoya Garland, Socioeconomic Issues, 10.

25. C. Ledo, Urbanización y Migración en Cochabamba, volume 1 (Cochabamba, Bolivia: OIT/PREALC, 1990), 57. Cited in Pérez-Crespo, Why Do People Migrate? 2.

26. Kevin Healy, "The Boom," 104, quoting José Blanes and Gonzalo Flores, ¿Dónde? 113.

27. See for example, Kevin Healy, "The Boom," 107–110; James Dunkerley, Political Transition and Economic Stabilization: Bolivia, 1982–1989 (London:

University of London, Institute of Latin American Studies Research Papers, 1990), 15–20; and appendices, Pérez-Crespo, *Why Do People Migrate?* 16–19.

28. M. Painter and E. Bedoya Garland, *Socioeconomic Issues*, 14.

29. James Dunkerley, *Political Transition and Economic Stabilization*, 15.

30. For a general treatment of the ensuing issues, see John Crabtree et al., *The Great Tin Crash: Bolivia and the World Tin Market* (London: Latin America Bureau, 1987).

31. See, for example, testimonies in John Crabtree et al., *The Great Tin Crash*. Most miners did not go to the Chapare, preferring to migrate to cities or to stay on as members of mining cooperatives either in their home areas or in the La Paz, Pando, and Beni departments, where there are small deposits of alluvial gold.

32. UNICEF, *The State of the World's Children 1991* (Oxford: Oxford University Press, 1990), 102.

33. Cited by James Painter, "Bolivia's Free Market Plan Sputters," *Christian Science Monitor*, 15 August 1991.

34. Quoted in Carlos Pérez-Crespo, "Tendencias migratorias en las areas de producción de coca en cochabamba, Bolivia"; Mimeo (Cochabamba: Circulated under the auspices of SARSA [Cooperative Agreement on Settlement and Resource Systems Analysis] and funded by USAID, March 1991), 16.

35. This suggests to some observers that farmers are striking a balance between a guaranteed minimum income from coca and the associated risks, such as police repression and price fluctuations.

36. M. Painter and E. Bedoya Garland, *Socioeconomic Issues*, 16.

37. J. C. Jones, "The Chapare: Farmer Perspectives on the Economics and Sociology of Coca Production"; working paper (Binghamton, NY: SARSA, Institute for Development Anthropology, 1990).

38. Carlos Pérez-Crespo, personal communication, October 1992.

39. J. Tolisano et al., *Environmental Assessment*, 28.

40. A. Rivera, *Diagnóstico socioeconómico de la población del Chapare* (Cochabamba, Bolivia: CERES, April 1990), 47; CIDRE, *Monografía del trópico: departamento de Cochabamba* (Cochabamba: HISBOL, 1990), contains a full list of all the schools, roads, and medical posts in the Chapare.

41. A. Rivera, *Diagnóstico socioeconómico*, 15–16.

42. Mario de Franco and Ricardo Godoy, "The Economic Consequences," 12.

43. As the authors stress, there is little indication of the assumptions behind the estimates relating to planting and clearing costs or net present values.

44. Quoted in Kevin Healy, "The Boom," 140.

45. Quoted in James Dunkerley, *Political Transition*, 44.

46. A. Rivera, *Diagnóstico socioeconómico*, 35.

47. José Antonio Quiroga, *Coca/cocaína*, 14, suggests a higher start-up cost of between U.S. $800 and $1,000, more than for coffee or citrus fruits. G. Justiniano, "La economía de la coca en Bolivia," in SEAMOS, *La economía de la coca en Bolivia: Análisis macro y microeconómico* (La Paz: EDOBOL [Editorial Offset Boliviana Ltda], 1992), 27, calculates a higher figure of U.S. $1,409 per hectare; whereas Samuel Doria Medina, in "Coca Por Desarrollo: Dos Años Después," in SEAMOS, *La Economía de la Coca en Bolivia, supra*, 84, suggests $522 a hectare for running costs once started.

48. One senior UNDCP official in Cochabamba said he assumed a yield of around 12 cargas a harvest, which would produce around 5,000 lbs or 2.26

tonnes a year. He calculated production costs at U.S. $1,000 a year, which would give a net income of around U.S. $800 to a farmer owning one hectare. Other UNDCP officials worked on a lower figure for gross income (just after the slump) of between U.S. $1,000 and $1,300.

49. Barbara Durr, "Where a Green Leaf Brings the Greenbacks," *Financial Times*, 22 August 1989. The minimum wage was raised to 110 bolivianos (U.S. $30) a month in August 1991, but many employers continued to ignore it.

50. Carlos Pérez-Crespo, *Why Do People Migrate?* 11.

51. A. Rivera, *Diagnóstico socioeconómico*, 36.

52. A. Rivera, *Diagnóstico socioeconómico*, 32.

53. Author interviews with Chapare farmers growing coca and cassava, September 1991.

54. D. Green, "Bolivian Coca Farmers Fight to Survive," *Guardian*, 19 May 1990.

55. A. Rivera, *Diagnóstico Socioeconómico*, 32.

56. LaMond Tullis, "Cocaine and Food: Likely Effects of a Burgeoning Transnational Industry on Food Production in Bolivia and Peru," in *Pursuing Food Security: Strategies and Obstacles in Africa, Asia, Latin America, and the Middle East*, W. Ladd Hollist, and LaMond Tullis, eds. (Boulder, Colorado: Lynne Rienner, 1987), 266–267.

57. *Los Tiempos*, "Profesores rurales derivaron en la fabricación de cocaína," 27 March 1985.

58. Mario de Franco and Ricardo Godoy, "The Economic Consequences," p. 13.

59. A. Rivera, *Diagnóstico socioeconómico*, 8. My own interviews with coca growers in late 1989 suggest that it was very rare for a day worker to earn as much as U.S. $4.

Notes for Chapter 2

1. U.S. Department of State, Bureau of International Narcotics Matters, *International Narcotics Control Strategy Report (INCSR)* (Washington, DC: U.S. Government Printing Office, March 1991), 86.

2. The official DEA view is that, prior to 1973, the cocaine industry was essentially based in Chile as a cottage industry transforming paste from Peru and Bolivia into cocaine and supplying a small market in the United States via Colombian middlemen. The coup of Gen. Augusto Pinochet in September 1973 is thought to have finished the participation of Chileans, who were soon replaced by traffickers based first in Medellín. See for example, Guy Gugliotta and Jeff Leen, *Kings of Cocaine* (New York: Simon and Schuster, 1989), 22.

3. Kevin Healy, "The Political Ascent of Bolivia's Peasant Coca Leaf Producers," *Journal of Interamerican Studies* 33, no. 1 (Spring 1991), 87–121.

4. For a full list of the bloqueos, see Rensselaer W. Lee III, *The White Labyrinth: Cocaine and Political Power* (New Brunswick, NJ: Transaction Press, 1989), 62; and James Dunkerley, *Political Transition*, 40–43.

5. Kevin Healy, "The Political Ascent," 91.

6. Sympathizers with the left-wing *Movimiento Bolivia Libre* were on the executive board of the FETCTC and FCCT in 1990, but support for most of

the country's main political parties can be found within the federations. See A. Rivera, *Diagnóstico socioeconómico,* 57.

7. It may seem facile to labor the distinction between coca and cocaine, but many Western observers still often equate cocaine traffickers and coca growers. Bolivians frequently point out that cocaine is essentially a problem for industrialized "consumer countries," whereas the acullico has been practiced for centuries in Bolivia without causing social or political problems.

8. President Paz Zamora estimated that increasing exports of coca tea to 5 percent of the world market would generate greater revenue than the country's gas exports to Argentina (worth U.S. $215 million in 1991). See Christopher Philipsborn, "Bolivia Sees Pots of Profit in Coca Cuppa," *Financial Times,* 3 June 1992.

9. The best known studies are L. Gill, "Commercial Agriculture and Peasant Production: A Study of Agrarian Capitalism in Northern Santa Cruz," Ph.D. dissertation, Columbia University, 1984; Latin America Bureau, *Narcotráfico y política, militarismo y mafia en bolivia* (Madrid: IEPALA, 1982); and René Bascopé Aspiazu, *La veta blanca, coca y cocaína en Bolivia* (La Paz, Bolivia: Ediciones Aquí, 1982).

10. Kevin Healy, "The Boom," 104–105.

11. Bascopé argues that the first phase of expansion of cocaine production occurred as a direct result of a deliberate policy of government promotion under the regime of Gen. Hugo Banzer from 1971 to 1978. James Dunkerley *Rebellion in the Veins* (London: Verso, 1984) recognizes the involvement of Banzer's close colleagues and relatives in drug trafficking offenses (Banzer's private secretary, son-in-law, and nephew were all arrested in the 1970s), but concludes (p. 315) that there was no firm evidence of a "concrete policy of unqualified state backing and patronage under Banzer rather than a generally benevolent attitude."

12. Kevin Healy, *The Boom,* 106–107.

13. See for example, Rensselaer W. Lee III, *The White Labyrinth,* 119.

14. For a detailed account of the García Meza regime, see James Dunkerley, *Rebellion,* 292–344. Arce Gómez was eventually expelled by the Paz Zamora government to Miami in December 1989; in March 1991 he was sentenced to thirty years' imprisonment by a court in Fort Lauderdale. His fortunes—and those of the García Meza regime—declined after a CBS TV program broadcast in March 1981 labeled him the "Minister of Cocaine." For more details on Arce Gómez, see "El Caso Arce Gómez," *Páginas, Ultima Hora,* 15 April 1991, and "Facetas," *La Razón,* 23 December 1990.

15. Rensselaer W. Lee III, *The White Labyrinth,* 119.

16. For further information on Roberto Suárez Gómez, see *Newsweek,* 28 July 1986, pp 28–29; *Criterio* (La Paz), 1 August 1988; C. Hargreaves, *Snowfields: The War on Cocaine in the Andes* (London: Zed, 1992), Chapter 3; and Dunkerley, *Rebellion,* p. 316.

17. *New York Times,* 27 October 1984. There are several versions of this offer. Another is that Suárez Gómez offered to pay off the debt and hand himself in, if the U.S. government released his son, Roberto Suárez Levy, who had been arrested in Florida on drug trafficking charges in 1981.

18. There are several interpretations of Suárez Gómez's arrest. Some say he was heavily in debt to Colombian organizations and was losing hegemony of Bolivian operations to his nephew, Jorge Roca Suárez. This may have softened his reluctance to go to jail. Suárez himself claims that he "had his suit-

cases ready and facilitated his capture" (*La Razón*, 8 December 1991). But interviews with the UMOPAR captain who made his arrest suggest that Suárez Gómez was indeed captured, and was keen to offer substantial bribes for his immediate release. He is currently serving a fifteen-year sentence in the Panóptico prison in La Paz.

19. Guy Gugliotta and Jeff Leen describe Pablo Escobar as a hired gun, kidnapper, and car thief of working-class origins; Jorge Luís Ochoa Vásquez was "a lower-middle class kid"; and Carlos Lehder, the youngest son of a construction engineer, was a petty criminal. Together with José Gonzalo Rodríguez Gacha ("The Mexican"), the four controlled more than 50 percent of the cocaine entering the United States in the middle of the 1980s. Guy Gugliotta and Jeff Leen, *Kings of Cocaine*, 18.

20. The U.S. Ambassador to Bolivia from 1988 to 1991, Robert Gelbard, used Bolivia's new ranking in part to justify the use of the Bolivian army to counter the drugs trade (see pp. 91–103). The Bolivian government never publicly acknowledged its new world status, perhaps fearing increased international pressure.

21. U.S. Department of State, Bureau of International Narcotics Matters, *INCSR* (Washington, D.C.: U.S. Department of State, Bureau of International Narcotics Matters, March 1991), 84.

22. This move to Bolivia should not be overstated. In the long run, most Colombian traffickers remained in Colombia because that was where they were safest.

23. Barbara Durr, "Where a Green Leaf Brings the Greenbacks," *Financial Times*, 22 August 1989.

24. *Independent*, 31 March 1992.

25. BBC World Service dispatch from São Paulo, Brazil, 18 June 1991, quoting Juan Carlos Antoniassi, Interpol's senior Latin American drug officer.

26. Author's interview with senior DEA official, La Paz, November 1991.

27. See James Painter, "Bolivian Military Leader Questions DEA's Role in Drug Bust Gone Awry," *Christian Science Monitor*, 12 July 1991, 6.

28. Wilson García Mérida, "El cuidadano: Techo de Paja," in *La Razón–Facetas*, La Paz, 23 December 1990, 4. The precise relationship between Roca Suárez and the Colombian cartels is difficult to establish. Some maintain that he was indeed successful in a significant break with them, others that he remained a major supplier.

29. Cable of the Spanish news agency, EFE, reproduced in *La Razón*, 16 December 1990. For details of Roberto Suárez's wealth, see pp. 58–59.

30. For a full list of the clan, see *Hoy*, 18 August 1991, 2.

31. It is significant that Bolivian drug trafficking organizations always seem to be called clans rather than cartels. This is because they often tend to be family-based, with many intermarriages, and they never control the market sufficiently to be called a cartel.

32. From 1988 Rivero Villavicencio in particular was sought by the U.S. government. He avoided at least two major operations to capture him in 1989 and 1991. The U.S. embassy said he had three ranches in the vicinity of Santa Ana—Santa Rosa, Donaciones, and India—whence he supplied Colombian traffickers.

33. Quoted in James Painter, "Bolivian Military Leader Questions DEA's Role in Drug Bust Gone Awry," *Christian Science Monitor*, 12 July 1991, 6. It is worth noting that DEA officials often spoke of a marked difference between

the period until the mid-1980s, when virtually all the major traffickers were ranchers or ex-ranchers. But it would seem that many of the younger traffickers to emerge in the 1980s were second-generation members of ranching or latifundista families who maintained their close links with each other.

34. *Ultima Hora*, 17 January 1989.

35. The full list read Roca Suárez, Gil, Barrientos, Rivero Villavicencio, Winston Rodríguez, José Cuellar, Guimbert Suárez, Carmelo Nuñez del Prado, José Luís Naciff, Rosa Romero de Humerez (La Chola Rosa), Mario Araoz ("The King of Insinuta"), and two Chávez brothers.

36. *Ultima Hora*, 12 January 1990.

37. For a fuller listing of different lists published since 1984, see *Hoy*, 18 August 1991.

38. Jessica de Grazia, *DEA: The War Against Drugs* (London: BBC Books, 1991), Chapters 2–5.

39. Jessica de Grazia, *DEA*, 49.

40. Jessica de Grazia, *DEA*, 49–51, and 81.

41. James Painter, "Colombians Elbow in on Bolivian Drug Trade," *Christian Science Monitor*, 10 December 1991, 3.

42. One other trafficker, Alcides Guardia ("The Mexican"), also turned himself in on 22 September under the terms of the decree, giving a total of eight. Guardia was from the town of Guayamerín in the Beni but probably had close links to the Santa Ana clan. Bismark Barrientos (and at least one other) reportedly offered to turn himself in, but may have been deterred by comments from the then U.S. ambassador, Richard Bowers, that the U.S. was not going to forgo its "right" to seek the extradition of top traffickers. See James Painter, "Colombians Elbow in on Bolivian Drug Trade," *Christian Science Monitor*, 10 December 1991, 3.

43. Author's interview with senior DEA official, La Paz, November 1991.

44. *Ultima Hora*, 19 September 1991.

45. *La Razón*, 25 September 1991, and *Ultima Hora*, 18 October 1991.

46. The government had some reason to be pleased. Of a list of ten top traffickers circulated by *Defensa Social* in May 1991, only one remained at large in December 1991. He was Isaac Echeverría, a pilot who had once been photographed campaigning with President Jaime Paz Zamora. Two other traffickers on the list—Humberto Gil and Micky Arrendondo—had been arrested earlier in the year in Buenos Aires, Argentina.

47. James Painter, "Colombians Elbow in on Bolivian Drug Trade," *Christian Science Monitor*, 10 December 1991.

48. P. MacFarren, *Bolivia's War on Drugs Becomes Airborne*, Associated Press, Chapare, Bolivia, 26 May 1992. The DEA also said the Colombians were bringing armed traffickers into the Chapare.

Notes for Chapter 3

1. See for example, José Antonio Quiroga, *Coca cocaína: Una visión boliviana*, 34.

2. One of the fullest lists is found in Mario de Franco and Ricardo Godoy, "The Economic Consequences of Cocaine Production in Bolivia: Historical, Local and Macroeconomic Perspectives," Table 4. USAID in La Paz regularly updates its estimates, as does UDAPE a semi-independent group of Bolivian economists working in La Paz. Two of the most useful

surveys have been written by José Antonio Quiroga, "The Economic Consequences" (although some of the data are now dated); and by Jeffrey Franks, "La economía de la coca en Bolivia: ¿Plaga o salvación?" *Informe Confidencial*, no. 64 (La Paz, June 1991), which is widely quoted in this chapter.

3. U.S. Embassy in La Paz, unclassified memo on the cocaine economy, 1991, 7.

4. U.S. Department of State, Bureau of International Narcotics Matters, *INCSR* (1991), 22.

5. Extrapolated from Jeffrey Franks, "La economía de la coca," 18.

6. Jeffrey Franks, "La economía de la coca," 5.

7. Mario de Franco and Ricardo Godoy, "The Economic Consequences," 14.

8. U.S. $501 million is the median of the range of $419 million and $583 million, arrived at by adding the value remaining in the country plus an income multiplier of 2.8.

9. CONALID, *Programa nacional de inversión de desarrollo alternativo* (La Paz, Bolivia: CONALID, 1991), 4. CONALID estimates the value of coca-cocaine production in 1989 at U.S. $726 million, of which $210 million stays in the country, or 26 percent of the value of formal exports.

10. There is universal agreement that this was the figure for 1989. Figures for membership of the five coca federations suggest a range of between 58,000 and 62,000.

11. A. Rivera, *Diagnóstico socioeconómico*, 7–9, 35–38.

12. One of the fullest lists is found in Mario de Franco and Ricardo Godoy, "The Economic Consequences," Table 3.

13. Jeffrey Franks, "La economía de la coca," 7; and Federico Aguiló, "Movilidad espacial y movilidad social generada por el narcotráfico," in *Efectos del narcotráfico*, Baldivia et al., eds. (La Paz: ILDIS, 1988), 53–73.

14. Jeffrey Franks, "La economía de la coca," 7.

15. Aguiló, *Movilidad*, 58–59.

16. Author interviews, 1988–1990.

17. USAID Update, "Estimates of the Economic Impact of Coca and Derivatives in 1990," Mimeo, La Paz, April 1991.

18. U.S. Embassy, unclassified memo, La Paz, 1991, 13.

19. See Jeffrey Franks, "La economía de la coca," Charts no. 7, 23 for full comparison.

20. USAID (interview with senior official, September 1991) assumes 22,000 families left, while Samuel Doria Medina uses the figure of 10,000 in "Coca por desarrollo: Dos años después," Mimeo, La Paz, October 1991.

21. Samuel Doria Medina, "Coca por desarrollo," section 2.

22. Quoted in *Hoy*, 5 September 1991.

23. Soya is not officially regarded as an alternative crop to coca and is not produced as such despite good international prices. U.S. farmers have mounted an effective lobby. J. G. Justiniano, "La economía de la coca," Mimeo for SEAMOS, Santa Cruz, October 1991, 4.

24. *La Razón*, 3 May 1991.

Notes for Chapter 4

1. LaMond Tullis, *Beneficiaries of the Illicit Drug Trade* (Geneva: UNRISD, March 1991), 7.

2. See, for example, José Antonio Quiroga, *Coca/Cocaína: Una visión Boliviana*, 38 ff.

3. Bolivia was only second country in Latin America after Chile to undergo a severe orthodox readjustment and free-market program of a type that would sweep the continent in the late 1980s.

4. See James Dunkerley, *Political Transition*, 32–39, for a fuller discussion of the model.

5. A similar point is made in Jeffrey Franks, "La economía de la coca," 18; and Quiroga, *Coca/cocaína*, 39. Quiroga argues that the Bolivian economy traditionally required a total liquidity of U.S. $680 million. In 1986, he calculates, the economy functioned with only U.S. $340 million, while an additional $200 million came directly or indirectly from cocaine trafficking.

6. Peter Andreas, "Coca Denial," in *Bolivia: The Poverty of Progress, Report on the Americas*, NACLA 25, no. 1 (New York, July 1991), 14–15.

7. Aguilar is quoted in *Ultima Hora*, 20 November 1988. Rensselaer Lee suggests that an increase in dollar reserves from U.S. $144 million in the second quarter of 1985 to $252 million in the third quarter of 1986 could have been due to the influx of cocaine dollars into the banking system. See Rensselaer W. Lee III, *The White Labyrinth*, 37.

8. Quoted in *Ultima Hora*, 14 December 1988. The interior minister under Paz Estenssoro, Juan Carlos Durán, even threatened to start legal proceedings against Roberto Jordán, a former planning minister, for suggesting that Bolivia was laundering cocaine money through this system. See *Presencia* (La Paz), 15 December 1988 and 27 January 1989.

9. Some analysts dispute whether the influx of cocaine dollars was the major cause of currency overvaluations, or even whether the currency is overvalued. Some of the inflows of foreign exchange can of course be attributed to the government's macroeconomic policies (and not coca revenue), particularly the high interest rates, that often cause large short-term inflows that overvalue the currency.

10. Mario de Franco and Ricardo Godoy, "The Economic Consequences," 21.

11. See Mario de Franco and Ricardo Godoy, "The Economic Consequences," 15 ff, for assumptions and discussion of their model.

12. Jeffrey Franks argues that coca production raises all incomes by an average of at least U.S. $43, or 6.4 percent, using a low estimate of the value of coca-cocaine revenue remaining in the country. See Franks, "La economía de la coca," 10.

13. Acetone, ether, sulfuric acid, and hydrochloric acid are brought in by road, river, or rail from Brazil, Argentina, and Chile.

14. Mario de Franco and Ricardo Godoy, "The Economic Consequences," 20–21. UDAPE uses a similar model and quotes similar results. UDAPE estimates every coca dollar exported required U.S. $0.04 worth of inputs, compared to $0.27 in modern agriculture, $0.07 in traditional agriculture, $0.10 in hydrocarbons, $0.13 in mining, $0.30 in industry, and $0.61 in construction. UDAPE, *Estrategia Nacional de Desarrollo Alternativo 1990* (La Paz: Presidencia de la República, 1990), 13.

15. See Kevin Healy, "The Boom."

16. A military-owned sulfuric acid factory near Oruro closed down in the mid-1980s.

17. Kevin Healy also notes that during a six-month period in 1981, 300 large trucks were purchased by peasant smallholders in the Chapare, "The

Boom," p. 115. Those days have long since passed, replaced by an influx of Japanese and U.S. jeeps bought and run by the large number of the employees of USAID, UNDCP, PDAR, and others who now regularly commute to the Chapare. In a chance meeting, a local Nissan representative told me in 1991 that sales had never been better.

18. A. Rivera, *Diagnóstico socioeconómico*, 48–49.

19. James Painter, "Bolivia Tries to Break Its Economic Addiction," *Christian Science Monitor*, 24 May 1991, 5.

20. José Blanes and Gonzalo Flores, *¿Dónde va el chapare?* and author interviews. Kevin Healy, "The Boom," 129, says extra income (earned in the early 1980s) was not invested in land and animals as it is in traditional peasant communities.

21. Rensselaer W. Lee III, *The White Labyrinth*, 36–37, gives an unusual picture of the Chapare when he says, "For rural dwellers especially, the cocaine industry offers a kind of instant introduction into modern life styles [*sic*]—the chance to enjoy color television [and] videocassette recorders." He must be referring to the early 1980s, as such trappings of modern consumer society are now few and far between.

22. Barbara Durr, "Where a Green Leaf Brings the Greenbacks," *Financial Times*, 22 August 1989.

23. See, for example, Rensselaer W. Lee III, *The White Labyrinth*, Chapter 1.

24. Quoted in *Ultima Hora*, 20 November 1988.

25. James Dunkerley, *Rebellion*, 316. Journalists who visited Suárez Gómez's estate near Santa Ana described it as not particularly luxurious.

26. Quoted in Clare Hargreaves, *Snowfields: The War on Cocaine in the Andes* (London: Zed, 1992), 72.

27. Hargreaves, *Snowfields*, 108. Chapters 3 and 5 provide details of Suárez Gómez and of the García Meza regime.

28. See *La Razón*, 19 December 1990, and 23 December 1990.

29. See *La Razón-Facetas*, 23 December 1990, for a full description of his network of supporters. (*Facetas* is a separate supplement accompanying *La Razón*—a daily paper—on weekends.)

30. U.S. Department of State, Bureau of International Narcotics Matters, (1991), 80.

31. See, for example, *Ultima Hora*, 28 April 1989.

32. It would be tempting to imagine that this influx of capital (and possibly cocaine dollars) released funds for banks to increase lending to stimulate economic activity. But such was the excess liquidity of the banks that bankers initially chose to place their excess funds in Central Bank CDs (*certificados de depósito*). The government set the rate of CDs high to attract dollars (to bolster international reserves), which in turn forced banks to set their rates high to compete.

33. They were, in order of importance, Finsa, Multiactiva, Orcobol, Comcer, Orbol, Cobol, and Vial. They were all based in Cochabamba, but many had branches in other cities. For a full account of the phenomenon of the *inmobiliarias*, see CEDOIN, *Inmobiliarias: La estafa del siglo* (La Paz, 1992).

34. Finsa was the savings company most closely associated with cocaine trafficking, but there were other examples of companies going bankrupt or their owners' fleeing. In 1988 Inmobiliaria Andina in Santa Cruz left thou-

sands of depositors in the street when its owners fled, as did Inmobiliaria Colón in La Paz in 1989. The three companies together defrauded their depositors of around U.S. $100 million. The owner of Vial in Cochabamba also fled in mid-1991, leaving nearly 4,000 depositors with little chance of recovering nearly U.S. $10 million. For a fuller account of the Finsa case, see, for example, Edwin Pérez, "Una Historia de Estafa, Narcotráfico e Inversión de Valores," *Presencia,* 24 March 1991.

35. There was considerable speculation in the Bolivian press that the DEA had pushed the Bolivian antidrug police into carrying out the raid. But private conversations with U.S. officials suggests that the DEA at least was concerned by the potential (and as it turned out, real) adverse publicity for them from angry Finsa depositors.

36. An internal audit revealed in November 1991 that of the U.S. $56 million deposited, $37 million had completely disappeared.

37. There was frequent speculation that some of the "big-time" depositors had recovered some of their money. See, for example, Ivan Canelas, "Prohibido dormir tranquilo cuando se presta dinero," *Presencia Reportajes,* 11 August 1991. (*Reportajes* is a separate supplement of newspaper [*Presencia*] on weekends.)

38. See Juan Javier Zeballos, "Financieras, el más grande fraude del ultimo tiempo," *La Razón,* 25 October 1991.

39. *Presencia,* 2 August 1991.

40. For example, Kevin Healy, "The Boom," 128–129, and LaMond Tullis, "Cocaine and Food," 247–283.

41. UDAPE, *Estrategia nacional del desarrollo alternativo,* 5.

42. Kevin Healy, "The Boom," 128.

43. Kevin Healy, in "Structural Adjustment, Peasant Agriculture and Coca in Bolivia," paper presented at the 16th International Congress of the Latin American Studies Association, Washington, D.C., April 1991, 6, uses a figure of 80 percent. Several other observers consider this to be too high, preferring 65 percent.

44. Mario de Franco and Ricardo Godoy, "The Economic Consequences," 22–23.

45. Taken from Muller Associates, *Estadísticas económicas 1991* (La Paz: Muller Associates, 1991), 63–64.

46. World Bank, *Bolivia Poverty Report,* internal document report no. 8646, 1990, quoted in Kevin Healy, "Structural Adjustment," 7–8.

47. CEDLA, *NPE: Recesión Económica* (La Paz: CEDLA, 1990).

48. Kevin Healy, "Structural Adjustment," 9.

49. UDAPE, *Estrategia nacional de desarrollo alternativo 1990,* 4.

50. Most notably these have been fruit from Chile; potatoes, barley, and some vegetables from Peru; rice and corn from Brazil; and potatoes and tinned foods from Argentina.

51. U.S. Congress, Senate Committee on Governmental Affairs, *Cocaine Production, Eradication, and the Environment: Policy, Impact and Options* (Washington, D.C.: U.S. Government Printing Office, 1990), *passim.*

52. The discussion and papers submitted to the Senate hearings covered 192 pages of findings, but Bolivia is hardly mentioned.

53. J. Tolisano et al., *Environmental Assessment,* Appendix F.

54. CEEDI-LIDEMA, *Evaluación ecológica de los cultivos de coca.*

55. M. Painter and E. Bedoya Garland, *Socioeconomic Issues,* 63.

56. Fires from land clearances to plant new coca in the Chapare can cause smoke to hang around in the atmosphere for days. See James Painter, "Breaking the Cocaine-growing Cycle Proves Too Costly for Bolivia," *Independent*, 21 December 1988.

57. U.S. Congress, Senate Committee on Governmental Affairs, *Cocaine Production*, 5.

58. M. Painter and E. Bedoya Garland, *Socioeconomic Issues*, 63.

59. News dispatch from the Spanish news agency, EFE, Rio de Janeiro, 4 June 1992

60. M. Painter and E. Bedoya Garland, *Socioeconomic Issues*, 63.

61. See James Painter, "The Rape of the Forest," in *South Magasine*, August 1989, 109. Bolivia's annual rate of forest depletion is estimated to be 0.35 percent, one of the worst in South America and only marginally slower than Brazil's 0.41 percent.

62. *La Razón*, 23 November 1991.

63. J. Tolisano et al., *Environmental Assessment*, 2.

64. U.S. Congress, Senate Committee on Governmental Affairs, *Cocaine Production*, 94.

65. D. Farrah, "Cocaine Makers Give the Amazon a Toxic Overdose," *Sunday Times*, 30 December 1990.

66. U.S. Department of State, *INCSR*, March 1991, 83.

67. See, for example, José Antonio Quiroga, *Coca/cocaína*, 48; and J. Baldivia et al., *Efectos del narcotráfico* (La Paz: ILDIS, April 1988), 86.

68. Quoted in *Presencia*, 19 June 1988.

69. *Presencia*, 27 June 1989.

70. U.S. Embassy, unclassified memo, La Paz, 1991, 10. [no title, no address].

71. Universidad Autónoma Gabriel René Moreno, *Universidad, sociedad, uso indebido de drogas* (Santa Cruz, Bolivia: Editorial Universitaria, 1991), 145.

72. Aguiló, "Movilidad," 67. Aguiló settles for a figure of 102,000 consumers of base and 138,000 consumers of HCL, although it is not clear where he gets these figures.

73. The same percentage is used by Jeffrey Franks, *La Economía de la Coca*, 11.

74. *Ultima Hora*, 26 June 1989.

75. Franklin Alcaraz, "Afterword," in *Effectos del narcotráfico*, Baldivia et al., eds. (La Paz: ILDIS, 1988), 110 ff.

76. See Alcaraz, "Afterword," and Universidad Autónoma Gabriel René Moreno, *Universidad, sociedad*, 147–148.

77. Universidad Autónoma Gabriel René Moreno, *Universidad, sociedad*, 347.

78. See, for example, Igor Tadic, "Afterword," in *Efectos del narcotráfico*, Baldivia et al., eds. (La Paz: ILDIS, 1988), 88–92.

79. Kathryn Leger, "Bolivians Awaken to Tragedy of Child Drug Addiction," *Christian Science Monitor*, 8 September 1986.

80. U.S. Congress, House Committee on Government Operations, *United States Anti-narcotic Activities in the Andean Region* (Washington, D.C.: November 1990), 41.

81. *DEA Review*, December 1989, 58, quoted in U.S. Congress, House Committee on Government Operations, *United States Anti-narcotic Activities*, 41.

82. U.S. Department of State, Bureau of International Narcotics Matters, *INCSR* (1990), 105 ff. The then U.S. Ambassador, Robert Gelbard, was so infuriated with the pervasive corruption within the navy that he threatened to cut off all aid to it until it cleaned up their operations.

83. U.S. Department of State, Bureau of International Narcotics Matters, *INCSR*, 1991, 80.

84. U.S. Department of State, Bureau of International Narcotics Matters, *INCSR*, 1992, 94.

85. James Painter, "Breaking the Cocaine-growing Cycle Proves Too Costly for Bolivia," *Independent*, 21 December 1988.

86. See *Informe R* (La Paz), nos. 119, 120, 121, 235, and 241; and WOLA, *Issue brief no. 4* (Washington, D.C.: WOLA, September 1991), 17–18, for a flavor of the full story of Huanchaca. At the time of writing, it was still not known who was responsible for the killings, nor for the shooting of Edmundo Salazar in 1987, who was a member of a parliamentary commission investigating the killings.

87. For a partial list, see Henry Oporto Castro, "Bolivia: El complejo coca-cocaína," in *Coca, cocaína y narcotráfico*, Diego Garcia-Sayan, ed. (Lima, Perú: Comisión Andina de Juristas, 1989), 178.

88. James Painter, "U.S., Bolivians Fall Out over Drugs," *Christian Science Monitor*, 18 March 1992.

89. Some of the more florid descriptions of the Capobianco case by top DEA officials in La Paz suggest that the receipt of drug money during the MIR government went further, involving very senior MIR officials. There is no published evidence of this, although it is hard not to believe that some officials must have known what their colleagues were doing.

90. M. Isikoff, "Blunt Assessment of Bolivia Ignored," *Washington Post*, 1 March, 1990, A4.

91. See James Painter, "Bolivian Right Plots Army Rule and Cocaine Economy," *Independent*, 13 January 1989; and *Informe R*, no. 165 for a full transcription of the tapes. Vargas Salinas says at one point that Banzer knew about the meeting, though Arce Carpio emphatically denies he was representing Banzer. The ADN won the 1985 election but ended up in alliance with the MNR under the presidency of Dr. Víctor Paz Estenssoro. In fact, the free-market model introduced by the MNR did allow narco-dollars to enter the formal economy and help to stabilize it.

92. Henry Oporto Castro, "Bolivia," p. 179. The MNR's *bete noir* was the Huanchaca case, in which Interior Minister Fernando Barthelemy was suspected of giving official protection to drug traffickers. The case against the MIR was not just Guillermo Capobianco's links, apparently through Carmelo Meco Domínguez. A so-called "narco-photo" showed Jaime Paz Zamora with a pilot, Isaac Echeverría, who regularly featured on lists of top suspected traffickers.

93. James Painter, "Drugs May Fund Bolivia Campaign," *Independent*, 6 June 1989. The La Paz–based weekly *Siglo XXI* reported that 10 percent of candidates in the 1989 elections had links with traffickers. Most suspicion, but no proof, surrounded Max Fernández, the multimillionaire head of the UCS (*Unidad Cívica Solidaridad*) party.

94. Some observers even suggest that the cocaine trade has indirectly bolstered democracy by increasing income and standards of living during hard times and providing an alternative "milk cow" for the military. See Mario de Franco and Ricardo Godoy, "The Economic Consequences," 1.

Notes for Chapter 5

1. José Antonio Quiroga, *Coca/cocaína,* 52 ff.

2. The aim of 50,000 hectares exceeds the estimate for the total hectares found in Table 1.1, but official figures of the time were using higher estimates.

3. María Laura Avignolo, "Bolivia: Coca Law Feeds Anti-U.S. Sentiments," *Latin America Press,* 15 September 1988; and Susannah Rance, "Bolivia: New Coca Control Law Aggravates Tense Situation," *Latin America Press,* 28 July 1988.

4. U.S. Department of State, Bureau of International Narcotics Matters, *INCSR* (1989), 7.

5. Although it was not spelled out in the law, the total amount to be reduced over a ten-year period was 35,000 hectares. New coca plantings were also banned in the Chapare. Farmers growing coca in the recent expansion area of the Yapacani in the Santa Cruz department were given one year of grace to reduce their plantings, during which time they would be compensated and eligible for credit.

6. CONALID is chaired by the foreign minister, and includes the ministers for defense, the interior, agriculture, and planning.

7. Anyone doubting this should read part 1 of J. de Grazia, *DEA: The War Against Drugs* (London: BBC Books, 1991), which though remarkably free of criticism of the DEA, should nevertheless be consulted because of the author's privileged access to DEA operations. The U.S. State Department tacitly accepted UMOPAR's (normal) subservience when it commented in 1991 on the "positive development [of] the demonstrated willingness of UMOPAR to initiate raids and operations; previously they would have left the initiative to USG advisors" (U.S. Department of State, Bureau of International Narcotics Matters, *INCSR,* March 1991, p. 80).

8. See U.S. Congress, House Committee on Government Operations, *United States Anti-narcotics Activities,* 77, for an indication of the level of hatred towards the DEA at times expressed by the navy.

9. U.S. officials accused Alderete of being corrupt, but Alderete was known for his strong anti-U.S. sentiments. He cited cases where the DEA and UMOPAR were both looking for the same known coca paste buyer in the Chapare but were pursuing two different people because of their failure to share intelligence.

10. J. Painter, "Bolivian Military Leader Questions DEA's Role in Drug Bust Gone Awry," *Christian Science Monitor,* 12 July 1991. The DEA was in fact never expelled. DEA officials have been accused several times of committing abuses against Bolivians, but no official has ever been found guilty and expelled from the country.

11. U.S. Congress, House Committee on Government Operations, *United States Anti-narcotic Activities,* 24–25. For evidence of the conflict between the DEA and U.S. army in Bolivia, see "The Newest War," *Newsweek,* 13 January 1992.

12. U.S. Congress, House Committee on Government Operations, *United States Anti-narcotics Activities,* 21.

13. U.S. Department of State, Bureau of International Narcotics Matters, *INCSR* (March 1991), Statistical Tables.

14. U.S. Department of State, Bureau of International Narcotics Matters, *INCSR* (March 1991), Statistical Tables.

15. James Painter, "Bolivian Military Leader," *Christian Science Monitor,* 12 July 1991. For a full description of the Santa Ana operation and the controversy surrounding it, see WOLA, *Issue Brief no. 4* (Washington: WOLA, September 1991), 14–17.

16. The most important of these clashes in recent years have been October 1986–UMOPAR attacked by the population of Santa Ana; October 1988—UMOPAR withdrawn from Guayamerín in the Beni after clashes with the population; June 1989—six killed in exchange of fire between UMOPAR and local navy detachment during operation to detain traffickers in Santa Ana; September 1990—DEA agent wounded in clash with traffickers.

17. James Painter, "In Bid to Curtail Violence Bolivia Moves to Suspend Extradition of Drug Lords," *Christian Science Monitor,* 22 July 1991. The government said it was afraid of the formation of paramilitary groups to protect traffickers.

18. The U.S. State Department list excluded "Ico" Rivero, but included Carmelo Rodríguez Roma. See U.S. Department of State, Bureau of International Narcotics Matters, *INCSR,* March 1992, 93.

19. James Painter, "Colombians Elbow in on Bolivian Drug Trade," *Christian Science Monitor,* 10 December 1991. The head of Defensa Social, Elías Gutiérrez, was fired in late 1991, in part for suggesting that the traffickers could still be managing operations from their cells.

20. P. MacFarren, "Bolivia's War on Drugs Becomes Airborne," Associated Press, Chapare, 27 May 1992; and U.S. Department of State, Bureau of International Narcotics Matters, *INCSR* (March 1992), 91.

21. The decision prompted strong opposition from some sectors on the grounds that the Supreme Court should have authorized the expulsion. But others, including some left-wing deputies, privately admitted that they were glad to see Arce Gómez leave the country, despite the illegal method of his departure.

22. U.S. Department of State, Bureau of International Narcotics Matters, *INCSR* (March 1992), 95, states that the U.S. government "continues to believe that the 1990 treaty should be concluded."

23. CONALID, Dirección Ejecutiva Nacional, *Programa nacional de inversión de desarrollo alternativo* (La Paz: CONALID, 1991), 13.

24. U.S. Department of State, Bureau of International Narcotics Matters, *INCSR,* Executive Summary (March 1989), 7.

25. James Painter, "Bolivian Coca Growers Voluntarily Eradicate Their Crops as Price Drops," *Christian Science Monitor,* 21 February 1990.

26. James Painter, "Bolivian Coca Growers Voluntarily Eradicate Their Crops as Price Drops," *Christian Science Monitor,* 21 February 1990. Some U.S. government officials even suggested that the invasion of Panama in December 1989, and the subsequent seizure of Gen. Manuel Noriega, also had some effect on coca prices, although this seemed fanciful.

27. U.S. Congress, House Committee on Government Operations, *United States Anti-narcotics Activities,* 20.

28. U.S. Department of State, Bureau of International Narcotics Matters, *INCSR* (March 1992), 93.

29. "U.S. Holds Back Part of Aid Package," *Latin American Weekly Report,* WR-92–26, 19 July 1992.

30. Much tension followed an announcement in June 1989 that the government was going to start forced eradication around Yapacani, an area west

of the main Chapare region in the Santa Cruz department that had been deemed illegal for coca growing by law 100. In any event, farmers were given more time to eradicate beyond a July deadline. See James Painter, "Bolivia to Crack Down on Coca," *Christian Science Monitor*, 21 July 1989.

31. U.S. Department of State, Bureau of International Narcotics Matters, *INCSR* (March 1991), 83. See also, U.S. Office of Inspector General, *Drug Control Activities in Bolivia, Audit Report 2-CI-001* (Washington, D.C.: U.S. Office of Inspector General, October 1991), 58.

32. See, for example, Guido Tarqui, a CSUTCB leader, quoted in *Ultima Hora*, 13 September 1991.

33. U.S. Department of State, Bureau of International Narcotics Matters, *INCSR* (March 1991), 87. The State Department recalculated the average yields for coca bushes from 1.6 metric tonnes per hectare to 2.7 metric tonnes per hectare (for bushes over two years old).

34. Institute of the Americas, *Seizing Opportunities: Report of the Inter-American Commission on Drug Policy* (San Diego, California: Center for Iberian and Latin American Studies, University of California, June 1991), 5.

35. Institute of the Americas, *Seizing Opportunities*, 32–33.

36. J. G. Justiniano, "La economía de la coca en bolivia," in SEAMOS, *La economía de la coca en bolivia* (La Paz: EDOBOL [Editorial Offset Boliviana Ltda], 1992), 14.

37. See José Antonio Quiroga, quoted in "Desarrollo Alternativo e Interdicción: Palos y Zanahorias," *Informe R* (La Paz), 1991, issue 219, 9.

38. Interview with UNDCP official, La Paz, September 1991.

39. Author interview with senior DEA official, La Paz, September 1991.

40. The results of the operation were that 20,000 people temporarily fled the area, and the coca price temporarily dropped, but no traffickers were arrested. Coca paste producing operations were temporarily moved to the upper Cochabamba Valley.

41. No active laboratories were found, few arrests were made, and little cocaine was seized. Coca prices did drop below the level of production costs but soon bounced back after the departure of the troops in November, although prices never reached their pre-operation levels. The use of U.S. troops provoked widespread protests against the Paz Estenssoro government. One of the more pertinent observations from José Antonio Quiroga (*Coca/cocaína*, 64) was that the U.S. Congress only approved the use of troops in antidrug operations in the United States in 1988.

42. For a good discussion of the domestic consequences of President Bush's war on drugs, see M. J. Blachman and K. E. Sharpe, "The War on Drugs: American Democracy Under Assault," *World Policy Journal* 7, no. 1 (Winter 1989–1990), 135–163. The two authors argue that the strategy erodes basic liberties, contributes to official abuses of power, and undermines the U.S. tradition of keeping the military out of civilian and police affairs.

43. For a full analysis of the Andean Strategy, see WOLA, *Clear and Present Dangers: The U.S. Military and the War on Drugs in the Andes* (Washington, D.C.: WOLA, 1991).

44. U.S. Office of Inspector General, *Drug Control Activities in Bolivia, Audit Report 2-CI-001* (Washington, D.C.: U.S. Office of Inspector General, October 1991), 4.

45. The Bolivian air force flies a fleet of U.S.-owned Vietnam-era UH-1H Huey helicopters (16 in 1991), and the navy operates U.S.-supplied patrol boats (8 in 1991), all in support of UMOPAR operations.

46. There was some disagreement over the final figure. The U.S. Embassy in La Paz gave the figure of U.S. $44.5 million, which included special dispensatory funds and aid not used by the Peruvian government. This represented a massive ninefold increase on 1989, and a spectacular jump from the amounts of military aid throughout the 1980s: U.S. $0.4 million in 1988, $1.2 million in 1987, $1.5 million in 1986, $3.4 million in 1985, and $0.1 million in 1984.

47. Senior army officers said that U.S. officials had "forced" them to accept a role by threatening to give the money earmarked for the army under Annex III to UMOPAR. However, the army was never unhappy at the thought of receiving a major inflow of new military equipment and training.

48. For Gelbard's controversial role in Bolivia, see Paul Knox, "Bolivia Uneasy with Alliance," *Toronto Globe and Mail*, 10 April 1991; James Painter, "Bolivian Military Leader Questions DEA's Role in Drug Bust Gone Awry," *Christian Science Monitor*, 12 July 1991; "Algunas Perlitas de Mr. Gelbard," *Informe R*, La Paz, no. 222, 12. There were several theories as to why Gelbard was so keenly in favor of law enforcement solutions. One of the more charitable was that he thought "they gave more bang for the buck" (quoted in J. de Grazia, *DEA: The War Against Drugs*, 83). The October 1991 Audit Report of the U.S. Office of Inspector General (*Drug Control Activities in Bolivia, Audit Report 2-CI-001*, 4) questioned in its findings whether "the Embassy could have adopted a lower profile style in achieving U.S. counternarcotics objectives."

49. Author interview with senior cabinet minister, La Paz, November 1991. The U.S. $196 million of U.S. economic aid earmarked for Bolivia for FY 1992 represented around 20 percent of planned central government spending. The World Bank and the IDB each budgeted over U.S. $100 million in loans to Bolivia every year.

50. See, for example, Gonzalo Torrico, subsecretary for the drugs fight, quoted in by Paul Knox, "Bolivian Army Joins Antidrug Battle," *Toronto Globe and Mail*, 8 April 1991.

51. *Presencia* and *Ultima Hora*, 7 March 1990.

52. U.S. Office of Inspector General, *Drug Control Activities in Bolivia, Audit Report 2-CI-001*, 39.

53. U.S. Office of Inspector General, *Drug Control Activities in Bolivia, Audit Report 2-CI-001*, 39.

54. Quoted in C. Hargreaves, *Snowfields*, 122. Another U.S. official told the U.S. Congress, House Committee on Government Operations (*United States Anti-narcotics Activities*, 45) that the Bolivian army was a major hindrance to narcotics control activities, and U.S. efforts would be more successful if the military were entirely excluded.

55. Don Ferrarone, then head of the DEA, was said to have been the last to hold out against the policy and Ambassador Gelbard. Other U.S. staff, including USAID officials and embassy staff, also privately admitted their fears about the policy on a number of occasions. Some pointed out that the U.S. people would probably not accept a role for the Bolivian army on U.S. soil. The DEA probably had the most to lose, because it would probably have had to surrender some of its control to an organization over which it had little influence, whereas in its view it had worked well with UMOPAR.

56. See, for example, U.S. Congress, House Committee on Government Operations, *United States Anti-narcotics Activities*, *passim*; briefings by the Washington Office on Latin America (WOLA); Institute of Americas, *Seizing*

Opportunities, June 1991; and, the U.S. Inspector General's October 1991 Audit Report (U.S. Office of Inspector General, *Drug Control Activities in Bolivia, Audit Report 2-CI-001).* Among the U.S. academics criticizing the policy were Melvyn Burke from the University of Maine, Eduardo Gamarra from the University of Florida in Miami, and Donald Mandy from the University of Mississippi. Alan Cranston was the most outspoken senator in the U.S. in opposition to the policy. He argued that the emphasis should be on economic aid for alternative development, adding that forcing the Andean countries to use their military forces against drug producers even exceeded what the U.S. government did in its own country.

57. Critics also pointed out that increased military aid to Bolivia in the early 1960s contributed to the end of civilian rule in 1964. The country did not fully emerge from military dictatorships until 1982.

58. See WOLA, *Issue Brief no. 4* (Washington, D.C.: WOLA, September 1991); and the Institute for the Americas, *Seizing Opportunities,* 5. Guillermo Richter, an MNR deputy from the Beni, complained that the United States "cannot solve the problem of cocaine taking in the U.S. by threatening Bolivia's social peace."

59. For generalized corruption, see pp. 70–74 above. In August 1991, a Bolivian air force light airplane was forced to make an emergency landing in neighboring Paraguay and found to have been carrying sixteen kilos of cocaine on board. The plane had previously been confiscated from drug traffickers and handed over to the air force to help antidrug activities. In 1989, an army general and three other officers were fired after accusations they were protecting drug traffickers in the Chapare—even though they had no formal role in antinarcotics activities.

60. *Presencia,* 26 March 1991.

61. *Presencia,* 24 March 1991.

62. *Ultima Hora,* 21 March 1990.

63. U.S. Congress, House Committee on Government Operations, United States Anti-narcotics Activities, 42.

64. Not all the arguments are included here. For example, some predicted that the policy would cause a weakening of popular support for antidrug operations and for cooperation with the U.S. in general. Others pointed out that very few drug traffickers in Bolivia had ever been captured as a result of antidrug operations against laboratories, which was the intended modus operandi of the army. Instead, most were seized away from their homes or laboratories as a result of intelligence work.

65. *Christian Science Monitor,* 29 November 1990.

66. It was widely suspected that the army was putting pressure on the government to accept the U.S. aid and its new role. See *La Razón,* 30 March 1991.

67. It was widely questioned why the U.S. was training recruits who would only stay in the army for a year. The first recruits to be trained at the Montero base were due to finish in December 1991. Officials said that the training of officers would give the program some continuity, while the recruits would be encouraged to join UMOPAR once they had completed their training and one-year military service.

68. For a fuller account of the training, see *Christian Science Monitor,* 25 June 1991.

69. *Ultima Hora,* 9 September 1991.

70. It is worth pointing out that several coca growers, including leaders, admitted privately that the army might not make that much difference because they were already the victims of constant harassment from UMOPAR.

71. See Evo Morales, quoted in *Newsweek,* 20 May 1991.

72. *Christian Science Monitor,* 17 May 1991. The CSUTCB had originally called a national blockade for 17 May, but this was called off at the last minute for further negotiations with the government.

73. One coca grower died as a result of an accident during the army and police breakup of the march, but the coca unions admitted that security forces had not in general used excessive force.

74. *Ultima Hora,* 23 October 1991.

75. *La Razón,* 9 and 10 October 1991; *Presencia* (La Paz), 11 October 1991; and *Hoy,* 9 October 1991.

76. *La Razón,* 17 November 1991.

77. *La Razón,* 17 November 1991.

78. The official U.S. verdict spoke of the effective coordination of the army and UMOPAR, and the government's resolve to press ahead with "this domestically controversial issue" (U.S. Department of State, Bureau of International Narcotics Matters, *INCSR,* 1992, 93).

79. Personal communication, June 1992.

80. Quoted in WOLA, *Andean Initiative—Legislative Updates* (Washington, D.C.: WOLA, July 1992), 4.

81. Quoted in *La Razón,* 20 July 1992.

82. Later, it emerged that even if the army were to participate in some antidrug capacity in the future, it would be the president who decided it—a principle endorsed by President Bush in a letter to President Paz Zamora in September. The reiteration of such a chain of command was apparently prompted by a huge row over the presence of 120 U.S. troops in the Beni department in 1992, without the authorization of Congress. A U.S. official said the troops were there to carry out civic action programs, but at least one report suggested that they were constructing a DEA base. See *Informe R,* no. 242, May 1992.

83. WOLA, *Clear and Present Dangers,* 3.

Notes for Chapter 6

1. Institute of the Americas, *Seizing Opportunities;* 1. The former Bolivian agriculture minister, Guillermo Justiniano, was responsible for much of the input on Bolivia.

2. See for example, USAID/Bolivia, *Alternative Development Strategy* (La Paz: USAID, 1991), 3. "Only under such conditions [of effective counternarcotics law to keep coca prices depressed] will the economic activities under the alternative development program succeed. . . ."

3. Author interview with senior USAID official, Cochabamba, October 1991.

4. Author interview, La Paz, September 1991.

5. See the criticisms expressed by C. Balderrama, assessor of the FETCTC and a researcher at CIDRE, in *Opinión,* 23 July 1991.

6. C. Balderrama in *La Razón-Facetas,* 8 December 1991, *passim.*

7. There were some grounds for concern. At the inauguration of a new road between Villa Tunari and Puerto San Francisco in 1986, one local

inhabitant told USAID officials that it had been so well-constructed that on the previous evening a small airplane had landed on it. See R. N. Rasnake and M. Painter, *Rural Development and Crop Substitution in Bolivia: USAID and the Chapare Regional Development Project* (Binghamton, New York: Institute for Development Anthropology, October 1989), 15. One of the most expensive highways to be built in Bolivia, from Yapacani to Villa Tunari, right through the middle of the Chapare, was undoubtedly used by light planes as a landing strip during its construction phase. The increase in traffic once the highway was completed in late 1988 (as the road now became the main route linking Cochabamba and Santa Cruz) made such landings hazardous, even at night. The road cost an estimated U.S. $90 million, funded in part by the Inter-American Development Bank and the World Bank. See James Painter, "Breaking the cocaine–growing cycle proves too costly for Bolivia," *Independent*, 21 December 1988.

8. James Dunkerley, *Political Transition*, 46.

9. USAID/Bolivia, *Alternative Development Strategy*, 1991, 1–4.

10. For a fuller description, see Samuel Doria Medina, in "Coca por desarrollo."

11. James Painter, "Bolivia Seeks U.S. Aid to Strengthen its Economy," *Christian Science Monitor*, 15 February 1990.

12. See, for example, C. Balderrama, in *La Razón-Facetas*, 8 December 1991. Observers also point out that UMOPAR is effectively paid for by the U.S. taxpayer.

13. Author interview, La Paz, September 1991. S. Wingert et al., "Review of USAID/Bolivia Development Assistance Support for Coca Eradication," Mimeo (Washington, D.C., 1988), 21, confirms the 60–40 percentage breakdown.

14. Author interview, Cochabamba, October 1991.

15. IBTA's budget in 1988, for example, was U.S. $1.5 million, although only $415,000 was actually released. S. Wingert et al., "Review of USAID/Bolivian Development Assistance Support," 4.

16. Quoted in *La Razón*, 6 December 1991. Moscoso was apparently including investments by UNDCP, which leaves little room for USAID money.

17. PDAR, *Informe técnico* (Cochabamba, Bolivia, May 1991), 237.

18. SUBDESAL actually budgeted U.S. $34.5 million for the Chapare in 1990, which broke down into the above quoted figures, plus $5.6 million from UNFDAC, $9.7 million for DIRECO, and $12.5 million for PL-480. This compares with its budget of U.S. $12.2 million for the AHV project. Author interview with SUBDESAL official, La Paz, December 1991.

19. An independent research center in Cochabamba, CIDRE, has calculated that from 1984–1990 the Bolivian and U.S. governments invested U.S. $131.3 million in all alternative development projects. The center calculated that this reached 1 percent of the coca growers, or an average U.S. $50 per farmer annually. See *La Razón*, 6 December 1991.

20. CONALID, *Programa nacional de inversión de desarrollo alternativo*, 15.

21. Author interview with Filemón Escobar, adviser to the coca federations, London, April 1992.

22. Author interview with Giovanni Quaglia, UNDCP assessor, the Chapare, September 1991.

23. Quoted in *La Razón*, 3 May 1991.

24. See R. N. Rasnake and M. Painter, *Rural Development and Crop Substitution in Bolivia*, 15–16.

25. R. N. Rasnake and M. Painter, *Rural Development and Crop Substitution in Bolivia*, 21.

26. M. Painter, *Institutional Analysis of the Chapare Regional Development Project (CRDP)* (Binghamton, New York: Institute for Development Anthropology, 1990), 7.

27. USAID/Bolivia, "Executive Summary of Internal Evaluation," Mimeo, La Paz, November 1990, 2.

28. Author interview with senior USAID official, Cochabamba, September 1991.

29. USAID/Bolivia, "Program Objectives Chapare," Mimeo, Cochabamba, September 1991, 3.

30. U.S. Office of Inspector General, *Drug Control Activities in Bolivia, Audit Report 2-CI-001*, 63.

31. M. Painter, *Institutional Analysis*, 17.

32. U.S. Office of Inspector General, *Drug Control Activities in Bolivia, Audit Report 2-CI-001*, 63; and A. Rivera, *Diagnóstico socioeconómico*, 63.

33. Figures from interview with USAID official, Cochabamba, September 1991.

34. See for example, a MIR leader from Cochabamba, Bernardo Rocabado, quoted in *La Razón*, 25 October 1991.

35. Evo Morales, leader of the FETCTC, quoted in *Opinión*, 19 December 1990.

36. A. Rivera, *Diagnóstico socioeconómico*, 64, has a list of the various IBTA prices for March 1992.

37. M. Painter, *Institutional Analysis*, 17.

38. U.S. Office of Inspector General, *Drug Control Activities in Bolivia, Audit Report 2-CI-001*, 65.

39. Author interview with a USAID official, La Paz, September 1991.

40. They included rubber, black pepper, colorants (achiote), macadamia nuts, hearts of palm, maracuya, cacao, corn, coffee, annatto, bananas, pineapples, oranges, coconut, papaya, guanabana, palm peach, cardamom, peanuts, turmeric, rice, beans, cassava, ginger, tea, vanilla, and various types of tropical fruit and flowers. Some observers say more than one hundred crops have been tried and all have failed. See K. Griffin, "The State, Human Development, and the Economics of Cocaine: The Case of Bolivia," Mimeo (University of California—Riverside, 1991), 28. Cynics noted that officials would change from one year to the next what crop was seen as the favored alternative.

41. Author interview, La Paz, September 1991. One version given by USAID advisers of where the idea of bananas came from is that a Bolivian businessman based in Cochabamba, who was importing tires from the port of Arica in Chile, wanted something to fill his empty trucks on the outward journey, and thought of bananas from the Chapare.

42. Two processing and cooling facilities and eighteen smaller collection and washing facilities were being planned for the Chapare, and a pineapple-packing operation was to be built near Maraposas.

43. Evo Morales, executive secretary of the FETCTC, quoted in *La Razón*, 5 October 1991.

44. C. Balderrama, "Bolivia to crack down on coca," in *Facetas, La Razón*, 8 December 1991.

45. See SUBDESAL, *Informa*, boletín de prensa, no. 3 (La Paz: SUBDESAL, July 1991), 5.

46. M. Painter, *Institutional Analysis*, 5–6.

47. The shift in thinking coincided with a period when it was becoming increasingly difficult to work in the Chapare; coca prices were high, alternative development policies had failed, and drug traffickers still enjoyed a strong presence. The change in priorities to the high valleys was certainly providential. Author interview with USAID official, La Paz, September 1991.

48. Author interview with USAID official, La Paz, September 1991.

49. M. Painter, *Institutional Analysis*, 6–7. M. Painter also argued on p. 7 that "USAID became the first donor to recognize explicitly the social and historical context in which that participation occurs."

50. Carlos Pérez-Crespo, *Tendencias migratorias*, 9.

51. USAID/Bolivia, "Executive Summary of Internal Evaluation," 1.

52. R. N. Rasnake and M. Painter, *Rural Development and Crop Substitution in Bolivia*, 23.

53. For full list of achievements, see USAID/Bolivia, *Alternative Development Strategy*, 4–5.

54. The same official said that it was only a couple of hundred because not that many people lived there in the first place, adding that "it was never anticipated that the AHV would have a major impact on migration."

55. USAID/Bolivia, "Executive Summary of Internal Evaluation," Mimeo, 4.

56. A. Rivera, *Diagnóstico socioeconómico*, 63.

57. Author interviews with representatives of NGOs, Cochabamba, September 1991.

58. PDAR, *Informe técnico* (May 1991), 34; USAID/Bolivia, *Alternative Development Strategy*, 3, claims 6,000 hectares have been planted in new crops as a result of the loans.

59. S. Wingert et al., "Review of USAID/Bolivia Development Assistance Support for Coca Eradication," 12.

60. Author interview with PL-480 official in Yapacani, June 1989.

61. U.S. Office of Inspector General, *Drug Control Activities in Bolivia, Audit Report 2-CI-OOU*, 66.

62. *Presencia*, 18 November 1991. The coca federations estimated that 13,000 farmers were eligible for credit, of whom 1,050 had received a loan.

63. James Painter, "Bolivia to Crack Down on Coca," *Christian Science Monitor*, 21 July 1989.

64. *La Razón*, 5 November 1991; and *Presencia* (La Paz), 18 November 1991.

65. See James Painter, *Christian Science Monitor*, 21 July 1989. A senior UNDCP official thought 10 percent was probably viable.

66. This was particularly true of the months in late 1989 and 1990 when farmers were keen to eradicate because the coca price was low. On at least one occasion, farmers who were sleeping outside DIRECO offices in the Chapare were told to return weeks later because DIRECO was unable to cope with the demand.

67. Author interview with senior USAID official, Cochabamba, September 1991.

68. M. Painter, *Institutional Analysis*, 33.

69. USAID/Bolivia, "Executive Summary of Internal Evaluation," 5.

70. M. Painter, *Institutional Analysis*, 33.

71. USAID/Bolivia, "Executive Summary of Internal Evaluation," 5.

72. PDAR, *informe técnica,* 33, said the change had already been effected, but USAID officials said it was still under discussion.

73. CEDOIN, "A Roof of One's Own," *Bolivia Bulletin* (La Paz) 7 (June 1991):3. It is interesting to record that one senior USAID official argued a credit policy was not needed at all in the Chapare, as the area was "awash with liquidity."

74. Bolivia was for some time a priority country for UNFDAC, along with Pakistan. Officially, since 1988, UNFDAC works under the direction of SUB-DESAL, in cooperation with the United Nations Office of Project Services, in the United Nations Development Program (OPS/UNDP).

75. The Bolivian government asked UNFDAC to continue working in the Yungas when 84/405 finished. Project AD/BOL/90/419, which started in 1990, called "Alternative Development for Transitional Areas in the Yungas," was expected to be in operation until late 1993, with the aim of reducing all the excess coca in the area.

76. UNFDAC, "Country Report on Bolivia," Mimeo, La Paz, 1991.

77. Econométrica, Resumen Ejecutiva, *Análisis del proyecto agroYungas: AD/BOL/84/405* (La Paz, 1990), 18.

78. Econométrica, *Análisis del proyecto agroYungas,* 18.

79. See, for example, the comments of Miguel Quispe, the president of a Yungas coffee producer association, in *Presencia* (La Paz), 22 January 1991. The credit terms were reasonably soft—three years of grace at 3 percent interest, and 5 percent for the remaining four years. The average loan was for U.S. $1,525.

80. Econométrica, *Análisis del proyecto agroYungas,* 28. The report also suggests that farmers growing the improved coffee increased their income four times over income from the traditional coffee.

81. See Peter MacFarren, "Productores de Coca Deciden Reemplazar sus Cultivos," *Ultima Hora,* 3 December 1990.

82. For a fuller description of the mayachasitas, and the agro-industrial schemes, see Econométrica, *Análisis del proyecto agroYungas, passim.* The Econométrica report suggests that if the families from the mayachasitas are included, a total of 3,900 families had benefited from Agro-Yungas, or 15 percent more than the original target. Government estimates said this represented 14 percent of the total population of the Yungas.

83. The La Paz–based newspaper *Presencia* and a local radio station gave particular prominence to criticisms of the Agro-Yungas project, often carrying articles or running programs, arguing that, for most farmers, coca still gave a better income. See, for example, *Presencia,* 9 August 1990, 16 February 1991, 26 June 1991, 1 August 1991. However, few farmers criticized the new social infrastructure built by UNFDAC, which included 500 kilometers of improved roads, more than 50 water systems, 21 repaired or new schools, and a controversial, brand-new, 40-bed hospital at Coroico.

84. See Gonzalo Flores, "Lo que deja agroYungas," *Ultima Hora,* 22 July 1990; and author interview with Econométrica researchers, October 1991.

85. M. Painter, *Institutional Analysis,* 7.

86. The official line is that "there is mutual respect on difference of approaches," but UNFDAC officials often complain that USAID does not really believe in putting money and permanent employees into the Chapare and invests far too high a percentage in the high valleys, makes too many promises, and imposes too much conditionality, particularly on its credit scheme. They point out they have seventy professionals, virtually all Bolivians,

working permanently in the Chapare (Villa Tunari, Chimore, and Ivirgarzama) on UNFDAC's three main projects.

87. UNFDAC officials said their unofficial aims are to preserve the ecological balance of the Chapare and to keep permanent farmers in the area.

88. UNDCP/MACA, *Proyecto de desarrollo alternativo del trópico de Cochabamba AD/BOL/88/412—Informe de Evaluación* (Cochabamba, Bolivia: UNDCP/MACA, 1991), 1–2.

89. The money was divided into U.S. $4 million for AD/BOL/88/411 (water supply and sanitation), $15.1 million for AD/BOL/88/412 (of which $6.9 million was for the electrification program, and $4 million for infrastructure, $1.5 million for agro-industry development), and $4.1 million for AD/BOL/88/415 (the dairy and associated projects at Ivirgarzama). In 1990 the source of funding for an estimated expenditure of U.S. $13.3 million on alternative development was roughly divided as follows: Italy 65 percent, Sweden 17 percent, United Kingdom 14 percent, and the EC 4 percent. Some European countries, notably Holland, had not granted any money, in part because of the problems surrounding the Agro-Yungas project.

90. UNDCP/MACA, *Proyecto de desarrollo alternativo,* has a fuller description of the achievements of the various projects. The glucose project, for example, was aiming to substitute the 105 tonnes of glucose imported every year, or about 35 percent of national demand.

91. Informe Final de la Comisión Agroindustrial Ante Coredal, Mimeo, Cochabamba, La Paz, August 1991, 14–15. Some observers also complained that other UNFDAC projects had not materialized—for example, a coffee-toasting plant, a jam-making plant, and a fruit juice processing plant (*La Razón,* 27 January 1991).

92. C. Balderrama, in *Facetas-La Razón,* 8 December 1991, makes a sharp distinction between multilateral and bilateral aid for alternative development, and argues that the former (i.e., money from UNFDAC) allowed the Bolivian state to have more autonomy, and thus to reach more farmers. Farmers often pointed out that UNFDAC projects carried less conditionality. A. Rivera (*Diagnóstico socioeconómico,* 66), reported that in 1990 PDAC projects were hardly known, largely because of the absence of any PDAC office in the Chapare.

93. CEDOIN, "Productores de coca: Il encuentro del trópico de Cochabamba," *Informe R* no. 244, June 1992, 4–5.

94. See Lupe Cajias, "¿Es posible el desarrollo alternativo o es parte de la guerra hipócrita?" *Hoy,* 30 June 1991.

95. Kevin Healy, "The Political Ascent of Bolivia's Peasant Coca Leaf Producers," *Journal of Interamerican Studies and World Affairs* (1991a): 99–100.

96. FONADAL formed part of the government's strategic plan to replace the whole coca economy. FONADAL was to form a bridge between the eradication and the maturing of long-term investments, providing short-term employment (for example, in public works projects) either in the Chapare or other areas. FONADAL's director said it needed U.S. $36 million from international donors in 1992, but at the time of writing it was unclear if even a quarter of that had been pledged.

97. See for example, Segundino Montevilla, quoted in *Presencia,* 29 May 1991.

98. The UNDCP has started a small farm complex so that women in the Chapare could improve nutritional levels and incomes by rearing hamsters

and other animals, but at the time of writing, only a handful of women were participating.

99. Quoted in "Desarrollo Alternativo Constituye un Rotundo Fracaso en el Chapare," *Opinión,* 19 December 1990.

100. *Presencia,* 27 December 1990. Not all government officials say the lack of funds is the problem. Samuel Doria Medina, the former planning minister, has argued it is Bolivia's lack of capacity to spend it that is the obstacle (Quoted in *La Razón,* 26 May 1991).

101. See, for example, U.S. Department of State, Bureau of International Narcotics Matters, *INCSR* (1991), 4.

102. USAID/Bolivia, *Alternative Development Strategy,* 4.

103. Quoted in "Frondoso personal en desarrollo alternativo impide más resultados," *La Razón,* 25 October 1991.

104. USAID/Bolivia, "Executive Summary of Internal Evaluation," La Paz, November 1991, 10.

105. USAID/Bolivia, "Executive Summary of Internal Evaluation," 10.

106. U.S. Office of Inspector General, *Drug Control Activities in Bolivia, Audit Report 2-CI-001,* 68; and *Presencia,* 25 June 1990.

Notes for Chapter 7

1. WOLA, *Issue Brief no. 4* (Washington D.C.: WOLA), September 1991; and WOLA, *Clear and Present Dangers,* 127.

2. See, for example, Carlos Toranzos, "Economía informal, economía ilegal: El papel del narcotráfico," paper presented at CERID Conference, La Paz, March 1991. Many despair, too, of U.S. overall priorities in attacking production and supply rather than demand and consumption. In the proposed U.S. federal budget for FY 1992, 70 percent of resources were devoted to programs for supply reduction (mostly interdiction and law enforcement), and only 30 percent to programs for demand reduction. See Institute of the Americas, *Seizing Opportunities,* 3.

3. The subdirector of FONADAL, Juan José Torrez, said in late 1991 that the Bolivian government needed U.S. $300 million to compensate for the coca eradicated.

4. CEDOIN, "Productores de coca: II encuentro del trópico de Cochabamba," *Informe R no. 244,* La Paz, 5.

5. Kevin Healy, "Structural Adjustment, Peasant Poverty and Coca in Bolivia," paper presented at the 16th Congress of the Latin American Studies Association, Washington, 4–6 April 1991.

6. This is the estimate of CONALID. Other government estimates suggest that the eradication of excess coca in eight years would need U.S. $434 million in the first year ($61 million for balance of payments, $25 million for a social compensation fund, and $348 million in general development funds) rising to $1.5 billion in the eighth year. These larger figures take into account both the loss of income from coca-cocaine production and the indirect effects. UDAPE, *Estrategía nacional de desarrollo alternativo 1990,* 38–39.

7. U.S. Office of Inspector General, *Drug Control Activities in Bolivia, Audit Report 2-CI-001,* 2.

8. Testimony of Peter Reuter before the Subcommittees on Legislation and National Security and Government Information, Justice and Agriculture, Washington, October 1989, quoted in U.S. Congress, House Committee on Government Operations, *United States Anti-narcotic Activities*, 33–35.

9. U.S. Congress, House Committee on Government Operations, United States Anti-narcotic Activities, 34.

10. Legalization is favored by such luminaries as Milton Friedman, and by the *Economist* and the *New York Times*. A useful summary of the arguments is found in Muller Associates, *La economía de la coca*, 13–14.

11. See, for example, Peter Bourne, a former adviser to President Carter, in "Bring Cocaine in from the Cold," *Financial Times*, 6 September 1989. He estimates less than one thousand die each year worldwide from the effects of cocaine, compared to the two million annually from the effects of tobacco.

Acronyms

• • •

ADEPA	Asociación de Productores de Algodón (Association of Cotton Growers)
ADN	Acción Democrática Nacionalista (Nationalist Democratic Action—a principal Bolivian political party)
AHV	Associated High Valleys Project (Valles Altos)
AIPE	Asociación de Instituciones de Promoción y Educación (Association of Promotion and Education Institutes)
CEDLA	Centro de Estudios para el Desarrollo Laboral y Agrario (Center for Studies of Labor and Agrarian Development)
CEDOIN	Centro de Documentación e Información (Documentation and Information Center)
CEEDI	Centro de Estudios Ecológicos y de Desarrollo Integral (Center for Ecological Studies and Integrated Development)
CEPB	Confederación de Empresarios Privados de Bolivia (Confederation of Bolivian Private Sector Businesses)
CERES	Centro de Estudios de la Realidad Económica y Social (Cochabamba) (Center for Economic and Social Studies, Cochabamba)
CERID	Centro par al Estudio de Relaciones Internacionales y el Desarrollo (Center for the Study of International Relations and Development)
CESE	Campaña Educativa Sobre Estupefacientes (Educational Campaign Against Drugs)
CID	Centro de Información para el Desarrollo (Center of Information and Development)
CIDRE	Centro de Invesigación y Desarrollo Regional (Center for Regional Information and Development)

173

CNPZ	Comisión Nestor Paz Zamora (Nestor Paz Zamora Commission)
COB	Central Obrera Boliviana (Bolivian Workers Central)
COFADENA	Corporación de las Fuerzas Armadas para el Desarrollo Nacional (the Bolivian Army's development corporation)
COLADAL	Consejo Local de Desarrollo Alternativo (Local Council on Alternative Development)
CONADAL	Consejo Nacional de Desarrollo Alternativo (National Council on Alternative Development)
CONALID	El Consejo Nacional Contra el Uso Indebido y Tráfico Ilícito de Drogas (National Council Against Illegal Use and Trafficking of Illicit Drugs)
CONAPRE	Consejo Nacional de Prevención Integral del Uso Indebido de Drogas (National Council on Drug Abuse Prevention and Education)
CORDECO	Corporación de Desarrollo de Cochabamba (Cochabamba Development Corporation)
COREDAL	Comité Regional de Desarrollo Alternativo (Regional Council on Alternative Development)
CRDP	Chapare Regional Development Project
CSUTCB	Confederación Sindical Unica de Trabajadores Campesinos de Bolivia (The Sole Sindical Confederation of Peasant Workers of Bolivia)
DEA	Drug Enforcement Administration (United States)
DIRECO	Dirección de Reconversión Agrícola (Directorate of Agricultural Reconversion)
EAP	economically active population
EGTK	Ejército Guerrillero Tupac Katari (Tupac Katari Guerrilla Army)
ESF	Economic Support Fund
FCCT	Federación de Colonizadores de Carrasco Tropical (Federation of Colonizers of Tropical Carrasco)
FECCh	Federación Especial de Colonizadores de Chimoré (Special Federation of Colonizers of Chimoré)
FETCTC	Federación Especial de Trabajadores Campesinos del Trópico de Cochabamba (Special Federation of Peasant Workers of the Tropics of Cochabamba)
FEYCh	Federación Especial de Yungas-Chapare (Special Federation of the Yungas-Chapare)
FINSA	Firma Integral de Servicios Arévalo (Arévalo Integral Service Company)
FONADAL	Fondo Nacional de Desarrollo Alternativo (National Fund for Alternative Development)

FUCU	Federación Unica de Centrales Unicas (Unitary Federation of Unitary Central Bodies)
IBTA-Chapare	Instituto Boliviano de Tecnología Agropecuario (An agricultural research and extension center)
IDB	Inter-American Development Bank
ILDIS	Instituto Latinoamericano de Investigaciones Sociales (Latin American Institute of Social Research)
INCSR	*International Narcotics Control Strategy Report,* published by the Bureau of International Narcotics Matters, U.S. Department of State
INE	Instituto Nacional de Estadísticas (Institute of National Statistics)
LIDEMA	La Liga de Defensa del Medio Ambiente (League for the Defense of the Environment)
MACA	Ministerio de Asuntos Campesinos y Agricultura (Ministry of Peasant Affairs and Agriculture)
MBL	Movimiento de Bolivia Libre (Free Bolivia Movement)
MIR	Movimiento de la Izquierda Revolucionaria (Movement of the Revolutionary Left—a principal Bolivian political party)
MNR	Movimiento Nacionalista Revolucionario (Revolutionary Nationalist Movement—a principal Bolivian political party)
NAU	Narcotics Affairs Unit (renamed NAS) (U.S. Embassy, La Paz)
OAS	Organization of American States
OIT	Organización Internacional de Trabajo (International Labor Organization—ILO)
ONDCP	U.S. Office of National Drug Control Policy
PACP	Plan de Acción a Corto Plazo (Short-term Action Plan)
PDAC	Proyecto de Desarrollo Alternativo de Cochabamba (Cochabamba alternative development project; subsumed by PDAR)
PDAR	Programa de Desarrollo Alternativo Regional (Program for Regional Alternative Development). Formerly known as PDAC (Proyecto de Desarrollo Alternativo de Cochabamba)
PIDYS	Plan Integral de Desarrollo y Substitución (Integrated Development and Substitution Plan)
PREALC	Programa Regional del Empleo para América Latina y el Caribe (Regional Employment Program for Latin America and the Caribbean)

PRODES	Proyecto de Desarrollo Chapare–Yungas (Chapare–Yungas Development Project)
SEAMOS	Sistema Educativo Antidrogadicción y de Movilización Social (Drug Addiction Prevention and Mobilization Program)
SNC	Servicio Nacional de Caminos (National Road Service)
SUBDESAL	Subsecretaría de Desarrollo Alternativo (Subsecretariat for Alternative Development)
UCS	Unidad Cívica Solidaridad (Union of Civic Solidarity)
UDAPE	Unidad de Análisis de Políticas Económicas (Unit of Analysis of Economic Policies)
UDP	Union Democrática y Popular (Democratic and Popular Unity)
UMOPAR	Unidad Móvil de Patrullaje Rural (Rural Mobile Patrol Unit)
UNDCP	United Nations Drug Control Program (formerly UNFDAC)
UNDP	United Nations Development Program
UNFDAC	United Nations Fund for Drug Abuse Control
UNRISD	United Nations Research Institute for Social Development
UNU	United Nations University
USAID	United States Agency for International Development
WOLA	Washington Office on Latin America
YPFB	Yacimientos Petrolíferos Fiscales Bolivianos (Bolivian State Petroleum Company)

Bibliography

• • •

Aguiló, Federico. 1988. "Movilidad espacial y movilidad social generada por el narcotráfico." In *Efectos del narcotráfico,* ed. Baldivia et al. La Paz: ILDIS.

Aguirre Badani, Alvaro, José Luís Pérez Ramírez, and Carlos Villegas Quiroga. 1990. *NPE: Recesión Económica.* La Paz: CEDLA.

Alcaraz, Franklin. 1988. "Afterword." In *Efectos del narcotráfico,* ed. Baldivia et al. La Paz: ILDIS.

Alvarez, Elena. 1992. "Opportunities and Constraints to Reduce Coca Production: The Macroeconomic Context in Bolivia and Peru." Paper prepared for the U.S. Congress, Office of Technology Assessment.

_____. 1990. "The Illegal Coca Production in Peru: A Preliminary Assessment of Its Economic Impact." Paper presented at the Project Hemispheric Cooperation for the Prevention of Drug Abuse and Traffic, at the Institute of the Americas and the University of California, April 19–21.

_____. 1988. *The Economics and Political Economy of Coca Production in the Andes: Implications for U.S. Foreign Policy and Rural Development in Bolivia and Peru.* Albany: Nelson A. Rockefeller Institute of Government.

Andreas, Peter. 1991. "Coca Denial." *Bolivia: The Poverty of Progress, Report on the Americas.* NACLA 25, no. 1 (July): 14–15.

Andreas, Peter, and C. Youngers. 1989. "Busting the Andean Cocaine Industry." *World Policy Journal,* Summer.

Antezana Malpartida, Oscar. 1990. *Bolivia: Exito macroeconómico, deficiencias microeconómicas.* Cochabamba: Los Amigos del Libro.

Antonil. 1978. *Mama coca.* London: Antonil.

Bagley, B. M. 1988. "U.S. Foreign Policy and the War on Drugs: Analysis of a Policy Failure." *Journal of Interamerican Studies and World Affairs* 30: 189–212.

Baldivia, José, Eric Roth, Federico Aguiló, and Daniel Caberas. 1988. *Efectos del narcotráfico.* La Paz: ILDIS.

Bascopé Aspiazu, Rene. 1982. *La veta blanca: Coca y cocaína en Bolivia.* La Paz: Ediciones Aquí.

Bedregal Gutiérrez, Guillermo, and Ruddy Viscarra Pando. 1989. *La lucha Boliviana contra la agresión del narcotráfico.* La Paz: Los Amigos del Libro.

Blanes, José, and Gonzalo Flores. 1984a. *De los valles al chapare.* Cochabamba: CERES.

_____. 1984b. *¿Dónde va el Chapare?* Cochabamba: CERES.

_____. 1982. *Campesino, migrante y colonizador.* La Paz: CERES.

Bruno, M., G. Di Tella, R. Dornbusch, and S. Fischer, eds. 1988. *Inflation Stabilization: The Experience of Argentina, Brazil, Bolivia, Israel and Mexico.* Cambridge, Mass: MIT Press.

Canelas Orellana, Amado, and Juan Carlos Canelas Zannier. 1982. *Bolivia: Coca cocaína.* La Paz: Los Amigos del Libro.

Carter, W., and M. Mamani. 1986. *Coca en Bolivia.* La Paz: Juventud.

CEDLA. 1990. *NPE: Recesión Económica.* La Paz: CEDLA.

CEDOIN (Centro de Documentación e Información). 1991. *Inmobiliarias: La estafa del siglo.* (December).

CEEDI-LIDEMA. 1990. *Evaluación ecológica de los cultivos de coca.* La Paz.

CIDRE. 1990. *Monografía del trópico: Departamento de Cochabamba.* Cochabamba: CIDRE.

———. 1988. *Estrategia y plan de acción para la formulación de un plan de desarrollo del trópico Cochabamba.* Cochabamba: CIDRE.

CONALID. 1991. *Programa nacional de inversión de desarrollo alternativo.* La Paz.

Crabtree, John, Gavan Duffy, and Jenny Pearce. 1987. *The Great Tin Crash: Bolivia and the World Tin Market.* London: Latin America Bureau.

Craig, R. 1987. "Illicit Drug Traffic: Implications for South American Source Countries." *Journal of Interamerican Studies of World Affairs* 29, no. 2: 1–34.

Curi, C., and C. Arze. 1990. *Estudio del impacto de los precursores en la producción de cocaína sobre el medio ambiente en Bolivia.* La Paz: USAID/Lidema.

Dávila, Sonia, Linda Farthing, and Susanna Rance. 1989. *Coca: The Real Green Revolution.* Volume 22 (March). New York: NACLA.

de Franco, Mario, and Ricardo Godoy. 1990. "The Economic Consequences of Cocaine Production in Bolivia: Historical, Local and Macroeconomic Perspectives." Mimeo. June. Harvard Institute for International Development.

de Grazia, Jessica. 1991. *DEA: The War Against Drugs.* London: BBC Books.

Doria Medina, Samuel. 1991. "Coca por desarrollo: Dos años después." In SEAMOS, *La economía de la Coca en Bolivia: Análisis macro y microeconómico.* La Paz: Editorial Offset Boliviana Ltda.

———. 1986. *La economía informal en Bolivia.* La Paz: Editorial Offset Boliviana Ltda.

Dunkerley, James. 1990. *Political Transition and Economic Stabilization: Bolivia 1982–1989.* London: Institute of Latin American Studies Research Papers, no. 22.

———. 1984. *Rebellion in the Veins.* London: Verso.

Durana, J., N. Anderson, and W. Brooner, 1987. *Population Estimate for the Chapare Region, Bolivia.* Washington, D.C.: Desfil.

Eastwood, D. A., and H. J. Pollard. 1987. "Lowland Colonization and Coca Control: Bolivia's Irreconcilable Policies." In *Singapore Journal of Tropical Geography* 8, no. 1.

ECLAC (Economic Commission for Latin America and the Caribbean). 1991. *Statistical Yearbook for Latin America and the Caribbean.* Santiago: ECLAC.

Econométrica, Resumen Ejecutiva. 1990. *Análisis del proyecto agroYungas: AD/BOL/84/405.* La Paz.

Escobar de Pabón, Silvia, and Carmen Ledo García. 1990. *Urbanización y migración en Cochabamba.* Cochabamba: CEDLA-CIDRE.

Franks, Jeffrey. 1991. "La economía de la coca en Bolivia: ¿Plaga o salvación?" *Informe Confidencial,* no. 64 (June). La Paz: Muller Associates.

García-Sayan, D. 1989. *Coca, cocaína y narcotráfico.* Lima: Comisión Andina de Juristas.

Gill, L. 1984. "Commercial Agriculture and Peasant Production: A Study of Agrarian Capitalism in Northern Santa Cruz, Bolivia." Ph.D. dissertation, Columbia University.

Gómez, Hernando J. 1991. "El impacto del narcotráfico en el desarrollo de la América Latina: Aspectos económicos." Paper presented to CERID conference, La Paz. March.

Griffin, K. 1991. "The State, Human Development, and the Economics of Cocaine: The Case of Bolivia." Mimeo. University of California.

Gugliotta, Guy, and Jeff Leen. 1989. *Kings of Cocaine: An Astonishing True Story of Murder, Money, and International Corruption.* New York: Simon and Schuster.

Gutiérrez, Elías A., and Jaime Céspedes. 1991. "Los efectos de la interdicción en los organismos nacionales de seguridad y en la institucionalidad del estado Boliviano." *Drogas: El debate Boliviano,* no. 1. August. La Paz: SEAMOS.

Hargreaves, Clare. 1992. *Snowfields: The War on Cocaine in the Andes.* London: Zed Books.

Healy, Kevin. 1991a. "The Political Ascent of Bolivia's Peasant Coca Leaf Producers." *Journal of Interamerican Studies and World Affairs* 33, no. 1 (Spring 1991): 87–121.

———. 1991b. "Structural Adjustment, Peasant Agriculture and Coca in Bolivia." Paper presented to the 16th International Congress of the Latin American Studies Association. April. Washington, D.C.: 4–6 April.

———. 1989. "Coca, the State and the Peasantry, 1982–1988." *Journal of Interamerican Studies and World Affairs* 30, nos. 2 and 3: 150–126.

———. 1988. "Bolivia and Cocaine: A Developing Country's Dilemma." *British Journal of Addiction* 33:19–23.

———. 1986. "The Boom Within the Crisis: Some Recent Effects of Foreign Cocaine Markets on Bolivian Rural Society and Economy." In *Coca and Cocaine: Effects on People and Policy in Latin America,* ed. Deborah Pacini and Christine Franquemont. Boston: Cultural Survival.

Institute of the Americas. 1991. *Seizing Opportunities. Report of the Inter-American Commission on Drug Policy.* San Diego, Calif.: Center for Iberian and Latin American Studies, University of California.

Joel, Clark. 1990. *"At What Price of Coca Is Our Compensation and Credit Program Effective in Inducing Eradication? And What Is the Relative Profitability of Alternative Crops?"* Mimeo. U.S. Embassy, La Paz.

Jones, J. C. 1990. "The Chapare: Farmer Perspectives on the Economics and Sociology of Coca Production." Working Paper. Binghamton: Institute for Development Anthropology (IDA).

Justiniano, J. Guillermo. 1992. "La economía de la coca en Bolivia." In SEAMOS, *La economía de la coca en Bolivia: Análisis macro y microeconómico.* La Paz: Editorial Offset Boliviana Ltda.

Latin America Bureau. 1982. *Narcotráfico y política, militarismo y mafia en Bolivia.* Madrid: IEPALA.

Lee, Rensselaer W. III. 1989. *The White Labyrinth: Cocaine Trafficking and Political Power in the Andean Countries.* New Brunswick, N.J.: Transaction Publishers.

Morales, Edmundo. 1989. *Cocaine: White Gold Rush in Peru.* Tucson: University of Arizona Press.

Morales, Juan Antonio. 1988. "Inflation Stabilization in Bolivia." In *Inflation Stabilization: The Experience of Argentina, Brazil, Bolivia, Israel and Mexico,* ed. M. Bruno, G. Di Tella, R. Dornbusch, and S. Fischer. Cambridge, Mass.

Morales, Juan Antonio, and Jeffrey D. Sachs. 1989. "Bolivia's Economic Crisis." In *Developing Country Debt and the World Economy*, ed. Jeffrey D. Sachs, 57–79. Chicago: The University of Chicago Press.

Morales, W. Q. 1989. "The War on Drugs: A New U.S. National Security Doctrine?" *Third World Quarterly* (London) 11 no. 3, 147–169.

Muller Associates. 1989, 1990, 1991. *Estadísticas económicas*. La Paz: Muller Associates.

OAS. 1984. *Integrated Regional Development Planning: Guidelines and Case Studies from OAS Experience*. Washington, D.C.: OAS.

Oporto Castro, Henry. 1989. "Bolivia: El complejo coca-cocaína," in *Coca, cocaína y narcotráfico*, ed. Diego García-Sayan. Lima, Perú: Comisión Andina de Juristas.

Painter, M., 1990. *Institutional Analysis of the Chapare Regional Development Project* (CRDP). Binghamton: IDA.

Painter, M. and E. Bedoya Garland. 1991. *Socioeconomic Issues in Agricultural Settlement and Production in Bolivia's Chapare Region*. Working Paper no. 70, Binghamton: IDA.

Pacini, Deborah, and Christine Franquemont (eds.). 1986. *Coca and cocaine: Effects on People and Policy in Latin America*. Boston: Cultural Survival.

Pando, Roger, and Jorge Lema Morales. 1991a. "Problemas jurídico-legales asociados a la aplicación de la ley 1008." *Drogas: El debate Boliviano*, no. 2. October. La Paz: SEAMOS.

_____. 1991b. "La economía de la coca en Bolivia: Análisis macro y microeconómico." *Drogas: El debate Boliviano*, no. 3. October. La Paz: SEAMOS.

PDAR. 1991. *Informe técnico 1990*. Cochabamba.

Pérez-Crespo, Carlos. 1991a. *Why Do People Migrate? Internal Migration and the Pattern of Capital Accumulation in Bolivia*. January. Working Paper no. 74. Binghamton: IDA.

_____. 1991b. Tendencias migratorias en las areas de producción de coca en Cochabamba, Bolivia. Mimeo. March. Cochabamba.

Quiroga, José Antonio. 1990. *Coca/cocaína: Una visión Boliviana*. La Paz: AIPE/PROCOM-CEDLA-CID.

Rasnake, R. N., and M. Painter. 1989. *Rural Development and Crop Substitution in Bolivia: USAID and the Chapare Regional Development Project*. Binghamton: IDA.

Rivera, A. 1990a. "El Chapare actual." In *Debate regional: El Chapare actual*; sindicatos y ONGs en la región. Cochabamba: ILDIS/CERES.

_____. 1990b. *Diagnóstico socioeconómico de la población del Chapare*. Cochabamba: CERES.

Sage, C. 1991. "The Discourse on Drugs in the Americas." *Bulletin of Latin American Research* (London) 10, no. 3:325–332.

_____. 1987. "The Cocaine Economy in Bolivia: Its Development and Current Importance." *Corruption and Reform* 2:99–109.

Sanabria, H. 1988. "Coca, Migration, and Differentiation in the Bolivian Lowlands." *Studies in Third World Societies* 37:81–124.

SUBDESAL. 1991. *Informa*, boletín de prensa, no. 3. La Paz: SUBDESAL.

Tadic, Igor. 1988. "Afterword." In *Efectos del narcotráfico*, ed. Baldivia et al. La Paz: ILDIS.

Thoumi, Francisco. 1994 (forthcoming). *The Political Economy of Colombia and the Growth of the Illegal Psychoactive Drugs Industry*. Boulder: Lynne Rienner Publishers.

Tolisano, J., Richard Bossi, Ray Henkel, Alberto Rivera, Chris Seubert, David Smith, John Sutton, and Jack Swagerty. 1989. *Environmental Assessment of the Chapare Regional Development Project, Bolivia.* Washington, D.C.: Development Alternatives Inc.

Toranzos, Carlos. 1991. "Economía informal, economía ilegal: El papal del narcotráfico." Paper presented at CERID Conference, La Paz, March.

Tullis, LaMond. 1991a. "Beneficiaries of the Illicit Drug Trade: Political Consequences and International Policy at the Intersection of Supply and Demand. Discussion paper no. 19. March. Geneva: UNRISD.

_____. 1991b. "Illicit Drug Taking and Prohibition Laws: Public Consequences and the Reform of Public Policy in the United States. Discussion paper no. 21. March. Geneva: UNRISD.

_____. 1991c. *Handbook of Research on the Illicit Drug Traffic: Socioeconomic and Political Consequences.* Westport: Greenwood Press.

_____. 1987. "Cocaine and Food: Likely Effects of a Burgeoning Transnational Industry on Food Production in Bolivia and Peru." In *Pursuing Food Security: Strategies and Obstacles in Africa, Asia, Latin America, and the Middle East,* ed. W. Hollist and L. Tullis, 247–283. Boulder: Lynne Rienner Publishers.

UDAPE. 1989. *Estrategia nacional de desarrollo alternativo 1990.* La Paz: Presidencia de la República.

UNDCP/MACA. 1991. *Proyecto de desarrollo alternativo del trópico de Cochabamba AD/BOL/88/412—Informe de Evaluación.* Cochabamba: UNDCP/MACA.

UNFDAC. 1991. "Country Report on Bolivia." Mimeo. La Paz.

UNICEF. *The State of the World's Children 1991* (Oxford: Oxford University Press, 1990).

Universidad Autónoma Gabriel René Moreno. 1991. *Universidad, sociedad, uso indebido de drogas.* Santa Cruz; Bolivia: Editorial Universertaria.

USAID/Bolivia. 1991. *Alternative Development Strategy.* La Paz: U.S. Embassy.

———. 1991. "Assistance for Alternative Development." Mimeo. La Paz.

———. 1991. "Program Objectives Chapare." Mimeo. Cochabamba.

_____. 1990. "Executive summary of internal evaluation." Mimeo. La Paz.

USAID Update. 1991. "Estimates of the Economic Impact of Coca and Derivatives in 1990." April. Mimeo. La Paz.

U.S. Congress. House. Committee on Government Operations. 1990. *United States Anti-narcotic Activities in the Andean Region.* Washington, D.C.: U.S. Government Printing Office.

U.S. Congress. Senate. Committee on Governmental Affairs. 1990. *Cocaine Production, Eradication and the Environment: Policy, Impact and Options.* Washington, D.C.: U.S. Government Printing Office.

U.S. Department of State. Bureau of International Narcotics Matters. 1986–1992. *International Narcotics Control Strategy Report.* Washington, D.C.: U.S. Government Printing Office.

U.S. Office of Inspector General. 1991. *Drug Control Activities in Bolivia. Audit Report 2–CI-001.* Washington, D.C.: U.S. Government Printing Office.

Wingert, Stephen, Helen Soos, Daniel Chaij, and Jerry Harrison-Burns. "Review of USAID/Bolivia Development Assistance Support for Coca Eradication." Mimeo. Washington, D.C., 1988.

WOLA. 1992. *Andean Initiative—Legislative Update.* July. Washington, D.C.: WOLA.

———. 1991. *Andean Initiative—Legislative Updates.* March, July, and October. Washington, D.C.: WOLA.

———. 1991. *Clear and Present Dangers: The U.S. Military and the War on Drugs in the Andes.* October. Washington, D.C.: WOLA.

———. 1990. *Andean Initiative—Legislative Update.* December. Washington, D.C.: WOLA.

———. 1989. *Andean Initiative—Legislative Update.* November. Washington, D.C.: WOLA.

Youngers, Coletta. 1991. "A Fundamentally Flawed Strategy: The U.S. War on Drugs in Bolivia." *WOLA Briefing Series* 3 (September).

———. 1990. "The War in the Andes: The Military Role in U.S. International Drug Policy" *WOLA Briefing Series* 4 (December).

Agencies, Newspapers, Magazines (Other Than Those in Bolivia)

Associated Press
Christian Science Monitor, Boston
EFE News agency, Madrid
Financial Times, London
Guardian, London
Independent, London
Latin American Press, Lima
Miami Herald, Miami
Newsweek, New York
New York Times, New York
South Magasine, London
Sunday Times, London
Toronto Globe and Mail, Toronto
Washington Post, Washington

Bolivian Publications

Bolivia Bulletin, La Paz
Conosur, Cochabamba
El Día, Santa Cruz
Hoy, La Paz
Informe R, La Paz
El Mundo, Santa Cruz
Opinión, Cochabamba
Presencia, La Paz
La Razón, La Paz
Los Tiempos, Cochabamba
Ultima Hora, La Paz

Index

• • •

183

About the Book
and Author

• • •

The domestic and international impacts of the production, trade, and use of coca in Bolivia have reached monumental proportions, as have the national and international efforts to suppress the country's drug trade. This book lucidly describes Bolivia's coca boom, the development of its cocaine industry, and the catastrophic consequences of both.

Painter explains how coca and cocaine are inextricably linked to Bolivia's long-term development problems, its internal political dynamics, the incipient militarization of its society, and a frantic search, at all levels of society, for a solution to the underlying problems of poverty. Considering the implications of various policies designed to curb the drug trade, he focuses on the "alternative development" approach proposed to reduce coca-crop production.

Although the final results of alternative development remain to be seen, Painter is not optimistic that even its success would materially alter Bolivian coca production. Nevertheless, he concludes, "even if a successful policy did little to stop the availability of cocaine, at least policymakers favoring alternative development could be left with the honorable objective of helping poor farmers in their efforts to escape poverty—which was, after all, why most of them started growing coca in the first place."

James Painter, currently a Latin America editor for the BBC World Service, was for several years the BBC's correspondent in Bolivia. His publications include numerous articles in both the popular press and scholarly journals, as well as books and monographs on Latin America.

The United Nations Research Institute for Social Development (UNRISD) is an autonomous agency that engages in multidisciplinary research on the social dimensions of contemporary problems affecting development. Its work is guided by the conviction that, for effective development policies to be formulated, an understanding of the social and political context is crucial. The institute attempts to provide governments, development agencies, grassroots organizations, and scholars with a better understanding of how development policies and processes of economic, social, and environmental change affect different social groups. Working through an extensive network of national research centers, UNRISD aims to promote original research and strengthen research capacity in developing countries.

Current research themes focus on the social dimensions of economic restructuring, environmental deterioration and conservation, ethnic conflict, the illicit narcotic drugs trade and drug-control policies, political violence, the mass voluntary return of refugees, and the reconstruction of war-torn societies, as well as ways of integrating gender issues into development planning.

A list of publications can be obtained by writing to the Reference Centre, UNRISD, Palais des Nations, CH-1211 Geneva 10, Switzerland.

 The United Nations University (UNU) is an international academic organization that provides a framework for bringing together the world's leading scholars to tackle pressing global problems of human survival, development, and welfare. It is an autonomous body of the United Nations, with academic freedom guaranteed under its charter to allow free collaboration with scholars worldwide. The University operates through a global network of its own research and training centers and programs and in association with individuals and other insitutions throughout the world.

Currently, the University works in five program areas, each related to an area of major global concern: universal human values and global responsibilities, the world economy and development, global life support systems, advances in science and technology, and population dynamics and human welfare.